Hollywood's 10 Greatest Actors: Humphrey Bogart, Cary Grant, Jimmy Stewart, Marlon Brando, Fred Astaire, Henry Fonda, Clark Gable, James Cagney, Spencer Tracy, and Charlie Chaplin

By Charles River Editors

Humphrey Bogart and Lauren Bacall in *Dark Passage* (1947)

About Charles River Editors

Introduction

Humphrey Bogart (1899-1957)

"All you owe the public is a good performance." – Humphrey Bogart

Americans have always loved movie stars, and there have been no shortage of Hollywood icons, but one man has long been considered the greatest male star. From the time he first became a leading man, Humphrey Bogart's screen image has resonated with viewers more than perhaps any other actor. At the end of the 20th century, when the American Film Institute assembled its list of the 50 Greatest American Screen Legends, Bogart was at the top of the list. His persona as a tough guy who manages to maintain his sense of virtue no matter how compromising the situation features in some of the most famous films ever made, including *Casablanca* (1942), *The Maltese Falcon* (1941), and *Key Largo* (1949).

Bogart's screen persona was not only desirable (everyone wanted to be like Bogart) but also highly approachable, in the sense that he played the everyman figure far more than Cary Grant or Laurence Olivier, for example. Bogart also had good timing, with some of his popularity due to the fact that he rose to fame in an era when the film industry was at its most potent. Bogart's prime coincided with the Golden Age of cinema; sound had been successfully integrated and the studio system ruled over the industry. Bogart was the biggest star at a time in which the medium itself held immense mass appeal, and he has been famous ever since.

People have long been familiar with Bogart's career and movies, but the differences between his persona and his real life are also interesting. Bogart's everyman screen persona belies the fact that he came from immense privilege, and his down-to-earth film roles are in many ways a rebellion against a family with which he was never close. There were traits that Bogart inherited from his parents, but his film career also offered Bogart to escape a family culture that was antithetical to his personality. Bogart's screen persona as a jaded but ultimately indestructible figure also obscures the fact that his life was filled with substantial tragedy, culminating in his own premature death at the age of 57. Separating Bogart's real life from his reel life is still a subject of great interest and debate.

Hollywood's 10 Greatest Actors profiles the life, career, and legacy of the man deemed by the American Film Institute as the greatest male star. Along with pictures of important people, places, and events, you will learn about Humphrey Bogart like you never have before, in no time at all.

Cary Grant (1904-1986)

"Everyone wants to be Cary Grant. Even I want to be Cary Grant." – Cary Grant

Movie stars are revered for their ability to captivate audiences, and perhaps no actor has done it as well as Cary Grant, the epitome of the suave, debonair actor who may have been rivaled only by dancer extraordinaire Fred Astaire. Grant offered a version of the male actor that stood in stark contrast with the gangster heroes and hard-boiled film noir detectives that populated the screen throughout his career. Impeccably groomed and always clad in dapper attire, Grant possessed a magnetism that was undeniably attractive, all while managing to come across as well-heeled and socially respectable. As a result, there was an archetypal quality to Cary Grant that endeared him to both male and female viewers. After all, he was able to star in major movies well into his 60s, and even after he retired, Grant never lost his charm and continued to maintain a universal appeal that has almost never been rivaled.

Cary Grant occupies an almost sacred place in American film history, but it is still important to recognize that the persona that has enchanted audiences for decades was in fact a creation. Grant was not born with the charm and elegance he later exuded, and the contrast between his upbringing and the man he would later become is arguably the most remarkable aspect of his life story. Born into a dysfunctional family, Grant had a tumultuous childhood that saw him tasked with perpetually overcoming major adversity. With a mother who was too ill to care for him and a father whose interests lay elsewhere, he was in many respects charged with raising himself, a dynamic entirely antithetical to the affluent characters he famously portrayed in films such as *The Philadelphia Story* (1939), *To Catch a Thief* (1953), and *An Affair to Remember* (1957). The progression from Grant's youth to his glamorous adult life was a complex transformation of its own, and it is a Hollywood rags-to-riches story of its own.

At the same time, Grant's rise to stardom was due to an intricate web of factors, including his own natural acting ability, developments in the motion picture industry, and the fortuitous opportunity to consistently work with gifted directors who molded his image. Like nearly every big star, Grant was an exceptionally gifted actor and someone who benefitted from a fortunate string of career opportunities that he took advantage of to full effect.

Hollywood's 10 Greatest Actors examines the life and career of Hollywood's most iconic leading man. Along with pictures of important people, places, and events, you will learn about Cary Grant like never before, in no time at all.

Publicity photo of Jimmy Stewart in *Anatomy of a Murder* (1959)

Jimmy Stewart (1908-1997)

"A feller came up to me the other day and said 'I don't know whether this means anything to you but you've given me and my family a lot of enjoyment over the years.' And I said to him, 'Does it mean anything to me? It means everything to me. That's the ballgame. That's it.' And I think that if I have done that to that man, and maybe a couple more…then I'm proud of that." – Jimmy Stewart

When the American Film Institute assembled its top 100 actors of all time at the close of the 20th century, Jimmy Stewart ranked third, behind only Humphrey Bogart and Cary Grant. There is a certain inevitability to these three actors ranking at the top of the list; after all, they were the dominant faces of Hollywood during the height of the era known as classical Hollywood cinema, a time before the onset of television when the movies still enjoyed relatively uncontested supremacy over American entertainment. The popularity of Stewart, Grant, and Bogart also extends well beyond the success of any of their individual films, reflecting their much broader cultural significance as monuments of Hollywood during its Golden Age.

In fact, if the list was reconstructed today, it is entirely possible that Stewart would rank first. Not only have movies such as It's a Wonderful Life (1946) and Vertigo (1958) continued to gain in popularity even into the 21st century, but Stewart has come to embody an accessible image of American values that is easy for everyone to embrace. The wholesome, happy-go-lucky persona he cultivated represents perhaps a more palatable image of American masculinity than the gritty realism of Bogart or the erudite but occasionally snobbish tendencies of Cary Grant. If there is any actor that embodies not only classical Hollywood but also American culture more generally, it's difficult to argue against Jimmy Stewart.

The phenomenon of Jimmy Stewart becomes even more remarkable when considering the incredible harmony between the characters he portrayed in his films and his personality off the movie set. Most actors and actresses cultivate a persona in order to achieve success, and in most cases it's an image that bears only a tangential relationship to an actor's true personality, but there was no such division for Stewart. The all-American image conveyed in films such as Mr. Smith Goes to Washington (1939) and It's a Wonderful Life corresponds seamlessly with Stewart's off-screen pursuits, which included a degree in architecture from Princeton and an extended tenure as a pilot during World War II. There were elements of his life story that resisted cultural norms - he waited until age 41 before marrying, and his very decision to pursue acting in 1930s America could be seen as a deviation from more characteristically masculine professions - but there was an almost seamless congruence between the Stewart that audiences saw on screen and the man he was in real life. Naturally, his defining traits developed out of and in response to the values instilled in him by his family and cultural background, and for this reason, examining his filmography alongside his life story paints a complete picture of the delicate unity of Jimmy Stewart's life.

This biography explores how exactly Stewart managed to parlay his boy-next-door image into international fame, and how his specific brand of American masculinity managed to generate tremendous approval not only from female viewers but men as well. At no point in his career was Stewart simply seen as a heartthrob (his gangly physique certainly precluded such a designation), nor was he viewed as someone specifically designed to cater to male viewers. Stewart's star image could also be modified and reworked, as proven in his films with Alfred Hitchcock and Anthony Mann. *Hollywood's 10 Greatest Actors* examines the life and career of one of Hollywood's most iconic actors. Along with pictures of important people, places, and events, you will learn about Jimmy Stewart like never before, in no time at all.

Marlon Brando with Eva Marie Saint in the trailer for On the Waterfront (1954)

Marlon Brando (1924-2004)

"He is the marker. There's 'before Brando' and 'after Brando'." – Martin Scorsese

Marlon Brando. Few names in the acting profession evoke such a strong, almost visceral reaction. Over the course of his long, prolific career, he was considered perhaps the greatest actor of the 20th century as well as one of the most complicated and misunderstood. Uniquely able to be both emotionally charged and technically constrained in the same performance, he single-handedly changed the direction of not only the American style of acting, influencing successors such as Robert De Niro, Al Pacino and even Johnny Depp, but the acting profession on a global scale. His iconic interpretations of characters such as Stanley Kowalski (A Streetcar Named Desire), Terry Malloy (On the Waterfront) and Vito Corleone (The Godfather) have been forever burned into the collective memory of film and theatre aficionados, scholars and critics for their immense passion, rage, love, defiance, vulnerability, cruelty and tenderness – basically, the full spectrum of the human condition. With several Oscars and Golden Globes to his name, Brando's contributions remain the gold standard of the acting craft, and the American Film Institute has listed him as the 4th greatest screen legend in history.

Brando was one of his generation's sex idols, its most versatile actors, and a political activist, but who was the person behind the legend? What propelled a young man from the Midwest to become such a powerful, capricious and dominating force in the acting arena? How was he able to penetrate the human condition, replete with all its multilayered emotional baggage, and convey its strengths, weaknesses and delicate nuances so successfully, often while plagued by his own personal tragedies and demons?

Hollywood's 10 Greatest Actors looks at the life and career of the acting legend and analyzes his enduring legacy. Along with pictures, you will learn about Marlon Brando like you never have before, in no time at all.

Fred Astaire (1899-1987)

"No dancer can watch Fred Astaire and not know that we all should have been in another business." – Mikhail Baryshnikov

Virtually all famous actors are regaled by the public, but even still, Fred Astaire occupies a privileged position in American pop culture. The specific films in which Astaire acted may not be especially famous in their own right - most people likely cannot recall the title of *Top Hat* (1935), his most decorated film - but Astaire's dancing prowess invariably creates a lasting impact on viewers. Instead of tying his fame to a single film, Astaire's genius lay in constructing his star persona around a specific set of iconographic imagery that has become embedded within American culture. Across his films, the recurring iconic images of the top hat, cane, and coat tails, as well as the image of Astaire dancing with Ginger Rogers, all constitute a timeless symbol for elegance that continues to captivate viewers who are unfamiliar with the plots of his films. There have been other film musical actors who were proficient dancers, Gene Kelly chief among them, but none were able to perform with the seamless elegance of Astaire, and none have been remembered nearly as well.

Astaire's dancing numbers epitomized grace and gaiety, making it seem as though he was carefree, but this was hardly the case. While it is easy to imagine Astaire being raised in an aristocratic family, his working-class background was so blue collar that his family eventually relied on him and his sister as the primary breadwinners in the family. Rather than being born and raised with wealth in a large city, Astaire came from a working-class neighborhood in Omaha, Nebraska, a setting so antithetical to the world of dance that it quickly became clear that the family would need to relocate. If anything, Astaire's unglamorous origins further demonstrate that the magisterial dancing and the effortlessly elegant image accompanying it were products of Astaire's tireless work ethic and insistence on perfection.

Astaire's popularity can in large part be tied to the escapism that his films offered to impoverished Depression-era American audiences, and yet Astaire was a working man, albeit one who labored in the studios of Hollywood rather than the factories of America. Considering the quiet life that he led off the movie set, it can be difficult to disassociate Astaire from his films, and while he may have attempted to project the same image off the screen, the era and his personal background were extremely important. As someone who was born just before the start of the 20th century, Astaire's life sheds light on the developments that occurred in American entertainment, from the stage (where he first performed during his youth) to cinema (the site of his greatest triumphs) and finally to television (a medium Astaire entered at the end of his career.) Astaire's career tends to obscure his all-American success story, one in which hard work transformed a Nebraska boy from a working-class family into America's most prominent symbol of grace.

Hollywood's 10 Greatest Actors profiles the life and career of one of America's most famous entertainers. Along with pictures of important people, places, and events, you will learn about Fred Astaire like you never have before, in no time at all.

Fonda in his Navy uniform during World War II

Henry Fonda (1905-1982)

"I must have had faith that day. When I went out, I was Henry Fonda again. An unemployed actor but a man." – Henry Fonda

Among all of Hollywood's iconic leading men, arguably none proved as versatile at acting as Henry Fonda, whose career spanned six decades and earned him Academy Awards for roles in various genres. After breaking into Hollywood in 1935, Fonda quickly rose the ranks, earning an Academy Award nomination in the classic *Twelve Angry Men* (1940), but Fonda had the kind of staying power that most actors could only dream of. In fact, Fonda had already received an honorary lifetime achievement award from the Academy (in 1980) before winning the Oscar for Best Actor for his role in *On Golden Pond* (1981), an award he earned when he was already well into his 70s and only about a year away from his death. Fonda would also earn Emmy nominations for his work on two different shows and even a Grammy for a spoken word album in 1977. And as if all that wasn't enough, he was also a critically acclaimed stage performer, winning a Tony for *Mister Roberts* in 1948.

A lot of Fonda's success could be attributed to the fact that he could convincingly play the all-

American man that everybody in the nation adored and/or wanted to be, to the extent that one magazine called him "the man we wished we lived next door to." At the same time, Fonda could portray characters like Tom Joad, who maintain their status as heroes even while breaking rules on-screen. His personal life also seemed to mirror his acting versatility; while his World War II service helped cement his all-American persona, his family life was also extremely troubled, even after he became recognized as the patriarch of a family full of famous actors, including Jane and Bridget Fonda. When Henry played an isolated father on-screen in *On Golden Pond* alongside his daughter Jane, the autobiographical elements of the film were apparent to those who knew him.

One of the remarkable aspects of Henry Fonda's career is that he was able to play vastly different roles despite not changing his style of acting. As Henry's distant personality would suggest, he hailed from an old-school breed of actors who didn't express emotions outwardly, and even as his progeny would become associated with Method Acting, Henry remained in the same mold as actors like Cary Grant and Jimmy Stewart. Of course, the seemingly effortless nature of Henry's acting only made him more endearing to contemporary audiences, even as his acting style would eventually go out of style.

Hollywood's 10 Greatest Actors examines the life and career of one of the Golden Era of Hollywood's biggest stars. Along with pictures of important people, places, and events, you will learn about Henry Fonda like never before, in no time at all.

Clark Gable and Vivien Leigh in *Gone with the Wind*

Clark Gable (1901-1960)

"The only reason they come to see me is that I know that life is great — and they know I know it." – Clark Gable

The 1930s were, without a doubt, the height of the classical Hollywood era. It is no accident that 1939 has historically been designated as the pinnacle of Hollywood film history. The era was known for its lavish studio productions, with MGM, RKO, Warner Brothers, Paramount, and 20th Century Fox all operating at the height of their powers. Every major studio possessed a long roster of contract players, with films released at such a rapid pace that it made for an especially competitive environment within the industry. Even while America remained in the throes of the Great Depression, the film industry continued to flourish, and movies easily supplanted the theater as the main attraction for American entertainment. Indeed, it would be no exaggeration to claim that the film industry reached its zenith during the decade precisely because it offered an affordable (if very temporary) escape from the anxieties of the economic woes of the era.

The 1930s were also a time in which Hollywood boasted an unprecedented array of famous leading men. Gary Cooper, Cary Grant, James Stewart, and Fred Astaire were just a handful of the A-list stars of the decade, and it is in this context that the achievements of Clark Gable are particularly remarkable. Best known for his role in *Gone with the Wind* (1939), Gable reached the ranks of the Hollywood elite well before the end of the decade through acting in films such as *It Happened One Night* (1934) and *Mutiny on the Bounty* (1935). Gable had a unique appeal that captivated Depression-era audiences; while Cary Grant offered a sophisticated charm and Fred Astaire was tied to the musical genre, Gable brought an air of sophistication that was less comical than that of Grant and appealed to both genders, unlike Astaire. At a time when so many Americans were financially destitute, Gable managed to appear classy without coming across as snobbish. At the same time, his virile masculinity was not overly macho or misogynist. For these reasons, Gable was able to captivate male and female viewers alike, and his mass appeal was a driving force behind the commercial success of *Gone With the Wind*, possibly the most beloved Hollywood film ever made. As iconic director John Huston once stated, "Clark Gable was the only real he-man I've ever known, of all the actors I've met."

Even if Gable is perhaps less widely-known than Grant or Astaire among 21st century audiences, examining the effect he had on viewers during the 1930s and 1940s allows a better understanding of Hollywood during its Golden Age. In conjunction with that, his career served as a sort of response to his upbringing and cultural background. In fact, there was a significant gap between his glamorous roles on the movie screen and the real-life adversity he faced from an early age. Gable faced great challenges throughout his entire career, from the death of his biological mother to the death of wife Carole Lombard in 1942. As with any famous actor, he was the recipient of great fortune, yet it is important to recognize that his many opportunities did not preclude him from experiencing great pain and tragedy.

Hollywood's 10 Greatest Actors examines the life and career of one of Hollywood's most iconic leading men. Along with pictures of important people, places, and events, you will learn about Clark Gable like never before, in no time at all.

Cagney in *G-Men* (1935)

James Cagney (1899-1986)

"You don't psych yourself up for these things, you do them...I'm acting for the audience, not for myself, and I do it as directly as I can." – James Cagney

When the American Film Institute assembled its top 100 actors of all time at the close of the 20th century, one of the Top 10 was James Cagney, an actor whose acting and dancing talents spawned a stage and film career that spanned over 5 decades and once compelled Orson Welles to call him "maybe the greatest actor to ever appear in front of a camera." Indeed, his portrayal of "The Man Who Owns Broadway", George M. Cohan, earned him an Academy Award in the musical *Yankee Doodle Dandy*, and as famed director Milos Forman once put it, "I think he's some kind of genius. His instinct, it's just unbelievable. I could just stay at home. One of the qualities of a brilliant actor is that things look better on the screen than the set. Jimmy has that quality."

Ultimately, it was portraying tough guys and gangsters in the 1930s that turned Cagney into a massive Hollywood star, and they were the kind of roles he was literally born to play after growing up rough in Manhattan at the turn of the 20th century. In movies like *The Public Enemy* (which included the infamous "grapefruit scene") and *White Heat*, Cagney convincingly and grippingly played criminals that brought Warner to the forefront of Hollywood and the gangster genre. Cagney also helped pave the way for younger actors in the genre, like Humphrey Bogart, and he was so good that he found himself in danger of being typecast.

While Cagney is no longer remembered as fondly or as well as Bogart, he was also crucial in helping establish the system in which actors worked as independent workers free from the constraints of studios. Refusing to be pushed around, Cagney was constantly involved in contract squabbles with Warner, and he often came out on top, bucking the conventional system that saw studios treat their stars as indentured servants who had to make several films a year.

Hollywood's 10 Greatest Actors examines the life and career of one of Hollywood's most iconic actors. Along with pictures of important people, places, and events, you will learn about Cagney like never before, in no time at all.

Tracy in *Fury* (1936)

Spencer Tracy (1900-1967)

"Know your lines and don't bump into the furniture." – Spencer Tracy

Of all the screen legends whose names remain synonymous with Hollywood, few took as long to become a star as Spencer Tracy, who is today recognized as one of the greatest actors ever but whose career did not truly take off until he was already in his mid-30s. After languishing with Fox for 5 years and over two dozen movies, one biographer had summed up his career to that point in time: "Tracy was scarcely a blip on the box office barometer in 1935, a critics' darling and little more."

However, after joining MGM in 1935, Tracy catapulted to fame with one of the most impressive runs in Hollywood history, winning Oscars for Best Actor in 1938 and 1939 after already being nominated in 1937. Over the next three decades, Tracy would appear in classics like *Captains Courageous* and *Judgment at Nuremburg*, appear in 9 films with Katharine Hepburn, and receive 9 Oscar nominations over a span of 32 years, including for his final film, *Guess Who's Coming to Dinner*. Several contemporaries considered Tracy the greatest actor of his era, a sentiment summed up by actor Richard Widmark, who once said, "He's the greatest movie actor there ever was...I've learned more about acting from watching Tracy than in any other way."

Tracy's career earned him an unbelievable number of accolades, and a place in the American

Film Institute's Top 10 actors of the 20th century, but it's also an open question how much more he could have accomplished without a litany of health problems brought on by alcohol. Even as he went years at a time without drinking, the effects gradually wore him down physically, and by his early 60's, he needed full-time care, provided mostly by his most famous co-star and lover, Katharine Hepburn. Ironically, his relationship with Hepburn has actually served to overshadow his own acting career among modern viewers, even as his acting abilities remain universally recognized.

Hollywood's 10 Greatest Actors profiles the life, career, and legacy of the man deemed by the American Film Institute as one of Hollywood's 10 greatest actors. Along with pictures of important people, places, and events, you will learn about Spencer Tracy like you never have before, in no time at all.

Charlie Chaplin (1889-1977)

"I remain just one thing, and one thing only — and that is a clown. It places me on a far higher plane than any politician." – Charlie Chaplin

Only a select few actors become international stars in their time, but none had as unique a career as Charlie Chaplin. Chaplin was the first true film star, and he managed to do so even when films were still silent. He has been honored with too many awards to count, and the fact that his name remains instantly recognizable nearly a century after his first film is a testament to his influence.

Even today, Chaplin's films are arguably more recognizable than those of perhaps any other actor or director; everyone is familiar with the famous "Tramp" costume and persona, and even the casual film enthusiast has likely seen films such as *City Lights* (1931) and *Modern Times* (1936). Chaplin is known for the singular blend of pathos and humor evinced by his films, and it is not uncommon for audiences to laugh and cry at alternate points of a Chaplin film, a trait that continues to endear audiences even to this day. For this reason, in his review of Stephen Weissman's biography of Chaplin, Martin Sieff noted, "It is doubtful any individual has every given more entertainment, pleasure, and relief to so many human beings when they needed it most."

As Sieff's comment suggests, Chaplin's career coincided with the two World Wars and the Great Depression, but while Chaplin the actor was popular, Chaplin the person became controversial in the final decades of his life. In fact, there is a wide discrepancy between the almost uniformly enthusiastic praise of Chaplin today and the subversive identity he cultivated toward the latter part of his career. Although accusations of being a communist sympathizer and Chaplin's confrontation with the House Committee on Un-American Activities have mostly become a footnote in the storied career of a man best remembered as an acting pioneer, it forced Chaplin to spend the last 15 years of his career working as an artist in exile, and the shifting viewpoints of Chaplin were instrumental in forcing people to evaluate the way in which they viewed celebrities, as well as what it means to be entertained. Indeed, it is impossible to substantiate the belief that Chaplin's later films are poorer in quality than his earlier ones, yet the public largely rejected his later directorial efforts. In the end, it must be acknowledged that, more than any other figure who had come before him, the public was aware of Chaplin's personal life in ways that were often upsetting and inconsistent with the persona effected through his films.

Due to the way Chaplin was vilified, relatively little is known about the final chapter of Chaplin's life, and one of the prevailing tensions concerning Chaplin is the way in which he is incredibly famous on the one hand but also a particularly mysterious and even unknown figure on the other hand. After Chaplin's body was stolen from his grave, Kenneth Schuyler Lynn pointed out that "the image of his empty gravesite came to symbolize his historic elusiveness, as a person no less than as a performer."

How is it that a director who is arguably more famous than any other also had such an "elusive" personality? *Hollywood's 10 Greatest Actors* comprehensively examines Chaplin's life and films, exploring the controversies and the ways in which his life and works are mutually informative. Along with pictures of important people, places, and events, you will learn about Charlie Chaplin like you never have before, in no time at all.

Humphrey Bogart

Chapter 1: Early Years

One of the most shocking aspects of Humphrey Bogart's life story is the discrepancy between his roles on screen and his family background. Humphrey was the eldest child of Belmont DeForest Bogart and Maud Humphrey, and he would later have two younger sisters, Frances and Catherine. Humphrey's father was a Presbyterian with Dutch and English ancestry whose last name was Dutch for "keeper of an orchard", but Belmont worked as a cardiopulmonary surgeon and came from a privileged family background. He had also descended from a family with historical ties to the landscape, as his family had arrived in Brooklyn from Holland in the 17th century. Humphrey's grandfather, Adam Watkins Bogart, ran an inn in the Finger Lakes region in upstate New York, and in 1853 the family had relocated to upstate New York from Brooklyn. Adam descended from a lineage of farmers, but Humphrey's paternal grandmother had come from a wealthy background herself.

Belmont was born in 1866, just one year following the death of his brother. His mother would die just two years after his birth and left all of her wealth to her son. But interestingly, in her will she asked that Belmont be removed from her husband's possession and placed in the custody of one of her sisters. Adam eventually sued her estate and won, regaining custody over his son. With his inheritance, Belmont was sure to enjoy a comfortable upbringing, and his father Adam made a fortune from creating a method for lithographing plates, but the unusual episode surrounding the will and Belmont's custody demonstrated the coldness of his parents' marriage. That lack of affection would also be especially relevant in Humphrey Bogart's life.

It is believed that Humphrey was born on Christmas Day in 1899, but the story has faced much dissension over the years because it seemed too good to be true. For a long time, many people thought Humphrey's Christmas Day birthday was a myth fabricated by Warner Brothers to add to his allure. The alternative theory was that he was born in late January 1900, but documents from the period suggest he was definitely born in December 1899. While movie studios often changed their stars' names and other pertinent information, based on his movie roles it would seem as though Bogart lacked the kind of sweet nature that would drive the studio to fabricate that story out of thin air.

Bogart's unusual first name was borrowed from his mother's maiden name. Maud Humphrey was of English origin and Episcopalian faith. She was also considered an extraordinarily beautiful woman, with vivid red hair. Her father was a wealthy shoe manufacturer, and she grew up even more privileged than her husband. Given the era Maud grew up in, she was a very strong and career-oriented woman, and she was also an avowed suffragette who never submitted to the male-dominated norms of the time period.

Maud's parents had sent her to art school, where she became an accomplished illustrator. After graduating from school and marrying Belmont, she worked as a commercial illustrator, where she earned a robust salary of $50,000 per year, more than double her husband's not-insignificant salary. Naturally, Maud drew pictures of her baby boy, one of which was featured in an ad campaign for Mellins Baby Food. Humphrey would later wryly note, "There was a period in American history when you couldn't pick up a goddamned magazine without seeing my kisser in it."

Maud and Humphrey

Humphrey as a boy

Since they were each so independently driven, Bogart's parents were never close or affectionate, and they sparred continuously, unleashing sarcastic quips on each other that made them seem more like rivals than loving parents. Humphrey clearly inherited his own caustic wit from his parents, but as a young child he suffered from lack of attention. As Humphrey put it, "I was brought up very unsentimentally but very straightforwardly. A kiss, in our family, was an event. Our mother and father didn't glug over my two sisters and me."

In fact, with his parents constantly working, Humphrey was largely raised by a collection of housekeepers and caretakers. His parents eschewed all manner of physical or verbal affection, keeping a cold distance from him that would never grow more intimate, even after their son rose to fame. Humphrey explained, "If, when I was grown up, I sent my mother one of those Mother's Day telegrams or said it with flowers, she would have returned the wire and flowers to me, collect."

Despite their professional strength and standing in the New York society realm, Humphrey's parents were physically fragile figures. Maud suffered from debilitating headaches, while Belmont was addicted to morphine, a condition that would later play a strong role in his demise. When both were at home, they continuously fought with one another, no doubt in part due to the fact that they often didn't feel well.

Of course, Humphrey's privileged upbringing had enormous advantages that were counterbalanced by significant disadvantages. He came from a highly respected family that lived in a posh Upper West Side apartment in Manhattan and was listed in *Dua's New York Blue Book*. The block Humphrey grew up on has since been ceremonially renamed Humphrey Bogart Place. Naturally there were aspects of his family's wealth that Humphrey enjoyed. Chief among these was the family's summer stays at their 55-acre estate in Canandaigua in upstate New York. The family held a prominent role in the summer community, and their arrival and departure was fodder for the newspaper. While summering, he was introduced to major society figures, including future president Franklin Delano Roosevelt.

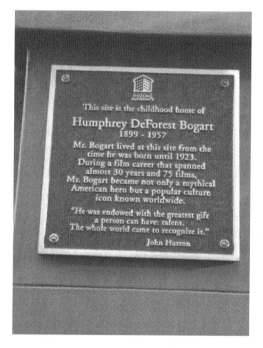

Plaque at Bogart's childhood home on W. 103rd St.

In 1913, when Bogart was still 13 years old, his family switched summer homes, relocating to Fire Island in order to be closer to Maud's job in New York City. In 1910, she had assumed the prestigious role of artistic director for the fashion magazine *The Delineator*. At Fire Island, Bogart became friends with the other residents, staged theatrical productions with them, and met his first girlfriend there. One of his closest friends was William Brady Jr., who would play an instrumental role later in his life. Brady was the closest friend Bogart would have during his youth, and the two were given free tickets to Broadway shows by Brady's father, entertainment mogul William Brady Sr. It has even been suggested that the friendship between Bogart and Brady was at times homoerotic. Most importantly, summering on the water engendered a deep love for boating, and Humphrey became particularly adept at sailing, a passion that would remain with him for the rest of his life.

Humphrey was quite happy during the summer, but he lived in relative misery during the other parts of the year. The thing that stood out most about young Humphrey was that his mother insisted on dressing him in precious clothes that had long become antiquated by the time he was born. Humphrey also grew to resent his name, which quickly became a source of ridicule among his classmates. Making matters worse, another source of self-consciousness stemmed from the fact that as a young child, Maud had illustrated her son in the nude from behind, a drawing that became famous and was disseminated throughout the country. Although Maud refrained from giving her son loving attention and their relationship was quite distant, it is also apparent that Humphrey was monitored too closely by his mother, who did not give him the agency to dress and present himself in a manner that would endear him to his classmates. His famous lisp, which would later become one of his trademarks as an actor, caused ridicule from his classmates, as did his curly hair. As a result, Humphrey was perpetually viewed as a pretty boy and an outsider; one classmate said of him, "Bogart never came out for anything. He wasn't a very good student... He added up to nothing in our class."

Given that his time at school was another source of discomfort, it is no surprise that Humphrey shunned his studies even at an early age. At first, he attended the Delancey School, where he matriculated until the 5th grade. Bogart then enrolled in Trinity School, an elite all-boys school that had already been in existence for 200 years by the time Humphrey went there in 1909. While attending Trinity School, Bogart was required to don a blue suit, a style of dress he would retain for the rest of his life. He attended Trinity for a full 8 years, during which time he performed poorly and was forced to repeat the 11th grade after having suffered from scarlet fever. After returning from school, Humphrey would pose for his mother, who would draw him in her studio. This curious dynamic, in which Humphrey was fodder for her illustrations, has led plenty of people to suggest that Humphrey's first experience as an actor was in his own home.

Despite attending prestigious schools, Humphrey always believed that school was not the appropriate environment for him. Even so, his parents had high aspirations that he would follow in his father's footsteps and become a doctor, so there was immense pressure on Bogart to perform well in school. The family also regularly entertained literary luminaries like Theodore Dreiser and H.L. Mencken, and Humphrey was an articulate and avid reader, so his lack of academic success greatly frustrated his parents. In a sense, his perpetual lack of achievement in school was a form of rebellion against his parents and his early years more than an expression of poor intelligence.

By the time Bogart neared the end of his high school studies, it was clear that he would need assistance in order to gain admittance to a prestigious college. Therefore, Belmont used his connections to have Humphrey admitted at Philips Andover Academy in Massachusetts, where Humphrey was to matriculate for his final year of high school and eventually attend medical school at Yale University. However, Belmont's best-laid plans were not realized, and the year at Andover was a tumultuous whirlwind of interactions between Humphrey, Belmont, and the school's headmaster. Ultimately, Humphrey was expelled just one month before graduating and was offered no option to repeat the year.

School was clearly a source of unhappiness for Humphrey, so his expulsion from Andover would come to be a welcome occurrence for him, especially because it effectively terminated his parents' delusional view that their son would grow up to be a surgeon. After failing to complete even the one year at Andover, they were finally forced to acknowledge that school was not the proper venue for their son. In this regard, the year at Andover was a sort of success for Humphrey.

Chapter 2: On His Own

"At 18, war was great stuff. Paris! French girls! Hot damn!...The war was a big joke. Death? What does death mean to a 17 year old?" – Humphrey Bogart

After his year ended prematurely at Andover, Maud secured her son a job working for a naval architect. Uninterested in this line of work, or in having his parents decide his profession, Humphrey lasted a very short time there; in fact, some people assert that he never actually worked there at all. In an act of youthful exuberance and rebellion against his parents, Bogart instead decided to enlist in the Navy.

Bogart in the Navy

For someone who had vehemently resisted authority all throughout his life, it may initially come as a surprise that he would choose to enlist in the Navy, which meant he would have to obey authority. However, Bogart knew that he loved ships, and he also wanted to travel overseas and explore the world. In the early summer of 1918, he enlisted and was stationed at the Naval Reserve Training Station in Pelham Bay, off the coast of New York.

While at Pelham Bay, Bogart was unable to progress through the ranks and eventually applied for a transfer to the Naval Aviation branch, but he was denied admission. In reality, Bogart's glamorous fantasies about World War I were ill-founded. By the time he enlisted, the Armistice had already been signed, and he eventually joined the USS *Leviathan*, where he spent 8 months transporting troops back and forth from overseas. It was the least glamorous naval job imaginable, but Bogart finally acquired a sense of discipline and commitment, and there is every indication that his experience there was vastly preferable to his time at Andover and Trinity.

Humphrey may also have received the scarred lip that became his trademark while serving on the *Leviathan*. The most common tale claims that a prisoner of war hit Bogart in the face with his handcuffs while being transferred to Kittery, Maine, but that story has not been verified and there are many conflicting reports, including one that asserts his lip was hit by a piece of shrapnel. Actor David Niven claimed Bogart told him his lip was scarred as a child and the Navy story was made up by movie studios to add to Bogart's persona. Either way, the scarred lip also contributed to Bogart's lisp.

In 1919, Bogart was transferred to the USS *Santa Oliva*, but he failed to show up for the boat's departure for Europe, a serious naval offense that earned him the label of Deserter. Bogart admitted to the transgression, but turning himself in to the authorities was not enough to overturn his punishment. He was forced to draw on more desperate measures. Relying on his family's connections with Franklin D. Roosevelt, who was then Assistant Secretary of the Navy, Humphrey contacted the future president. Taking pity on his family acquaintance, Roosevelt exercised his authority and had Bogart's punishment changed to Absent without Leave. For his actions, he was stationed in solitary confinement for three days, the standard punishment for going AWOL, but the lighter punishment allowed Bogart to be honorably discharged. Bogart was even given a medal for his efforts in the service.

After returning from the Navy, Bogart was still just 19 years old, and he still did not possess even a high school education. Making matters worse, his family's economic situation was in shambles. His father's addiction to morphine had become more severe, and he had begun to lose his mental acuity. In a bizarre move, his father had invested in a foolish business opportunity involving timber, losing the family fortune and falling massively into debt. As a last resort, Belmont was relegated to serving as a ship doctor. Nevertheless, Belmont's travails and the collapse of the family's wealth didn't particularly devastate Humphrey; outside of the family's summer home, he had always resented their upper class trimmings. Bogart had never cared for the pretentious ways the family's wealth had provided for the family, even though he had used money and connections to pull strings a few times himself.

Even if his father was unable to subsidize him, Belmont did use his influence to secure his son a job as a bond salesman. After this occupation proved unsuccessful, Humphrey called upon William Brady Sr., the father of his childhood friend. By this point, Brady had become immensely powerful and was looking to spread his empire from the theater to the motion picture industry. He had founded the motion picture company World Films, where he made a fortune capitalizing on the popularity of the seventh art. Brady offered Bogart a position in his office, where he was paid $35 per week, $5 more than he had made as a bond salesman.

Bogart committed himself to the job with greater diligence than any prior period in his life, and he was immediately successful. After just one month in the office, Humphrey was promoted to the role of production manager, a shift that earned him a salary increase to $50 per week. While with World Films, Bogart conducted a number of tasks, including arranging for props and paying the actors. Eventually, he even served as producer and director, and did screenwriting as well.

Although he enjoyed his time at World Films, Bogart was always more interested in acting. As the 1920s progressed, Bogart began appearing in theatrical productions in New York City. It was clear to everyone, including his reluctant parents, that Bogart was a natural actor; in one of his first performances, Belmont noted of his son, "The boy's good, isn't he?" Still, Bogart was unpolished enough at first that it was also apparent he had plenty of work to do yet.

Bogart was drawn to city life, and the acting lifestyle suited him perfectly. He had begun drinking while in high school, but acting allowed him to drink heavily without losing his job. Bogart spent ample time in speakeasies and became increasingly attached to drinking bourbon and smoking cigarettes. He would later quip, "The whole world is three drinks behind. If everyone in the world would take three drinks, we would have no trouble. If Stalin, Truman and everybody else in the world had three drinks right now, we'd all loosen up and we wouldn't need the United Nations."

Bogart had watched his parents drink heavily, but his own heavy drinking was likely due more to his youth and rebellious personality. The fact that Prohibition was just going into effect only encouraged Bogart to drink more. Bogart and William Brady Jr. became notorious for spending most of their nights at speakeasies in New York, and Bogart was able to partially fund his drinking by challenging bar patrons to chess games for $1 each. When he was strapped for money, the young man frequently managed to talk his way into having the owners put his drinks on a long-running tab. Bogart spent so much time at bars that he constantly fell asleep in them, and some contemporaries claimed his scarred lip came from a barroom brawl.

To Bogart's credit, the long nights and heavy drinking didn't stop him from securing relatively consistent acting opportunities. But Humphrey was repeatedly cast in roles that he found disagreeable, performing in what he would later refer to as "White Pants Willie" roles. Ironically, these stage roles represented the antithesis of the rugged characters he would later portray on film, and it seems his family background made it difficult for him to shed the soft, unmasculine roles he kept being assigned on stage.

Bogart may have thought his career was still less than satisfactory, but his personal life underwent significant developments during the 1920s. While acting in a performance of *Drifting* at the Playhouse Theatre in 1922, he met actress Helen Menken, who he would later marry on May 20, 1926 at the Gramercy Park Hotel in New York City.

Helen Menken

Their marriage was doomed from the start and would last roughly 18 months. Menken was 10 years older than him, and her domineering personality clashed with young Bogart's independent streak. The time he spent at bars made adultery much easier, and he admitted, "I had had enough women by the time I was 27 to know what I was looking for in a wife the next time I married."

Despite what he said, the second marriage didn't go much better. Following his divorce, Bogart met Mary Philips, another actress. Philips was closer in age to Bogart and could drink nearly as much as him, something that was actually considered an asset by her husband, but she was similar in many respects to Menken too, particularly her quick temper. Bogart and Philips had known each other since before he had married Menken, after they performed together in a production of *Nerves* at the Comedy Theatre in 1924. He and Mary would remain married for nearly a decade, but their marriage was hardly a happy one. Bogart was perpetually unfaithful and slept with many women, a dynamic that would continue until he met Lauren Bacall nearly two decades later. More noteworthy, the marriage between two strong-willed individuals reproduced the unhappy marital dynamic that had compromised his parents' own marriage. For whatever reason, Bogart's early marriages were filled with the same friction that had subsumed Belmont and Maud, and he was unable to adhere to the strict routines of domestic life.

Mary Philips

Bogart's career was less than ideal during the 1920s, but it was still possible for a stage actor to earn a decent living during most of the decade. However, this would change with the stock market crash and the onset of the Great Depression. Suddenly, the upper-middle class demographic that the industry had relied upon was gone, and stage actors were forced to search for new opportunities. Fortunately, the collapse of the theater coincided with the emergence of the Motion Picture industry, which by this time was in the process of converting to synchronized sound.

There were many reasons for the emergence of film and its ability to flourish even during the Great Depression. First, film had always marketed itself as a more democratic medium than theater; although film borrowed from theater, it also had roots in more traditionally working class forms of entertainment like the circus and the vaudeville stage. From an economic standpoint, movies were cheaper to attend, and even those who were strapped for money were able to save up and see at least one movie a week. Moreover, the inherent dreamlike quality of film, with spectators sitting in a dark movie house, afforded viewers a sense of escape that was not possible in the theater.

At first, Bogart was unsuccessful in finding consistent employment in the movies. He was able to secure minor roles in two Vitaphone shorts, *The Dancing Town* (1928) (which also starred Mary Philips) and *Broadway's Like That* (1930). In the first film, a 20-minute two-reel production, Bogart plays himself. Meanwhile, *Broadway's Like That* involves a girl finding out on the night before her marriage that her husband (played by Bogart) is already married. Despite these two roles, lasting employment evaded him, and Bogart grew increasingly depressed. He was trapped in an unhappy marriage and lacked consistent acting opportunities.

Finally, Bogart was hired by the Fox Film Cooperative in 1930, where he earned a lucrative salary of $750 per week, a substantial amount of money during the Great Depression. He began to appear in films on a continuous basis, but he also acted in the theater as well. He appeared in John Ford's early film *Up the River* (1930), during which he met then-unknown actor Spencer Tracy, who would later become one of his closest friends. The next year, he acted in *The Bad Sister*, playing a minor role in the film, which starred Bette Davis.

Spencer Tracy

However, after his contract with Fox expired, Bogart again found himself without work and he spiraled into a deep depression. For the next four years, he would alternate between theater and cinema, but he suffered from extended bouts of unemployment the entire time. Bogart continued to drink heavily, and conditions were made even worse when his parents separated and his father died. Belmont's death left Bogart with substantial debt, placing him in a position of outright economic desperation. One friend later recalled seeing Bogart drinking himself into a stupor at a low-scale bar in the city and saying to her friend, "Poor Humphrey, he's finally licked."

Chapter 3: Breakthrough

By 1934, Bogart's life had reached its nadir. He had incurred his father's debt, was involved in a loveless marriage, and could not find consistent employment. In light of these circumstances, it is worth asking exactly how Bogart was able to catapult himself to fame.

One answer is that the poverty he experienced throughout the latter part of the decade effectively shed his label as a spoiled youth. Bogart had always shunned the title, but after actually experiencing poverty, he was finally able to capture the essence of a hardened everyman. Additionally, the advent of sound cinema played an integral role in transforming Bogart's identity. If vestiges of the spoiled, bourgeois young adult remained in his appearance, they were swiftly counteracted by his throaty voice, which grew increasingly coarser through his persistent smoking habits. Bogart's appearance eventually became iconic, but his voice played at least an equal role in catapulting him to fame.

It was not until 1934 that Bogart earned his breakthrough role, and it was on the stage. While Bogart acted in the Broadway play *Invitation to Murder* at the Theatre Marque in 1934, stage producer Arthur Hopkins learned of his role. Bogart auditioned for a role in Hopkins' *The Petrified Forest* completely hungover and looking like he had just spent all night at a bar, which he had. But the scruffy look was exactly what Hopkins was looking for, so he decided to cast Bogart to play an escaped convict in the theatrical production of *The Petrified Forest*. Hopkins mentioned just how different Bogart looked compared to the previous roles he had performed, "When I saw the actor I was somewhat taken aback, for he was the one I never much admired. He was an antiquated juvenile who spent most of his stage life in white pants swinging a tennis racquet. He seemed as far from a cold-blooded killer as one could get, but the voice (dry and tired) persisted, and the voice was Mantee's."

The play enjoyed a long run, with 197 performances at the Broadhurst Theatre in New York City, and Bogart received critical acclaim for his realistic portrayal of a madman. His role was substantially different from the film roles that would make him famous. After all, he played a man with no moral compass and was celebrated for his ability to shock audiences, leaving viewers terrified by him rather than identifying with him. Bogart was well aware that it was his breakthrough role, claiming that the role "marked my deliverance from the ranks of the sleek, sybaritic, stiff-shirted, swallow-tailed 'smoothies' to which I seemed condemned to life."

The show's enduring run also led to *The Petrified Forest* receiving a film adaptation from Warner Brothers, but casting for the film adaptation was not as simple as transferring the actors from the stage to the screen because there were studio politics at work. Warner Brothers felt obligated to feature their premium talent; because of the play's success, the studio envisioned the film as a major box office hit and intended to deploy their most famous actors. During this period, every studio had a different niche that was aligned with a particular genre. MGM was renowned for its musicals, but Warner Brothers was associated with gangster and crime films. The studio's most notable actors were Edward G. Robinson, George Raft, James Cagney, and Paul Muni, and all of them were associated with the gangster genre. For the film version of *The Petrified Forest*, the studio had originally wanted Edward G. Robinson to play Bogart's role. Given their substantial differences in appearance and star image, it is easy to retroactively deride the studio for intending to cast Robinson, but at this time there were few actors in Hollywood with more renown, and audiences expected to watch a Warner Brothers film with at least one major gangster actor in it.

Nevertheless, Bogart was dejected after learning that he was not going to be included in the film. In an act of desperation, he contacted Leslie Howard, with whom he had starred in the play and who was also set to star in the film, and informed him of the news. Howard had been fond of Bogart in the play and contacted Jack Warner, after which Bogart was given the role.

Publicity still shot of Bogart in *The Petrified Forest*

The film version of *The Petrified Forest* (1936) proved to be an even greater career milestone for Bogart than the play had been, not because the film garnered any acclaim but because it solidified Bogart's place with the studio. He would remain with Warner Brothers for roughly the next 15 years. Beginning with a salary of $550 per week, he would keep rising through the studio's ranks until he became the highest-paid actor in Hollywood in 1946. Bogart terrified audiences in his role as Duke Mantee, the escaped convict who takes customers at a roadside diner hostage. The film is hardly remembered today, but it was a relatively significant production that starred Bette Davis in addition to the aforementioned Bogart and Leslie Howard.

Leslie Howard and Bette Davis

One of the more interesting developments that took place during the production of *The Petrified Forest* is that Jack Warner attempted to get Bogart to adopt a stage name, but he refused. Considering his ambivalence toward the name "Humphrey," it is surprising that Bogart did not adopt a new moniker, and there is no ready explanation as to why he kept the name. After all, the reasons why the studio suggested a name change were the same reasons why Bogart had always despised his first name: it was not masculine enough. It is possible that Bogart kept his name as an act of deference toward his mother, but he never spoke fondly of her and it doesn't seem likely that he would have felt any obligation toward her. Moreover, at this point in his career, Bogart held absolutely no leverage within the film industry, particularly considering the fact that he was only in the film because the leading star had forced the studio's hand. Perhaps the best explanation is that by 1936, Bogart was no longer young and it would have been too drastic a change for someone in the middle of his life.

In a sense, the rest of the decade would prove to be Bogart's most prolific period. He had not yet reached the popularity that he would later enjoy, but there was no busier period of his career. Over the course of his career, Bogart would act in over 80 films, and the vast majority of them came during the latter half of the 1930s. As a result, it is important to remember how substantially different the film industry was during the 1930s from how it is today. After an actor signed a contract with the studio, they effectively operated as indentured servants, appearing in an unlimited number of films at the discretion of the studio, who could drop them at any point in time. For this reason, from 1936-1940, Bogart averaged a film every two months, and it was not uncommon for him to appear in multiple films at once.

Bogart was typecast as a gangster villain, which ensured that he had constant work but also prevented him from becoming a star. He was a subordinate to actors like Robinson, Cagney, and Raft, who had been involved in the gangster genre for a longer period of time. Therefore, while the 1930s were the busiest phase of his career, being relegated to a narrow character type meant that he was unable to truly display his acting talents. Bogart claimed, "I can't get in a mild discussion without turning it into an argument. There must be something in my tone of voice, or this arrogant face—something that antagonizes everybody. Nobody likes me on sight. I suppose that's why I'm cast as the heavy."

Many of the films Bogart acted in from 1936-1940 are largely forgotten, but by the end of the decade he had appeared in some of the most acclaimed films in the genre. In 1938, he appeared in *Angels with Dirty Faces* alongside James Cagney, and in 1939 he held substantial roles in *The Roaring Twenties* (also with Cagney) and *Dark Victory* (with Bette Davis). In these films, there is no mistaking that Bogart was not the leading star, but he became a more recognizable face, albeit one who was forced to assimilate within the character norms of the gangster genre.

Bogart and Cagney in *The Roaring Twenties*

During the latter half of the 1930s, major changes occurred within Bogart's personal life as well. In 1937, he divorced Mary Philips, ending their perpetually tumultuous relationship. The following year, he married Mayo Methot, another stage actress whose heavy drinking was coupled with a fiery temper. Methot was yet another woman with a personality like his mother's, but Bogart's third wife had an even more erratic temper. While at times she could be quite charming, she was also prone to immense bouts of anger and was often abusive to Bogart. Over the course of their marriage, she committed a number of incidents that in most any other marriage would have been grounds for divorce, including stabbing Bogart, threatening to kill him, and setting their house on fire. Bogart could be just as abusive, and one friend quipped, "The Bogart-Methot marriage was the sequel to the Civil War". Even the press was well aware of the marital troubles, dubbing them "the battling Bogarts", and their household also became known as Sluggy Hollow. It was one of the few places Bogart and Methot could go after awhile, because places started to ban them to avoid public fighting.

Mayo Methot would drink herself to death by the age of 47.

It is difficult to determine why Bogart was drawn to such women, but some of it may have stemmed from his inherent dislike for the bourgeois nuclear family. With nontraditional wives, Bogart prevented his life from falling into the staid rhythms of the upper crust lifestyle he had always shunned. For his part, Bogart often played it off, claiming that he liked having a jealous wife and asserting, "I wouldn't give you two cents for a dame without a temper." Besides, Bogart also had a reputation for being prickly, to the extent that plenty of people in Hollywood went out of their way to avoid him, even as the media lapped up his candid statements. He explained, "All over Hollywood, they are continually advising me, 'Oh, you mustn't say that. That will get you in a lot of trouble,' when I remark that some picture or writer or director or producer is no good. I don't get it. If he isn't any good, why can't you say so? If more people would mention it, pretty soon it might start having some effect."

Chapter 4: Hollywood Stardom

"An actor needs something to stabilize his personality, something to nail down what he really is, not what he is currently pretending to be." – Humphrey Bogart

It would not be until 1940 that Bogart caught his big break. That year, he was given a prominent starring role in *They Drive by Night* (1940). Directed by Raoul Walsh, the film cast Bogart and George Raft as brothers who operate their own truck-driving business. The film marked a dramatic shift away from gangster films and toward a more socially realistic style that portrayed Bogart with greater pathos than his earlier roles. One scene in particular, in which he falls asleep behind the wheel while transporting an overloaded truck filled with cargo, is especially suspenseful and conveys Bogart and Raft as everymen forced to go to extremes to make ends meet. Although the film's chief romantic grouping is between George Raft and Ida Lupino, Bogart serves as a sympathetic co-star rather than simply acting as a foil for the leading actor, and the role is substantially more significant than his earlier ones. With *They Drive By Night*, audiences finally became exposed to a more sensitive side to the actor, a dimension that would obviously emerge even further as the decade progressed.

Bogart's next film was even more significant. After starring with him in *They Drive By Night*, Ida Lupino cast him in *High Sierra* (1941), another film that deployed elements of the gangster genre while portraying its heroes in a sympathetic light. In the film, Bogart plays a man who has just been released from prison (a motif that recalls his role in *The Petrified Forest*) and is forced into reentering the mob since they engineered his release. He is then asked to take part in a major heist and acquiesces out of desperation. The heist fails, and Bogart falls in love with Ida Lupino's character, ultimately sacrificing himself to save her at the film's conclusion. The tragic hero is a trope of the gangster film, and in this regard Bogart's death would appear to make the film a classic example of the genre. However, in most gangster films the death of the criminal signals the victory of justice, whereas in *High Sierra*, Bogart's death elicits sympathy from the viewer. Consequently, *High Sierra* had a nuanced portrayal of morality, in which the viewer is forced to think outside traditional notions of good vs. evil and consider the obstacles facing a convict who is relegated to serving in the mob even after he has outgrown it and is ready to reform.

High Sierra was not a box office sensation, but it did show Hollywood that Bogart was capable of playing a leading role. Moreover, his experience acting in the film had placed Bogart in contact with John Huston, who had written the script for Lupino's film. Although he would later enjoy a famously prolific career, at the start of the 1940s Huston had not yet directed. Fortunately for him, he had the opportunity to direct *The Maltese Falcon*, a film based on a superlative pulp fiction novel by Dashiell Hammett and for which he wrote the script. Huston knew that he wanted Bogart for the starring role of Sam Spade, a world-weary detective who cannot trust anyone and is forced to solve a mystery in which nothing is as it appears.

Huston

With *The Maltese Falcon*, Bogart fully portrayed the screen persona for which he would become an icon. Although Bogart's Sam Spade is a member of law enforcement, he also defies conventional standards of behavior and morality, as evidenced by his famous quote, "I stick my neck out for nobody." In particular, his disregard for chivalry enables him to suspect that the leading female character (played by Mary Astor) is the individual responsible for the murders that take place. In his essay "The Hero", Manny Farber offers a perceptive analysis of Bogart's character and the complications associated with the star persona:

> "The hero played by Mr. Bogart, which grew out of the gangster film and Dashiell Hammett detective novels, looks as though he had been knocked around daily and had spent his week-ends drinking himself unconscious in the back rooms of saloons. His favorite grimace is a hateful pulling back of the lips from his clenched teeth, and when his lips are together he seems to be holding back a mouthful of blood. The people he acts badly toward and spends his movie life exposing as fools are mainly underworld characters, like gangsters, cabaret owners and dance-hall girls (and the mayor whom he puts into office every year). Everything he does carries conflicting quantities of hatred and love, as though he felt you had just stepped on his face but hadn't meant it….He is the soured half of the American dream, which believes that if you are good, honest and persevering you will win the kewpie doll".

Bogart's role renewed the focus on psychological realism that was initiated in *They Drive By Night* and *High Sierra*. While the traditional law enforcement character works to maintain the façade of the American Dream, there is the sense that Bogart's character has undergone too much suffering to subscribe to such an idea. It is as though he sees the world as it is rather than how it should be. Bogart was especially proud of the film, calling it "practically a masterpiece" and adding, "I don't have many things I'm proud of...but that's one."

Trailer image from *The Maltese Falcon*

After the success of *The Maltese Falcon*, Bogart's stock had soared, and he was now nearly on top of Hollywood. Another helpful factor for him was that the United States was fighting World War II, and many of the leading actors were fighting overseas. While actors such as Kirk Douglas, Douglas Fairbanks, and Henry Fonda were gone abroad, Bogart was too old to join in the war effort, and he took full advantage of his opportunity. At the same time, Bogart provided a challenge for the Warner Brothers studio because he offered more versatility. Stars like Edward G. Robinson, James Cagney, and George Raft were all major box office attractions, but the studio basically reprised the well-worn formula of casting them as psychotic villains. Meanwhile, with Bogart the studio had a more valuable commodity, but also one who appeared too smart to believably cast as the flawed villain.

Bogart's next film, *Casablanca* (1942), would be one of the more ambitious films for Warner Brothers, as well as a major financial commitment. Hailed as an all-time classic, *Casablanca* was recognized as the number two Hollywood film of the 20th century by the American Film Institute when they comprised their list at the century's conclusion. There are many reasons for the film's continued acclaim, and chief among these was that the film perceptively captured the nation's ambivalence about going to war while at the same time recognizing that war was unavoidable.

Trailer screenshot of Bogart and Ingrid Bergman in *Casablanca*

As mentioned earlier, Warner Brothers was not only recognized for its gangster films but also for its social realist slant, and on the surface *Casablanca* would appear to clash with this framework. There is no on-location shooting, and the interiors are easily discernible as studio sets. The film does not portray the gritty scenes of working-class life that characterized *They Drive By Night* or *High Sierra* either. Bogart played the role of Rick Blaine, an American expatriate operating a nightclub in Casablanca. After coming into possession of two tickets that grant permission to leave the country, he initially intends to take his ex-lover with him (Ilsa, played by Ingrid Bergman), but instead he eventually decides to give the tickets to Ilsa and her husband Victor (played by Paul Henreid), who the police want to arrest on specious charges. By refusing to leave the country with his beloved Ilsa, the film forgoes the classical narrative trope of the protagonist and heroine uniting at the film's conclusion. Instead, Bogart's character ends the film in much the same way as in *Maltese Falcon*: alone and world-weary.

The plot borrows heavily from other genres. First, the reconciliation between Rick and Ilsa superficially resembles the comedy-of-remarriage films that involved a romantic couple reuniting. Meanwhile, the cat-and-mouse game between the virtuous Laszlo and the villainous

Vichy Captain Louis Renault recalls the Warner Brothers gangster films of the preceding decade. As Manny Farber writes, "Before allied troops made it more famous, Casablanca served as a jumping-off spot to America for many of Europe's refugees—therefore a timely place to carry on Warner's favorite cops and robbers." Still, while it borrows from many different genres, the film derives its power through its ability to avoid the good vs. evil dichotomy that characterizes most gangster films. The zaniness of gangster films and screwball comedies is eschewed, and the film pours on as much emotion as possible.

One of the confounding (and appealing) aspects of *Casablanca* is that it achieves a level of psychological realism that few films have captured, yet it does so while adhering to an immense number of clichés. According to Umberto Eco, it is precisely through invoking an endless supply of clichés that *Casablanca* acquires its power: "But precisely because all the archetypes are here, precisely because *Casablanca* cites countless other films, and each actor plays a part played on other occasions, the resonance of intertextuality plays upon the spectator…When all the archetypes burst in shamelessly, we reach Homeric depths. Two clichés make us laugh. A hundred clichés move us."

The effect described by Eco has become even more pronounced in the years following the film's release. When the film is now screened, the audience is not only moved by the emotions specific to the film itself but also by the way in which archetypal scenes in the film (the famous "Play it Again, Sam" musical number, for example) have become embedded within American culture. For this reason, there is arguably no film that is more beloved in America, and the film completed the seemingly impossible task of outdoing *The Maltese Falcon* in terms of building Bogart's legend.

For *Casablanca*, Bogart was nominated for an Oscar, but he didn't win it. Bogart claimed he was fine with that, stating, "The best way to survive an Oscar is to never try to win another one. You've seen what happens to some Oscar winners. They spend the rest of their lives turning down scripts while searching for the great role to win another one. Hell, I hope I'm never even nominated again. It's meat-and-potato roles for me from now on."

Following *Casablanca*, Bogart finally broke his streak of successes, acting in four films of relatively minor acclaim. His next significant film was *To Have and Have Not* (1944), a film that was directed by Howard Hawks and co-starred his future wife, Lauren Bacall. Despite an age difference of nearly 25 years, Bogart and Bacall were instantly smitten with each other, and Hawks would claim "Bogie fell in love with the character she played, so she had to keep playing it the rest of her life."

Like many films of the 1930s and 1940s, the film was adapted from a book by a major literary giant, this one having been borrowed from Ernest Hemingway's novel of the same title. Even so, it would be misleading to simply declare Hawks' film as a straight adaptation of the famous book, because Hawks and Bogart applied their own trademarks to the film.

Bacall

Any analysis of Bogart's filmography must not only examine the actor himself but also the directors with whom he worked. To this end, it is important to note that the films Bogart acted in with John Huston are vastly different from those with Howard Hawks, reflecting the extent to which Bogart cannot be considered the sole author of his films. Where Huston's films are highly stylized and filmed with violence and virtuoso camera movements, Hawks' films are lighter in tone and deploy comedy to dramatic effect. In *To Have and Have Not*, Bogart and Bacall star as lovers who meet in Martinique after the collapse of France in 1940. Bogart plays a fishing-boat captain who transports members of the French resistance. While stationed in Martinique, he meets Marie "Slim" Browning (played by Bacall), with whom he falls in love.

Unlike *Casablanca*, Bogart ends the film with the love of his life, as it is implied that he and Bacall will spend the rest of their lives together. Another difference between *To Have and Have Not* and the earlier films is that Bogart displays a lighter side of his personality, referring to Bacall by the nickname "Slim" and engaging in courtship banter with her (most famously, when Bacall's character asks him if he knows how to whistle) that is reminiscent of the screwball comedy. In a sense, Hawks cast Bogart in the most desirable way imaginable; Bogart's role is playful enough to assume the role of a traditional leading man, but also rugged enough as a sailor and hard drinker that his masculinity is also on full display.

Moreover, despite the massive age difference between Bogart and Bacall, their witty repartee reflects a dynamic in which they treat each other as equals. In fact, Bacall is the character who more aggressively pursues the other, and her physique is more athletic and domineering as well. To this end, one of the most notable aspects of the film is the way in which Bogart is able to withhold his masculinity while also treating Bacall as his equal rather than his subordinate. Part of this was a conscious effort on Bogart's part to let Bacall steal scenes. The dynamic between the two of them was so appealing to audiences in *To Have and Have Not* that parts of their second film together, the classic *The Big Sleep*, were reshot to be racier.

The flirtatious dialogue of *To Have and Have Not* is not only characteristic of Hawks' style but also particularly apropos in light of the fact that Bogart and Bacall were also in love with one another off the film set. Despite still being married to Mayo Methot, Bogart and Bacall continued to date even after the film's production. Their courtship was not well-received by Howard Hawks, who was also in love with Bacall despite being married himself. Finally, Bogart and Methot divorced each other in 1945, something that was well overdue, and a few weeks later he married Bacall. Despite being just 45 years old, Bacall was his fourth wife. They moved into a gigantic white brick mansion in the posh neighborhood of Holmby Hills, California, and Bogart was happily married for the first time in his life.

Working with Hawks proved to be a wise move, and despite their conflict over their shared love interest, the Bogart, Hawks and Bacall triumvirate reunited once again for *The Big Sleep* (1946). Adapted from a novel by Raymond Chandler, the plot borrows elements from *The Maltese Falcon*. Bogart again played a detective (Philip Marlowe), and again he is non-committal. Nevertheless, there are significant differences between the two films, extending beyond the aesthetic tendencies of the two directors. While the plot of *The Maltese Falcon* is slow and protracted, *The Big Sleep* progresses at a breakneck speed that makes it difficult for viewers to keep track of the plot developments. Bogart's Philip Marlowe saves Bacall's character, Vivian, from being prosecuted for a murder she did not commit. At the same time, Vivian is the daughter of Bogart's client, which also serves as a reminder of the age discrepancy between Bogart and his much younger wife. The film concentrates on the romance between Bogart and Bacall to the extent that the murder plot becomes almost trivial, and in this vein, Pauline Kael notes that "sophisticated sex talk became the link for the movie, and the incidents and talk were so entertaining that audiences didn't care about the solution of the murder plot." In fact, one legend claimed that Raymond Chandler, the man who wrote the novel, couldn't answer who killed the limousine driver.

In the end, the film was another enormous success, and Humphrey Bogart was now the highest paid actor in Hollywood, commanding an unparalleled salary of $460,000. Furthermore, he commanded greater leverage in deciding on the films he appeared in. After appearing in three minor films, his next significant film was *Dark Passage* (1947), in which he plays the role of Vincent Parry, a man who has been convicted of murdering his wife and who subsequently escapes from the San Quentin Prison through a delivery truck. After meeting Irene Jansen (Bacall), Vincent falls in love with her, and they make plans to escape to South America together. It is easy to see why Bogart might have been attracted to take on the role, as there were similar plot elements to his earlier films. The escaped convict role recalls Bogart's character from *The Petrified Forest*, while the delivery truck calls to mind scenes from *They Drive By Night*. Ultimately, the film is above all a failed romance like *High Sierra*, as the romantic union between Bogart and Bacall will almost certainly be disrupted when Bogart is captured.

After the polished, fast-paced films with Hawks, it might seem surprising that Bogart would return to the grittiness of his earliest films, and in that regard *Dark Passage* is a somewhat perplexing film. At the same time, it is worth noting that Bogart had always preferred the dramatic style of John Huston over the zaniness of Howard Hawks. For this reason, it should come as no surprise that Huston would direct three of Humphrey's final films, all of which rank among the actor's most famous.

After *Dark Passage*, Bogart returned to Huston and appeared in *The Treasure of the Sierra Madre* (1948). It had been seven years since Bogart and Huston had joined forces in *The Maltese Falcon*, and now they were both giants in Hollywood. In light of this, it may come as a surprise that *The Treasure of the Sierra Madre* does not have the polish of the earlier film, but similar to *Dark Passage*, Bogart draws from the manic energy that had characterized his earliest films. In the film, he plays Dobbs, a man who goes to the Sierra Madre Mountains in Mexico with a friend to look for gold. Although he finds an ample amount of gold, he is consumed by paranoia and later killed. The film's methodical pace raises suspense in a manner similar to *The Maltese Falcon*, but the two films are quite different. While the earlier film featured Bogart in the smartest role, the later film casts him as someone who is psychologically weak enough to let himself become overrun with irrational fear. Consequently, much of the film's success depends on whether the viewer is able to convincingly accept Bogart as capable of such mental instability. Not surprisingly, the film is more divisive than Bogart's other acclaimed works, since it was a daring departure away from the traditional Hollywood narrative structured around the formation of the romantic couple.

Publicity still from *Treasure of the Sierra Madre*

The final film Bogart appeared in with Warner Brothers was *Key Largo* (1948), another film directed by John Huston. He played Frank McCloud, who had been a Major in World War Two. McCloud arrives at the Hotel Largo in Southern Florida, where he falls in love with Nora Temple (Lauren Bacall), the hotel owner's daughter. Nora's husband died in Italy during World War II, and it is revealed that Frank knew him during the war.

Key Largo is a methodical suspense film in the manner of *The Maltese Falcon*. As the plot unfolds, Frank becomes aware that the other guests in the hotel are affiliated with gangster Johnny Rocco (Edward G. Robinson), who also stays at the hotel but refuses to see anyone. Rocco wishes to return to Cuba, where he had been exiled, and he takes Frank, Nora, and her father hostage and orders Frank to transport him and his associates to the island nation. Ultimately, Frank acquiesces but kills them while traveling on the boat.

Key Largo is very much a post-war film that addresses the horrors of killing (it is ambiguous how many men Frank has killed, but the experience has left him weary), as well as the difficulties associated with losing a spouse in the war. However, the film is also remarkably similar to *The Maltese Falcon* in its slow pacing and casting of Bogart in a role where he is outnumbered by villains whom he ultimately defeats. Additionally, the film serves as a commentary on the fall of the gangster genre, a motif that makes the film feel as though it were made a decade earlier. By defeating Johnny Rocco, who is played by an actor who had dominated Bogart early in his career, Bogart effectively usurps his early gangster roles and turns the tables on the subservient role he had played throughout the 1930s.

Bogart and Bacall in *Key Largo*

In addition to becoming more involved in selecting his film roles, Bogart also started his own production company, called Santana Productions. Bogart's decision was met with hostility by Jack Warner; after all, the late 1940s and the 1950s were a difficult time for Hollywood studios because the emergence of television limited the box office totals and fewer major stars were willing to attach themselves to studios. For Bogart though, the idea of operating his own production company was understandably appealing. For years, he had served as a cog in the Warner Brothers machine, taking on many roles he didn't care about. Starting Santana Productions was also in line with the independent-minded characters he portrayed.

During the late 1940s, Bogart also became more politically active. He had always shunned the conservative politics of his parents, even after becoming incredibly rich himself, and the liberal ideology prevalent in Hollywood at the time cohered with his own views. Humphrey advocated on behalf of his colleagues in defense against the House Committee on Un-American Activities, which grew powerful during the Red Scare in the 1950s. At the same time, Bogart was quick to distance himself from the Hollywood Ten, a move that was instrumental in preserving his good name within the industry. He wrote an article for *Photoplay* in which he took pains to point out, "I'm no communist."

The late 1940s also saw Bogart become a father for the first time. In 1949, Bacall gave birth to Stephen Humphrey Bogart. In 1952, they would have a daughter, Leslie Howard, who was named after Bogart's co-star in *The Petrified Forest*. By the standards of the time period, he was particularly old to raise children, and the decision to start a family reflects his satisfaction with his marriage and position of security within the film industry.

Chapter 5: Final Years

"When I chose to be an actor I knew I'd be working in the spotlight. I also knew that the higher a monkey climbs the more you can see of his tail. So I keep my sense of humor and go right on leading my life and enjoying it. I wouldn't trade places with anybody." – Humphrey Bogart

In 1949, Bogart's first films from Santana Productions were released: *Knock on Any Door* (1949) and *Tokyo Joe* (1949). They were followed in 1950 with *Chain Lightning* (1950). These were all relatively unremarkable films, but *Knock on Any Door* put Bogart into contact with Nicholas Ray, a precocious young director who blended the punchy style of John Huston with more expressive formal techniques. Huston was an "actor's director" who favored a motionless camera, while Ray was fond of experimenting with camera angles, heights, and, in his later films, color. Satisfied with the experience of *Knock on Any Door*, Bogart's would again appear in a film directed by Ray, and the film, *In a Lonely Place*, stands as one of his most renowned performances. Bogart's character, Dixon Steele, is an alcoholic writer with a tendency toward acting abusive. He is accused of committing a murder he did not commit, but his erratic behavior draws suspicion from those around him, including his girlfriend. The film juxtaposes scenes in which Steele behaves endearingly with those in which he is abusive. Even though he is eventually exonerated from the crime, his behavior ultimately ruins his relationship.

In a Lonely Place harkens back to the pre-Bacall films in that the film does not end with romantic union. Instead, the film explores the effects of a violent temper both professionally (affecting Steele's productivity as a writer) and personally (he cannot sustain a relationship.) Bogart's character resonates as someone with a utopian desire to escape the constraints of his own paranoia and the conflicts (most notably, the murder accusation that has been leveled towards him) that are imposed on him from the outside world. It sounds somewhat autobiographical too, something actress Louise Brooks picked up on in noting, "[H]e played one fascinatingly complex character…in a film whose title perfectly defined Humphrey's own isolation among people. *In a Lonely Place* gave him a role that he could play with complexity because the film character's, the screenwriter's, pride in his art, his selfishness, his drunkenness, his lack of energy, stabbed with lightning strokes of violence, were shared equally by the real Bogart."

The duality between Bogart's calm and angry temperaments in the film corresponds with Richard Schickel's belief that beneath his gruff façade, Bogart always had a romantic side that was underexplored in his films. Schickel wrote, "In many of these pictures he was woefully miscast as a 'tough guy,' rather than what he was—a romantic hiding his true nature under a gruff and sardonic shell." Certainly, the dichotomy that Schickel sees between the hardened, tough individual and the sweet romantic is on display with *In a Lonely Place*, but it is ultimately Bogart's violent side that overcomes him in the film.

Still photo from *In a Lonely Place*

After *In a Lonely Place*, Bogart teamed up with John Huston one last time, in a film that was not produced by Santana Productions but instead by United Artists, a studio that had been founded roughly three decades before by a group of actors that included Charlie Chaplin. The ambitious film, *The African Queen* (1951), was the first Technicolor film in which Bogart appeared and featured him alongside Katherine Hepburn. The plot involved sinking a German gunboat on the rivers of German-controlled East Africa during World War I. Bogart plays Canadian Charlie Allnut, while Hepburn's character is Rose Sayer, a British missionary. Over the course of the film, they become romantic while also managing to sink the German boat through a plot engineered by Rose.

More than *In a Lonely Place*, *The African Queen* conveys Bogart's romantic side. In fact, the plot line is based around Charlie shedding his tough exterior. By collectively sinking the German boat, the film displays the romantic belief that love between two people can solve any obstacle. The film builds on the romantic side of Bogart that had emerged with through *In a Lonely Place*. Hepburn and Bogart were an interesting pairing too, since she had spent much of her career appearing in screwball comedy films and he had acted in gangster films. They were thus equals and opposites at the same time, two individuals who finally united at a time in which they were beginning to grow old in front of the camera. Consequently, *The African Queen* contains an unusual balance between being an action film on the one hand (shot on location in Africa), while also a sentimental romance between two aging stars.

Hepburn and Bogart in *The African Queen*

The African Queen was a major success for Bogart, and he was awarded his first Academy Award for that performance. However, the film's production was exhaustive and took its toll on the actors. The crew lived on canned food and became ravaged by disease. Hepburn had serious difficulties with the conditions. Nevertheless, the setting on the water rekindled Bogart's love for boats, and he bought a large boat upon returning to the United States. The boat immediately became an integral part of his lifestyle, and he went on short trips nearly every day, balancing work with play in his own singular style.

After *The African Queen*, the next major film in which Bogart appeared was *The Barefoot Contessa*, directed by Joseph Mankiewicz and co-starring Ava Gardner. The film built on the autobiographical bent of *In a Lonely Place*, again casting Humphrey as an artist. He plays Harry Dawes, a film writer and director who works for an oppressive producer. Dawes directs Maria (played by Gardner), and the conflict involves Maria's discontent with being pregnant. In the end, the film is a tragedy, and Dawes is unable to prevent Maria from being killed. As with *In a Lonely Place*, Bogart is an unlikely choice to play the part of an artist. After all, it is difficult to envision Sam Spade or Philip Marlowe watching a movie, let alone writing or directing one. Even so, it is also true that even in his "tough guy" roles, Bogart has a dignified face and an articulate manner of speaking. Critic Stefan Kanfer noted that no matter how far he tried to dissociate himself from his parents, Bogart was never able to full cast aside vestiges of his bourgeois upbringing. He wrote:

> "For all his rebellions against Maud and Belmont, for all his drunken sprees and surly postures, Humphrey could not escape the central fact of his life. He was the scion of straightlaced parents whose roots were in another time. Their

customs and attitudes may have become outmoded, but they were deeply ingrained in their son no matter how hard he tried to escape them. They showed in his upright carriage and in his careful manner of speaking, in his courtesy to women and his frank dealing with men."

In many respects, Bogart was the quintessential modern hero, exhibiting a sometimes precarious balance between desirable and detrimental qualities. However, roles such as *The Barefoot Contessa* attest to the validity of Kanfer's claim. While he still assumes the world-weary feel of his earlier films, he also exudes an eloquence that recalls his privileged upbringing.

Also in 1954, Bogart appeared in the big-budget film *The Caine Mutiny*. In the film, which was Bogart's last major box-office success, he plays Lieutenant Commander Phillip Queeg, a disciplinarian who takes control over the eponymous World War II minesweeper. Queeg's harsh conduct forms the basis for the narrative's conflict, which centers on whether he is insane. Despite the obvious plot differences, Bogart's performance resembles that of *In a Lonely Place* through the instances of unrestrained (and psychotic) rage. Again, the film eschews the romantic grouping characteristic of classical Hollywood narration, as Bogart is relegated to a psychologically disturbed role that gestures to his early gangster performances for Warner Brothers. Still, it is worth noting that Bogart had eagerly sought out the role, demonstrating how he preferred performances that were psychologically unsettling and deviated from the standards for a Hollywood leading man.

The final two years of Bogart's career did not contain any legendary performances. In 1955, he sold his stake in Santana Productions for over $1 million, and he began to develop an even higher profile social life, something largely attributable to Bacall's more outgoing nature. Bogart and Bacall were founding members of the Rat Pack along with Frank Sinatra and a select group of other entertainers. The group would rise to fame after Bogart's death, highlighted by the film *Ocean's Eleven* (1960), and they developed a legacy of hard drinking and easy living.

Dean Martin and Frank Sinatra were both part of the Rat Pack

Bogart's last film was *The Harder They Fall* (1956), directed by Mark Robson. A notable director in his own right, Robson specialized in social realist films during the 1940s, and his style would have been an ideal match for a younger Bogart. In *The Harder They Fall*, Humphrey plays Eddie Willis, an impoverished sportswriter who becomes involved in fixing boxing matches and eventually becomes ashamed and publicizes the seedy injustices of the sports gambling industry.

The Harder They Fall was particularly difficult for Bogart, as he had become quite ill by the time the film was made. Always a heavy bourbon drinker and cigarette smoker, he developed cancer of the esophagus, the effects of which were worsened by the fact that he refused to see a doctor until January of 1956. By this point, the cancer had rapidly progressed, and Bogart's health went into swift decline. In March 1956, he had his esophagus, two lymph nodes, and a rib removed.

Unable to make any more films, his life and career ended in concert. Instead of making any additional films during that year, 1956 was spent saying farewells to his family and acquaintances. He took his poor health in stride, and even had his dumbwaiter custom designed so that he could ride in a wheelchair up and down to get around: "Put me in the dumbwaiter and I'll ride down to the first floor in style."

Bogart lasted for one year after his diagnosis, finally passing away on January 14, 1957. By then, his 57 year old body had withered to just 80 pounds. Huston gave the eulogy at Bogart's family and said:

> "Bogie's hospitality went far beyond food and drink. He fed a guest's spirit as was well as his body, plied him with good will until he became drunk in the heart as well as his legs…Himself, he never took too seriously—his work most seriously. He regarded the somewhat gaudy figure of Bogart, the star, with an amused cynicism; Bogart, the actor, he held in deep respect...In each of the fountains at Versailles there is a pike which keeps all the carp active; otherwise they would grow overfat and die. Bogie took rare delight in performing a similar duty in the fountains of Hollywood. Yet his victims seldom bore him any malice, and when they did, not for long. His shafts were fashioned only to stick into the outer layer of complacency, and not to penetrate through to the regions of the spirit where real injuries are done...He is quite irreplaceable. There will never be another like him."

Bogart died a premature death, just three years after being nominated for an Academy Award in *The Caine Mutiny*, but it is worth considering whether his career would have remained successful. By the mid-1950s, Bogart's tough, unsentimental acting style was becoming outdated by a more sensitive acting style, a development attributable to the popularity of the Actors Studio headed by Lee Strasberg in New York City. While Bogart displayed little emotion, actors like Marlon Brando and James Dean won audiences over with sweeping portrayals of sensitive, disturbed characters. Had Bogart's career continued, he almost certainly would have continued to find consistent employment, but it is likely that his days as a leading man were coming to an end, regardless of his cancer.

Bogart's legacy has only grown in size since his death, and today it extends well beyond his iconic character type and roles in films like *The Maltese Falcon*, *Casablanca*, and *Key Largo*. While those movies inextricably linked with the crime genre as a whole, Bogart's subsequent characters (from the 1940s onward) behaved with honor but also an understanding that traditional views of morality were inadequate in the context of modern life. This helped solidify Bogart as an iconic modern hero who not only behaves virtuously but does so in an approachable, psychologically realistic manner that understands the difficulties of life. In his pseudo-obituary on Bogart, Andre Bazin describes Bogart thusly: "Humphrey Bogart was a modern hero. The period film—the historical romance or pirate story—didn't suit him. He was the starter at the race, the man who had a revolver with only one bullet, the guy in the felt hat that he could flick a finger with to express anger or gaiety." This description in particular, treating anger and joy as twin emotions, reflects the monumental effect that he had on audiences.

In a similar vein, Bogart and his roles continue to be relevant today because of the individualistic nature that his characters had. As actor Rod Steiger put it, "Bogart has endured because in our society the family unit has gone to pieces. And here you had a guy about whom there was no doubt. There is no doubt that he is the leader. There is no doubt that he is the strong one. There is no doubt with this man that he can handle himself, that he can protect the family. This is all unconscious, but with Bogart you are secure, you never doubt that he will take care of things." This also extended to the man himself, as friend and biographer Nathaniel Benchley wrote of him, "He achieved class through his integrity and his devotion to what he thought was right. He believed in being direct, simple, and honest, all on his own terms, and this ruffled some people and endeared him to others."

Ultimately, Bogart showed people how to respond in a modern way to a modern world, and that even an ordinary man can navigate the challenges of life.

Bibliography

Bazin, Andre. "A Portrait of Humphrey Bogart." *The Films of My Life*. Cambridge: Da Capo Press, 1994.

Brooks, Louise. "Humphrey & Bogey." *Sight and Sound* 36.1 (Winter 1967). Accessed from http://www.psykickgirl.com/lulu/bogey.html.

Dyer, Richard. *Stars*. London: BFI, 1986.

Eco, Umberto. "Casablanca, or, The Cliches are Having a Ball," *Signs of Life in the U.S.A.: Readings on Popular Culture for Writers*, Eds. Sonia Maasik and Jack Solomon, Boston: Bedford Books, 1994, 260-264.

Farber, Manny. *Farber on Film: The Complete Film Writings of Manny Farber*. Ed. Robert Polito. New York: Library of America, 2009.

Gledhill, Christina. "Signs of Melodrama." *Stardom: Industry of Desire*. Ed. Christine Gledhill. New York: Routledge Press, 1991.

Kael, Pauline. "About Comic-Strip Style, from a Sense of Disproportion." *For Keeps: 30 Years at the Movies*. 103-105.

Kanfer, Stefan. *Tough Without a Gun: The Extraordinary Life and Afterlife of Humphrey Bogart*. New York: Random House, 2011.

McArthur, Colin. *Underworld, USA*. London: Secker & Warburg, 1972.

Meyers, Jeffrey. *Bogart: A Life in Hollywood*. London: Deutsch, 1997.

Porter, Darwin. *The Secret Life of Humphrey Bogart: The Early Years (1899-1931)*. New York: Blood Moon Productions, 2003.

Schickel, Richard. *Bogie: A Celebration of the Life and Films of Humphrey Bogart*. London: Aurum Press Ltd., 2006.

Thomson, David. *Humphrey Bogart*. New York: Faber and Faber, 2009.

Cary Grant

Chapter 1: Rejection and Rebellion

"My formula for living is quite simple. I get up in the morning and I go to bed at night. In between, I occupy myself as best I can." – Cary Grant

The first clue that Cary Grant was not born into a life of wealth and luxury can quickly be deduced due to the fact that was not his real name. On January 18, 1904, he was born Archibald Alexander Leach, and while his screen name connotes a sense of suave respectability, Archie Leach is a name that conjures up images of a working class street-tough. Indeed, he was born in the outskirts of Bristol, England, the second child of Elsie Marie Kingdon and Elias James Leach. Although Archie was born four years after his brother John, his older sibling died before his birth, so he was ultimately raised as an only child. John's death had an indelible effect on Archie's own upbringing because his mother was never able to recover emotionally from the death of her first child.

A statue of Cary Grant in Bristol today

The fact that Archie had no younger siblings hints at the turmoil that existed between Elias and Elsie, who were largely incompatible even before their first child died. First, the two came from different social classes and mores; while Elsie was not born into a wealth family, her father was a shipwright who could provide a comfortable existence for the family. Conversely, Elias was the son of a potter, a profession squarely situated in the working class (Eliot). In addition to their different backgrounds, Elias was a full six years older than her, and while this was not especially unusual for the era, the age difference reflected very different motives for marrying. While Elsie married with the full intention of raising a family and being supported by her husband, Elias welcomed the financial security of marrying a woman from a higher social class. In effect, they each got married in the interest of acquiring security that their spouse was ultimately incapable of providing. Given that he was already 27 years old by the time they married, Elias had already carried on a long string of affairs, and the opportunity to marry (particularly to someone from such a respectable family) was attractive: Biographer Marc Eliot explains, "By the time he walked his twenty-one-year-old wife down the aisle, he had already played through the field of Bristol's most (and least) eligible women, using his good looks to insinuate himself into their beds if not their lives. When he met Elsie, he sensed that her father might provide a rich dowry and, later on, a comfortable inheritance. It was enough to lure him to renounce her wild ways and seek Elsie's hand in marriage." (Eliot 24).

Clearly, Elias's motives for marrying were largely selfish. While Elsie's rationale was hardly selfless herself, she certainly made an inaccurate assessment about her future spouse. As someone who was never financially successful and had never shown himself capable of committing to a long-term relationship, she had plenty of evidence in front of her to suggest Elias would be the husband she desired.

The marriage between Elias and Elsie proved every bit as unsteady as one might guess. Elsie's shy demeanor bored Elias, who also struggled with his wife's chaste attitude toward sex. Meanwhile, Elias found work in a clothing factory and the couple moved into their home in the working-class neighborhood on the outskirts of Bristol, but Elsie routinely criticized her husband for his inability to adequately provide for her and their child. (Schickel).

While the region offered little in the way of entertainment options, it was known for its vaudeville venue, and the never-ending string of female vaudevillians were ideally suited for satisfying Elias's sexual promiscuity. The marriage between Archie's parents continued to deteriorate over their first few years together, with Elias constantly out of the house and Elsie still in mourning over the death of John. Consequently, their doctor suggested to them in 1904 that they have another child, in the interest of salvaging their marriage and compensating for John's death (McCann). In the 21st century, the prospect of having a child in order to save a marriage might seem like a ludicrous proposition, but in an age in which therapy did not exist, the decision was not entirely out-of-place. Thus, it was this context in which Archie was born on January 18, 1904.

Of course, after their son was born, neither Elias's boisterous lifestyle nor Elsie's depression subsided, and the couple's situation was only exacerbated by the fact that they were charged with raising a child they weren't capable of properly parenting. Furthermore, they took opposite approaches when interacting with their son. Elias remained out of the household whenever possible, spending a lot of his time working, while Elsie smothered him with attention but not necessarily affection. In fact, she dressed him in girl's clothing and suffocated him with motherly care out of a desperate need to do everything in her power to prevent another infant tragedy from occurring. As Archie grew older, he began to notice his mother becoming increasingly withdrawn from the outside world, remaining in the house and rigorously adhering to her established routine. It's possible she would have been diagnosed as obsessive-compulsive had the term existed back then.

Cary's interactions with his father were more joyous, and it was through his father that he acquired a love for the vaudeville stage. Both Elias and Elsie took their son to the cinema, but Elias frequented the more seedy venues, which was cheaper and provided more action. (McCann). Elias worked hard and was not afraid to show his son his work environment, as Eliot notes: "Whenever Elias did get to spend time alone with his son, it was that much more fun for the both of them. When Archie was just five, his father began taking him to the pressing factory on Saturdays, where the boy loved to stand amid the loud machinery until closing time, then walk through town holding his hand above his head to reach his father's big one as Elias made the rounds of the local pubs and traveling cribbage games." (Eliot 27).

The contrast between Elsie and Elias's interactions with their son demonstrate the cultural divide that was in full force in England during the early 20th century. Elsie had a Puritanical, late Victorian sensibility that privileged religion and virtue, while Elias was more modern and enjoyed leisurely pursuits. Nevertheless, it would be a mistake to simply declare that all of Archie's entertainment talents stemmed from his father. Through Elsie, he became an adept piano player, and his grandfather purchased a piano for the household.

As it turned out, Archie's piano skills were so good that the young child gained admission to the prestigious Bishop Road Junior School in Bishopton. However, after matriculating there, he focused more on sports and other leisurely activities in lieu of his studies. Meanwhile, Elsie continued to suffer more heavily from depression, and while she remained a strong presence in her son's life, her influence began to wane. By this time, Elias had accepted employment at a clothing factory in Southampton (80 miles away), where he lived with his mistress and helped raise her child.

One day, 9 year old Archie returned from school to find his mother missing. Two of his cousins had been living in the house, and they informed him that she had gone away to live in a resort, but Elias informed his son that Elsie had passed away. The truth was that he had arranged for her to live in a mental institution. Regardless, the sudden absence of his mother caused

Archie to feel extreme guilt, and after her departure he was largely left to shoulder the responsibility of raising himself.

After his mother left, Archie became even more rebellious in school. He began to steal minor items and paid little attention to his schoolwork (Eliot). In spite of this, he was still awarded a scholarship to the well-regarded Fairfield Secondary School, but he continued to disregard his education. One distraction at Fairfield came in the form of his first girlfriend. By the age of 13, he was already 6'1, and while he had always possessed dark, cutting eyes, his growth spurt rounded out his attractive appearance. From that point forward, he would always be considered a heartthrob for women.

During his adolescence, Archie followed in his father's footsteps, working menial jobs during the summers like his father had always done. But even though the absence of his mother might have suggested his father would assume a more involved role in his upbringing, this was not the case. Since Elias had a family of his own to help raise in Southampton, he spent little time with Archie, and when Archie moved to Southampton for the summer of 1914 with the intent of staying with his father, he was disappointed to learn that there was no room for him. As a result, he turned to working as a messenger on the docks and often resorted to sleeping on the street (Eliot). While this sounds gruesome, that was not entirely the case for the young kid, who had no problem working jobs that required great physical toil. At the end of the summer, he returned to Bristol for his schooling, and even though he had not grown closer to his dad over the summer, he did prove himself to be no stranger to harsh, difficult work. In fact, in an interview months before his death, Cary Grant would tell his interviewer he hoped to be a sailor:

> "I had no definite ambition. One has to go through one's education before forming thoughts about what one wants to do. Unless you've got some mad ideas about being a fireman or a great boxer or a football player. But I had none of those…I had no ambition toward acting…I had ambition to travel. I was born in a city—Bristol— from which there was a great deal of travel. It was a very old city, and in those days the ships came and left all the time from the port. I was constantly interested in what was going on down there and in those ships that took people all over the world."

Archie may have returned to school in 1915, but he failed to commit himself to his studies any more than he had done over the past several years. Thus, he was fortunate that his science teacher's assistant took a liking to him. The man had a side job working for the Bristol Hippodrome, a theater that could show Archie all the inner workings that go into a production. For many, learning how the sausage is made ruins the appeal of the show, but Archie was drawn to producing and became infatuated with the production of theatrical entertainment. The assistant to the science professor used his connections at the Hippodrome to allow Archie the opportunity to assist with the stage production for some of the shows, and he greatly enjoyed this experience, until one night when he made a lighting error that inadvertently revealed the secret to a magician's trick. At the behest of the magician, he was no longer allowed to work at the Bristol Hippodrome, which devastated the teenager.

Although he was now denied the opportunity of working at the Bristol Hippodrome, a benefit to living in Bristol was that the town did not lack other entertainment venues. Archie quickly found an opportunity to work at other establishments, and shortly thereafter he caught a break when he was hired as a young actor in Bob Pender's troupe of young comedians. Pender, whose name was actually Bob Lomas, ran the company with his wife Margaret, and Archie proved to be an adept comedic performer. From Lomas, he learned many standard vaudeville tricks, including the ability to walk on his hands and on stilts (Eliot).

Working for Lomas was as enjoyable as his schooling was loathsome, and it was clear to Archie from even this early age that he would work as an entertainer in some capacity for the rest of his life. However, Elias was less than enthusiastic when learning of his son's activities, and he removed Archie from Pender immediately thereafter. In a large sense, Pender had assumed the role of a surrogate father to Archie in Elias's absence, but Elias had no interest in handing his son off to another father figure. Elias intended for his son to receive a full education, and the vaudeville arena did not have the high-class reputation of the dramatic theater. Thus, from Elias's point of view, Archie's work as a comedy performer was a sign that he was not progressing beyond his own social class.

Archie begrudgingly agreed to return to school, but with the knowledge that he would never be able to remain in an academic setting for an extended period of time. After reentering Fairfield Secondary School, he plotted a way through which he would be expelled. It's believed that in order to accomplish his dismissal, he drilled a hole into the girl's bathroom, making it seem as though he were a peeping tom (Eliot). His actions were obviously frowned upon, and after that he was expelled. Now his father could not prevent him from returning to Lomas' comedy group. He signed a three-year contract, and even though he possessed little in the way of an education (how much of his studies he had actually absorbed is ambiguous), he did have the security of employment.

Even if he was less than pleased by his son's actions, Elias was suffering his own stigma over the fact that his son was not living with him (Eliot). Thus, Archie's three-year contract worked well for everyone, as Archie could pursue his chosen profession and Elias was relieved of having to be a better father figure.

Considering his impoverished upbringing and two incapable parents, it is easy to leap to the conclusion that Archie's entry into vaudeville was the only way he could rise toward a higher social class. But throughout his childhood, he was enrolled in high-profile schools that offered best quality education he could have hoped to receive. Had Archie Leach committed himself to his studies, it's possible he could have succeeded as a professional in another industry. That said, while there is no telling what might have happened had he been raised with a more active and supportive set of parents, Archie Leach's eventual success as Cary Grant testifies to his natural ability in the performance arena.

Chapter 2: A Vaudeville Comedy Career

"I really am a happy, amusing fellow at heart. Trouble is I seem the only one left." – Cary Grant

Archie's second stint with Bob Pender's Comedy Troupe was just as engrossing as his first. Lomas never exploited his young actors, and he continued to serve as a benevolent figure over the next several years. It was with Lomas that Archie perfected his physical comedy and worked hard to lose his strong Bristol accent. The comedy troupe gained a sterling reputation, and by the time Archie was 16 he had risen to the top of the company. As he excelled, so too did the group, and in 1920 they were invited to travel to New York City. Only eight of the actors were selected for the trip, and Archie was one of those chosen.

It would be impossible to overstate the importance of Archie's first trip to the United States in 1920. The comedy troupe was quite talented, and by the time they arrived in the United States, they had already performed together for years, so they experienced great success. The troupe did encounter adversity early in their stay when they were invited to perform an opening act for the famous vaudeville star Fred Stone at the 42nd Street Globe Theater. Fearing that Lomas and his players would upstage his own act, Stone came up with the spurious reasoning that the Globe Theater would not be able to accommodate the stilts used in one of Lomas's routines. After the troupe was removed from the program, they were able to secure continuous employment and performed a longstanding routine at the Hippodrome in New York. The show ran on Broadway for 9 months, after which they left New York and toured the American vaudeville circuit.

The troupe's run ended in January of 1922 when Lomas decided to return to England, but Archie was on the verge of turning 18 years old. No longer an adolescent, he had his own future to consider, so he joined together with several of his fellow players and decided to stay put in New York City. The split from Lomas was amicable, and Archie now had assumed full control over his performing career. He explained in an interview, "When the troupe went back to England, I remained here. I liked this country very much, and gradually I got into musicals. In those days, a musical generally only lasted a year, so there weren't very many. But I was in musicals before I came to film."

When Archie separated from Lomas, he was paid all of the money that his boss owed him, as well as a small bonus sum of money. These funds lasted him through much of the year, but by Fall he was broke. Eventually, he teamed up with his former colleagues, and they formed their own company, the aptly named Lomas troupe. Archie served as both manager and performer, and the group was successful, with their show running for six months at the Hippodrome. He had proved that his talents in vaudeville comedy could be successful in either Europe or the United

States.

That same Fall, Archie moved in with actor George Orry-Kelly. The relationship is well-documented in biographies of Grant, and it is widely believed that it was homosexual in nature, though Grant never openly acknowledged that. (Eliot). At the time, Orry-Kelly was a successful stage actor and a significant figure in the queer theater scene, while Archie was finding it difficult to get a job. Vaudeville was hardly the most prestigious theatrical genre, and his history as a vaudeville performer did not make him particularly marketable in either dramatic theater or the burgeoning motion picture industry. Furthermore, despite all of the practice he had conducted with Lomas to overhaul his accent, his voice still reflected his working-class origins, and it would be years before the last traces of his accent disappeared.

Orry-Kelly

Archie toiled in theater jobs during the mid-1920s, but he hadn't yet had a career breakthrough, and as his relationship with Orry-Kelly soured over the course of the decade, he found himself living in poverty yet again. It was not until spring of 1927 that things improved. Frustrated with his lack of career prospects, he reached out to Orry-Kelly, who subsidized a small apartment for him on East 80th Street (Eliot). More significantly, Orry-Kelly used his connections to place him in contact with Reginald Hammerstein, who was, like Orry-Kelly, strongly involved in the queer theater scene. After meeting Archie, Hammerstein was physically attracted to him and gave him a role in the production of *Golden Dawn*. He was compensated at the respectable rate of $75 per week, with the contract renewable in predetermined increments that could send the contract up to $800 per week.

Golden Dawn was a major breakthrough for Archie, mainly due to the financial security associated with it. The show itself possessed little substance and was essentially a vehicle for displaying lavish set designs and musical numbers, as well as topless chorus girls, the first time this had ever happened on film. Set in Africa, the plot involved a white goddess who assumes control over an African tribe, and Archie was cast in the lesser role of a young Australian prisoner-of-war. Unsurprisingly, the play received harsh reviews and was roundly panned for its shallow plot, but one of the benefits of acting in such a high-profile production is that a large audience saw it anyway.

Ultimately, Archie's performance made a positive impression on talent agent Billy Grady, who worked for William Morris. Grady contacted the Hammersteins and was successful in getting Archie a part in *Polly*, a musical adaptation of the 1917 stage comedy *Polly with a Past*. In a role more befitting of the ones he would later portray, Archie was cast as a wealthy playboy, but he was unable to get along with the play's headlining star, June Howard-Tripp, who arranged for Archie to be cut from the production.

Luckily, Archie did not have to wait long before finding another opportunity; in fact, there would be competition for his services. Florenz Ziegfield was impressed by his work and intended to sign him for the national tour of the Broadway production *Rosalie*. Archie liked the opportunity, but it required the blessing of the Hammersteins, who disliked Ziegfield and thus refused. At around this time, J.J. Shubert bought out the remainder of his contract from the Hammersteins, and Archie was then cast to star in the Shubert's Broadway comedy *Boom, Boom*, starring alongside Jeanette MacDonald.

The play received mixed reviews and closed after 72 performances, but once again the exposure to large audiences helped Archie draw plenty of notice. After the production, he received an audition with Paramount, and even though the studio turned down his services, Archie began making connections in the film industry. He next acted in *Nikki*, a play about World War I that earned $375 per week, less than he had made for his previous performance, but his performance earned praise from Ed Sullivan. That praise would mean more than his salary. After the play ended its run, Archie was given a role in *Singapore Sue* (1932) with Paramount, and from that point forward he would be a fixture in the film industry.

Ed Sullivan

Chapter 3: From Theater to Cinema

After the completion of *Singapore Sue*, Archie moved to Hollywood, where Orry-Kelly had recently earned a job as a costume designer for Jack Warner. He and composer Phil Carig made the trip together, arriving in January of 1932 and sharing a small apartment in California. Shortly after the move, Archie earned an audition with Paramount, the same studio that had cast him in *Singapore Sue* but also previously turned down his services.

Fortunately for Archie, Paramount was in a fragile state by the early 1930s. The studio had built its reputation by producing classy genteel comedies, as well as the films of international heartthrob Rudolph Valentino, but the emergence of Clark Gable and Gary Cooper mandated that they find an actor who could compete with them. With his well-groomed appearance, Archie offered an attractive alternative to the more serious Gable or Cooper, and Paramount signed him to a salary of $450 per week.

The studio's only stipulation was that he change his name. During his entire theatrical career, he had still performed under the name Archie Leach, a name the studio found unpalatable for a man who was to be groomed into a major star. Cary Grant did not officially change his name until 1942, but he was known and credited as Cary Grant immediately after signing with Paramount. He personally came up with the name Cary Lockwood, named after one of the characters he had previously played, but the studio insisted on not using that last name, and he wound up using Grant because the initials C and G were being used by Clark Gable and Gary Cooper as well.

Clark Gable

Gary Cooper

Like most new actors, Grant kept a strenuous schedule during his opening year, acting in 8 films in 1932 alone. The most significant of these films was *Blonde Venus*, which paired him with Paramount's other major find, Marlene Dietrich. Although a screwball comedy with Marlene Dietrich and Cary Grant might sound like an attractive proposition, the film was a melodrama that featured Dietrich as a housewife who becomes a stage performer as a means of paying for her ill husband's medical bills. As the husband, Grant appears as a handsome, likable figure, but more than a little bit bland when compared with his later roles. Consequently, Dietrich appears as the more significant character.

Grant and Diedrich in *Blonde Venus*

More instrumental for Grant than *Blonde Venus* was *She Done Him Wrong* (1933), in which Grant starred with Mae West. The film cast Cary in the role of a Federal agent who investigates illicit activities conducted in a saloon but becomes attracted to West, who stars as a performer at the club. The plot is built around the romance between Grant and West, and the efforts of Grant to remove her from the club so that they can live happily ever after together. The film is most known for West's many double entendres, making it a representative example of the films that were made immediately before the Hays Code censorship began being enforced more vehemently. Even though Hollywood would adopt censorship regulations that were far more stringent immediately thereafter, there is no doubting the box office appeal of the racy content featured in films such as *She Done Him Wrong*. Before the film, Paramount was approaching financial ruin, and the film is often credited with saving the studio from bankruptcy (Eliot). It was also a critical success, nominated for the Academy Award for Outstanding Production (Best Picture).

Mae West

Building on the success of the Grant-West pairing, Cary's next significant film was *I'm No Angel*, and as the provocative title suggests, the film was another attempt to capitalize on the success of *She Done Him Wrong*. The film again showcases West as a nightclub performer and Grant as the respectable man who marries her and gives her respectability. *I'm No Angel* was an even greater success than the earlier West-Grant pairing, and another example of the daring pre-Hays code films. Due to the strict censorship standards that developed over the decade, West became less marketable, and the film was the final one that featured her and Grant together.

Cary remained busy throughout the mid-1930s, but it was not until 1937 that he began appearing in the types of comedic films for which he is now remembered. There is still merit to his films from 1935 and 1936; of these films, *Sylvia Scarlett* (1935) is the most noteworthy because it paired Grant with Katharine Hepburn for the first time. Although Grant and Hepburn would later form one of the most memorably screwball comedy duos of all time, their first film together was a less outrageous romantic comedy. Hepburn plays the eponymous character, a female con artist who develops a friendship with Grant's character, a jewel thief. The film was a major box office flop, but this is largely attributable to the inherent challenge for a 1930s American audience to witness a female actress in drag.

Grant with Katharine Hepburn in *Sylvia Scarlett*

As one of Hollywood's most eligible bachelors, Grant was a female heartthrob but was also past the age at which most men married and raised a family. During the production of *She Done Him Wrong*, he began dating actress Virginia Cherrill, who gained an international reputation for her starring role in Charlie Chaplin's *City Lights* (1929). Although she is now scarcely remembered, Cherrill was even better known than Grant at the time, ensuring their romance was high-profile. They were married on February 10, 1934, but at the same time, it has been widely alleged that Grant also had a long-term affair with the actor Randolph Scott. Cherrill and Scott did not get along, and Grant's friendship with Scott greatly compromised his first marriage. Just over a year after the wedding, they were divorced, on charges that Grant had been physically abusive toward Cherrill. Although they were incompatible as man and wife, they remained on friendly terms following the divorce.

Virginia Cherrill

Randolph Scott

During the late 1930s, there were other important off-screen developments for Grant. Since the age of nine, Cary had been under the impression that his mother was dead, but in 1937 he was informed of her actual whereabouts and visited her at the mental institution. By the late 1930s, she had grown even more withdrawn than before, and Grant was always aware of her inability to control anxiety, but they remained friendly from that point forward and communicated through long-distance correspondence. Eventually, Grant arranged for her release and purchased a property for her in Bristol. In addition to helping Elsie, Cary began dating Phyllis Brooks, an actress and model. The two were eventually engaged but never married, and he remained single until 1942.

Chapter 4: Professional Independence and Stardom

By 1937, Cary Grant was squarely in the ranks of Hollywood's leading men, yet he still lacked a clear niche. He could play the male lead in a romantic melodrama or light romantic comedy, but his most famous films had been vehicles for Mae West more than showcases for himself. Paramount never quite discovered how to best utilize his talents, and in 1937 Grant broke away from the studio following the termination of the five-year contract he had signed in 1932.

For an actor to go independent was exceedingly rare for the time period, and Cary (along with Charlie Chaplin) helped legitimize the idea of the film star as an independent contractor, a dynamic that continues to this day. Freed of any obligation to Paramount, he began to diversify and appeared in films for a number of studios in 1937. The most famous of these films was *The Awful Truth*, which was directed by Leo McCarey and co-starred Irene Dunne.

Irene Dunne

The Awful Truth is now credited for catapulting Grant to the top of Hollywood. The genius of *The Awful Truth* lay not so much in the particularities of the script itself but in casting Cary Grant in the screwball comedy genre, which fit his acting style like a glove. *The Awful Truth* remains one of the quintessential films of the genre, as well as an example of the subgrouping of screwball comedy films known as the comedy of "remarriage" (Cavell). In these films, the plot features a married couple who has divorced or become estranged, with the narrative resolution involving their reconciliation. In *The Awful Truth*, Cary and Irene Dunne play a married couple who divorce and begin dating on their own, only to realize at the conclusion that they belong together. By looking at divorce and remarriage, the films call into question the value of marriage, and it is important to note that the conditions of the remarriage differ significantly from those of the initial one. While the first marriage is dominated by the male, the second is more equal, and thus it is Grant and not Dunne who at the conclusion of *The Awful Truth* admits to having been foolish. Cavell thus notes that the remarriage films were instrumental in challenging the ultra-conservative gender politics of classical Hollywood, noting that "the subject of the genre of remarriage is well described as the creation of the woman, or of the new woman, or the new creation of the human" (139). While one might guess that these films would be rejected by male viewers, this was hardly the case, because Grant's charm appealed to both genders. The film was a tremendous success, as it was nominated for the Academy Award for Best Picture and McCarey won an Oscar for Best Director.

Grant in *The Awful Truth*

Following the success of *The Awful Truth*, Grant resisted working again with Columbia and instead signed with RKO to appear in *Bringing Up Baby* (1938), one of the films for which he is best remembered. The film reprised Grant's working relationship with Katharine Hepburn, but by 1938 both of their reputations had changed drastically from when they starred together in *Sylvia Scarlett*. Grant's stock had risen substantially, while Hepburn's reputation had fallen considerably; the box office failure of *Sylvia Scarlett* had certainly not helped her career. Fortunately for both stars, *Bringing Up Baby* was considerably different from their earlier film together. It was made by a different director (Howard Hawks), and as a screwball comedy it was closer in nature to *The Awful Truth*. Even though the film was not a remarriage film, it contained the zany plotline of the genre, as well as the progressive gender portrayal. Grant plays a tight-laced paleontologist, while Hepburn stars as a fun-loving girl unafraid to buck societal norms; she is introduced while playing golf and eventually owns a pet leopard. Over the course of the film, Hepburn's character helps Grant loosen his disposition, and the film ends with the two of them solidifying their romance.

If *The Awful Truth* offers a subversive interaction between genders, *Bringing Up Baby* was even more extreme. The film sees Grant cede the patriarchal authority conferred by his scientific profession as he allows himself to become overtaken by Hepburn. This undermining of gender roles is at the heart of both the screwball comedy and the directorial style of Howard Hawks; in this vein, Cavell argues, "Hawksian comedy, through its characters' struggles for consciousness, remembers that a society is crazy which cedes it, that the open pursuit of happiness is a standing test, or threat, to every social order" (129). This dynamic represented a significant turn away from the Hollywood comedies of past decades, as Benshoff and Griffin noted, "Many of the male stars of screwball comedies were similar to those softer, more romantic, and good-looking stars of the 1920s…What marks these films as different is that the silent comedies almost always affirmed masculinity in their final reels, while screwball comedies barely returned to patriarchal norms."

Given the undermining of patriarchy surfacing in films such as *Bringing Up Baby*, it is noteworthy that Cary Grant's character still resonates as a confident, attractive figure at the film's conclusion. *Bringing Up Baby* is a prime example of Grant's uncanny ability to poke fun at himself while still retaining his poise. To this end, when discussing *Bringing Up Baby* in the context of Grant's screwball comedies from the late 1930s, Andrew Britton astutely claims, "The films are united, remarkably, by their affirmation of a feminized hero and of a couple whose validity and vitality are continuous with his feminization. Hawks's film, as the most extreme…demands closer consideration here: the way in which it redefines a process we might be tempted to describe as "emasculation" is fundamental to our sense of the value of the Grant persona." (10).

Today, *Bringing Up Baby* is recognized for the chemistry of the Grant-Hepburn grouping, but contemporary audiences heavily preferred the pairing of Grant and Irene Dunne in *The Awful Truth*. The Depression-era audience did not care for Hepburn's snobbish reputation, and the film was actually a box office failure. It was not nominated for any Academy Awards, and it would be years before it was considered a classic.

Grant and Hepburn in *Bringing Up Baby*

Cary Grant and Katharine Hepburn starred in three famous screwball comedies together, all from 1938-1940. The second was *Holiday*, directed by George Cukor and produced by Columbia. The studio initially wanted to pair Grant with Irene Dunne, and it was only through Cukor's insistence that Hepburn won the role. As with *Bringing Up Baby*, the plot casts Hepburn as a rich young woman and Grant as a comfortably affluent man from a more humble background. As a screwball comedy, the film involves the romance between this apparently antithetical pair, and at the end of the film, Grant decides to quit his job in order to be with Hepburn's character.

That said, the relationship between the two resembles that of a brother and sister. In one famous scene, the two play with children's toys in Hepburn's family's house while a dinner party is held downstairs. However, this notion that the characters favored play over hard work did not appeal to the impoverished audience of contemporary Depression-era America, and the film was another in a string of box office disappointments for Hepburn. Certainly, the film has the potential to alienate working-class viewers, but the film's attitude toward wealth is more nuanced than it appears. According to Andrew Britton, the wealth of Hepburn's character does not support the wealthy so much as it serves as a device that distances the characters from social conventions: "The wealth of the screwball couple, like its childlessness, is a means of detaching the partners from any social function: it is a precondition for the destruction of the gender roles which are defined by their social function" (23). In this regard, wealth facilitates the film's progressive gender equality.

The theme of opposites attracting is fundamental to the gender dynamics of both *Bringing Up Baby* and *Holiday*, and both films reflect the screwball comedy presentation of the man and woman as engaged in a sort of sparring dynamic that not only sees them as equals but also as playful competitors. Willett argues that the first two Hepburn-Grant screwball comedies suggest marriage as the reconciliation of differences: "As Hepburn repeats in *Bringing Up Baby*, love manifests itself in conflict, or in what I am calling dialectic. In Hollywood, then, marriage is that unity of two extreme characters where each character undergoes an educative process in order to learn to communicate with a prospective spouse" (19-20). These films, therefore, portray gender equality through presenting marriage as a union between equals rather than patriarchal control.

Grant and Hepburn in *Holiday*

The last of the Hepburn-Grant screwball comedies, *The Philadelphia Story*, was made in 1940 and remains arguably the most famous of the trio. Again directed by George Cukor, the film featured both Cary Grant and James Stewart as suitors vying for Hepburn's hand in marriage. The film is another famous example of the comedy of remarriage, since Hepburn and Grant's characters were once married but then divorced. While Grant's character comes from a wealthy background, Stewart plays the role of a middle-class newspaper reporter. Eventually, Hepburn is reunited with Grant. Pairing Hepburn and Grant was nothing new, but the incorporation of the everyman newspaper reporter was instrumental in soliciting a positive response from American viewers. Stewart's character served as a surrogate for the viewer, and the interaction between Hepburn and Stewart showed that the famous actress could tone down her haughty image. As a result, *The Philadelphia Story* was the film that salvaged Hepburn's career, and it was both a commercial and critical success, winning Oscars for Best Screenplay and Best Actor (given to James Stewart) and nominated for several others.

The Philadelphia Story was the last of the Hepburn-Grant films, but Cary continued to appear in screwball comedies. In 1940, he appeared in arguably his most famous one, *His Girl Friday*, which reunited him with Howard Hawks and co-starred Rosalind Russell. Grant plays a ruthless newspaper editor, Walter Burns, who is willing to go to any lengths in search of a great story. Russell stars as the female romantic lead, playing the role of Hildy Johnson. *His Girl Friday* is another example of the comedy of remarriage, as Walter and Hilde were previously married, only to divorce after Walter's excessive commitment to his job compromised their relationship. The narrative, therefore, works toward Walter and Hilde rekindling their romance, and although Walter begins the film as the dominant figure, by the film's conclusion their dynamic is reconfigured so that Hildy has an equal voice. As with the earlier screwball films, there is a countless number of witty exchanges between the two.

Given that he was such a lucrative figure and films such as *The Philadelphia Story* and *His Girl Friday* received great acclaim, it is somewhat surprising that Grant was not nominated for any Oscars during this period. This can most likely be attributed to his decision to leave the Academy of Motion Picture Arts and Sciences at the time of his departure from Paramount. The Academy did not feel it was proper to give their biggest award to someone who actively went against the structure of the studio system. Moreover, Grant did not improve matters by ardently and vocally asserting that denying him an Oscar resulted in a tremendous loss of revenue both for himself and the studios. (Eliot). While Grant was certainly talented enough to win multiple Academy Awards, he would not win any until after his retirement.

Grant and Rosalind Russell in *His Girl Friday*

Chapter 5: The 1940s

By the 1940s, Cary Grant had solidified his status as one of the premier actors in Hollywood, matching stars like Clark Gable, Gary Cooper, and Spencer Tracy, and over the next decade, he began to diversify by appearing in films with a more dramatic bent. One of these was *Penny Serenade*, a melodrama made by Columbia that cast Grant and Irene Dunne as a married couple who salvage their failing marriage by adopting a child. A major difference between *Penny Serenade* and Grant's films from the previous five years is that he plays an impoverished character. Playing someone who was not wealthy ingratiated him to viewers and critics alike, and he was nominated for an Academy Award (though he did not win).

Grant's biggest professional move during the 1940s was his decision to appear in a pair of films with Alfred Hitchcock, who had just arrived in the United States in 1939. Grant's first Hitchcock film was *Suspicion* (1941), a suspense film featuring Grant and Joan Fontaine as a married couple. The marriage is a study in contrasts; Grant's character has an irresponsible background, while Fontaine is far more prudish. This contrast recalls the central differences that compromised the marriage between Grant's own parents. In the film, the marriage is not one of mutual love so much as the fact that Grant represented the polar opposite of Fontaine's father, thus continuing a long line of Freud-inspired Hollywood films that saw the husband as a replacement for the woman's father (Modleski). Fontaine suspects that her husband is plotting to kill her for her life insurance, and the film reaches a dramatic conclusion when Grant takes her for a dangerous car ride while speeding along tortuous roads, but he prevents his wife from falling out of the car when her door inadvertently opens. The film prepares the viewer for an actual murder and the happy ending feels forced, yet the drama of the plot compensates for the tacked-on ending, and the film is still possible to enjoy.

Suspicion was nominated for an Academy Award for Best Picture, Best Score, and Best Actress, and though it would be several more years before Hitchcock and Grant collaborated again, their first film was a major success. When asked about his memories working with Hitchcock, Grant had only good things to say in an interview: "I have only happy ones. They're all vivid because they're all interesting. It was a great joy to work with Hitch. He was an extraordinary man. I deplore these idiotic books written about him when the man can't defend himself. Even if you defend yourself against that kind of literature, it gets you nowhere."

Alfred Hitchcock

In the early 1940s, Grant officially changed his name to Cary Grant from Archie Leach, which by this point was a mere formality anyway. On June 26, 1942, he became an American citizenship, a move that was motivated by his relationship with Barbara Hutton, who he married on July 8, 1942. By this point, Grant was 38 years old, and Hutton was eight years younger. Unlike his first wife, Hutton was not an actress, but she had been born into one of the wealthiest families in the country. By 1942, Hutton had already been married on two occasions and had one son, so Cary became a father to her child. The marriage began successfully but began to dissolve; Grant was not accused of spousal abuse, but he and Hutton proved incompatible. They divorced in 1945, but as with his first marriage, he and Hutton remained good friends.

Hutton

Grant's most notable film from 1943 and 1944 was *None But the Lonely Heart* (1944), which saw Grant play a very different role from his past ones. This time, he played a troubled Cockney man who is unable to settle into a life of domesticity, and it is only after his mother passes away that he is able to reform. The film ends with the suggestion that Grant will leave to fight for the Allies in World War II, and the dramatic plotline (as well as the patriotic support for the Allied war effort) held great appeal, even if the film is not remembered as one of his more decorated films. In recognition for his performance, he was nominated for an Academy Award.

Far more famous than *None But the Lonely Heart* was Grant's second collaboration with Hitchcock: *Notorious* (1946). The plot involves the daughter of a Nazi spy (played by Ingrid Bergman) who is contacted by a government agent (Grant) to reveal secrets about a group of Nazis residing in Brazil. Over time, Grant and Bergman develop a mutual affection, and the film is one of the most romantic of all time, highlighted by a show-stopping two-and-a-half-minute kiss that got around the Hays Code by stopping the kiss every 3 seconds and restarting it. The film also contains a number of suspenseful sequences, mainly revolving around Bergman's efforts to evade her father's friend, Sebastian (Claude Rains), who attempts to silence her through uranium poisoning. As with many of Hitchcock's films, the movie contains a deft balance of suspenseful scenes and more lighthearted, dryly comedic ones. Grant was not nominated for an Academy Award, but this was due mainly to his acrimonious relationship with the Academy. Regardless, the film was a great success.

Grant and Bergman in *Notorious*

The late 1940s did not include any of Grant's most famous films, but he remained a major box office attraction even as he aged into his mid-40s. After not starring in any films in 1945, he acted in three the following year (including *Notorious*) and two in both 1947 and 1948. The end of the decade saw the release of *I Was a Male War Bride* (1949), which was directed by Howard Hawks and paired Grant with Ann Sheridan. The film is interesting for the manner in which it combines the war film (a genre that had emerged in full force during World War II) with the screwball comedy. Grant plays a war officer who must cross-dress and pass himself off as a war bride in order to return to the United States with Sheridan's character, a Women's Army Corps officer. In the screwball comedy tradition, the film ends with marriage between the two main characters, but only through the undoing of the patriarchal authority of the male character.

Also in 1949, Grant married actress Betsy Drake, his third wife. The year before the marriage, the two had acted together in *Every Girl Should Be Married* (1948), and they would again appear alongside one another in *Room for One More* (1952). The marriage would prove far more enduring than his past (and future) ones by lasting until 1962. Drake is not only remembered for being the spouse with whom Grant was wedded the longest, but also for introducing Cary to

LSD, a drug that provided him great therapeutic relief. In an interview late in life, he discussed his LSD use and admitted to using it "100 or 150 times." He claimed that he stopped using it after the drug was banned, stating, "I'm conservative. I'm not recommending anyone else try it, though it certainly was helpful for me…I took small doses under the supervision of a physician, both here and in England…The whole point is to get pure again, to be born again, to be as pure as when we were little babies, to drop off all the barnacles and misconceptions we've built up."

Room for One More proved to be the last film in which Grant and Drake co-appeared. The most memorable and critically acclaimed films of the decade for Cary involved renewed collaborations with past directors, namely Howard Hawks, Alfred Hitchcock, and Leo MacCarey. In 1952, he starred in *Monkey Business*, playing a scientist who consumes a potion that prompts him to behave like a schoolboy. The film was not hailed as a masterpiece by contemporary critics, but it has subsequently been recognized as a complex meditation on the anxieties of aging and the stifling effects of marriage.

Grant and Marilyn Monroe in *Monkey Business*

More memorable than *Monkey Business* were Cary's two collaborations with Alfred Hitchcock during the decade. The first was *To Catch a Thief* (1955), which paired Grant with Grace Kelly. The plot centers on Grant in the role of John Robie, a famed jewel thief who is accused by the police of being responsible for a series of jewel robberies. As he defends his innocence and works toward discovering the identity of the true jewel thief, he becomes romantically involved with Kelly's character. Shot on location in the French Riviera, the film doubles as a travelogue of sorts, with many glamorous sequences featuring Grant and Kelly in two-shot set against scenic backdrops. The film's impressive production elements resulted in an Academy Award for Best Cinematography, as well as nominations for Best Art Direction and Best Costume Design.

With Hitchcock, Grant, and Grace Kelly all working together, the film was virtually guaranteed a positive reception from the American public and despite the $2.5 million budget, it turned a strong profit. For his part, Grant called Grace Kelly the best actress he ever worked with, saying, "I've worked with many fine actresses. But in my opinion, the best actress I ever worked with was Grace Kelly. Ingrid, Audrey and Deborah Kerr were splendid, splendid actresses, but Grace was utterly relaxed - the most extraordinary actress ever. Her mind was razor-keen, but she was relaxed while she was doing it. I appreciated that. It's not an easy profession, despite what most people think."

Nearly 10 years separated *Notorious* from *To Catch a Thief*, and Hitchcock used Grant very differently from the 1940s films. *Notorious* and (especially) *Spellbound* showcase Grant in roles that are almost sinister, but in the 1950s films his characters are more lighthearted and romantic, accentuating his suaveness. In *To Catch a Thief*, viewers can immediately sense that Cary Grant and Grace Kelly were Hitchcock's favorite stars, and as the Academy Award nominations attest, they were never more attractive than in the 1955 film. Grant proved to be the ideal actor for Hitchcock's singular ability to combine suspense, romance, and comedy, and there may be no better example than *To Catch a Thief*.

Grant and Grace Kelly in *To Catch a Thief*

One of the great accomplishments of Cary Grant's career was his ability to age gracefully before the camera; the 1950s were one of his most successful decades, and yet he was already reaching his 50s, an age in which many male stars become unable to command starring roles. He later made note of the fact people always told him he looked good for his age in a self-deprecating manner: "I think it has become a thing to say to me how good I look. Sometimes I wonder if what's really behind it all is that people are amazed I'm still around. You know, when I was just getting started in the business, there was an actress named Claire Windsor, and it became a regular thing to say to her that she looked so young for her age. The papers picked it up, and everyone repeated it. Well, I think people are doing the same thing with me. I don't think it's that I look so young; it's that other people let themselves look older."

In 1957, Cary continued his trend of working with directors with whom he had already collaborated, starring in Leo McCarey's *An Affair to Remember* (1957). The film remade the director's 1939 film *Love Affair*, and as the title alludes, the plot revolves around an affair between Cary Grant and Deborah Kerr. *An Affair to Remember* did not receive the critical accolades of Grant's films with Hitchcock and Hawks, but it is remembered for being one of the most romantic films of all time.

The most famous of Grant's 1950s films is undeniably *North by Northwest* (1959), which co-starred Eva Marie Saint. The espionage plot, a precursor to the James Bond films, features Grant as Roger Thornhill, a businessman who is confused for being a spy named George Kaplan. As with *To Catch a Thief*, the action-filled plot is matched by a memorable romantic pairing between Grant and Eva Marie Saint, replete with highly deliberate sexual innuendos and Freudian symbolism. For her part, Saint stands as one of the premier examples of the icy "Hitchcock blonde," and the romantic scenes between the two exemplify Hitchcock's ability to convey scenes that are filled with erotic energy while at the same time remaining remarkably dignified. The film thus resists charges of overly explicit sexuality, a trait separating it from the more sexually overt films of Marilyn Monroe, Jane Russell, and others that were made during the time period.

Grant in *North by Northwest*

Grant and Eva Marie Saint in *North by Northwest*

Given that he appeared in *Suspicion*, *Notorious*, *To Catch a Thief*, and *North by Northwest*, it's clear that Cary Grant was one of the most prolific stars to work with Hitchcock, and the only other actor who comes to mind is James Stewart. That is indicative of the fact that Grant and Stewart were rivals on screen during their entire careers, and they each held longstanding working relationships with the master of suspense. That said, they were used in very different ways by the famous director. In his interview with Hitchcock, French director Francois Truffaut identifies the central difference in the way in which the two stars were used: "It might seem as if Cary Grant and James Stewart were interchangeable in your work, but you actually use each one in a different way. With Cary Grant the picture is more humorous, and with James Stewart the emphasis is on emotion" (228). This distinction highlights how every film that Cary Grant appeared in was to some extent a comedy; one of the similarities between the film and the Bond movies it influenced is that even when Grant's character is placed in dangerous situations (such as the famous crop-duster scene or the sequence on Mount Everest), he never abdicates his slightly comedic, suave demeanor. Whether it was an inevitable result of his vaudeville training or simply the result of his charm, even Grant's more dramatic films, such as *Notorious*, contain moments of spirited romance and playful banter.

Another difference between Hitchcock's treatment of Cary Grant and James Stewart is that Grant is romantically successful, whereas the director is unafraid to make Stewart suffer at the hands of women, like in *Vertigo* (1958). This frustration leads Stewart to resort to violent behavior, while Grant forever maintains his calm veneer. Comparing the manner in which Grant is used by Hitchcock vis-a-vis Stewart, Robin Wood argues that "he may lie to and manipulate women (*Suspicion*), but he doesn't try to dominate them. When he is given something like the Stewart domination image, Hitchcock plays the effect for comedy…The Hitchcock films with Grant move toward an equalized male/female relationship" (365). Considering that Hitchcock is not a director viewers typically associate with gender equality, the fact that this theme surfaces in the Hitchcock-Grant films testifies to the way in which Grant's screen presence tended to correspond with a more favorable depiction of women.

Chapter 6: Retirement

North by Northwest proved to be the final collaboration between Grant and Hitchcock, and Cary's output lessened substantially during the 1960s, culminating with his retirement in 1966. He did appear in five films during the decade, including a string of three consecutive ones for which he was nominated for the Golden Globe Award for Best Actor, but the most well-known of the 1960s films by far is *Charade* (1963), which featured Cary alongside Audrey Hepburn. The film, directed by Grant's close friend Stanley Donen, borrows elements of *North by Northwest*. Grant stars as a government agent whose identity is misunderstood throughout much of the film, as viewers are led to believe he's a famous thief. And despite Grant's age, in 1963 viewers could hardly get a more glamorous pairing than Hepburn and Grant. The suspenseful plot gestures toward Grant's Hitchcock films, but Hepburn's natural talent for romantic comedy transforms the film into even more of a comedy than films such as *North by Northwest*.

Grant and Audrey Hepburn in *Charade*

After the completion of *Charade*, Grant appeared in just two additional films: *Father Goose* (1964) and *Walk, Don't Run* (1966). Both are more unabashedly comedic than Grant's earlier films, demonstrating his undying ability to poke fun at himself. In the first film, Grant plays a gruff coast watcher for the Royal Australian Navy who becomes romantically involved with a

French woman who cares for seven young children. There is an element of self-parody to the role, as it is plainly evident that it is not the sort that he played during his younger years. Grant's final film similarly deviates from his typical roles, as he plays a British businessman who attempts to set up a female acquaintance with an eligible bachelor. Cary shows his age in a couple of respects. Most notably, he no longer plays the male romantic lead, and by 1966, he was no longer quite as thin or athletic as he had been even as recently as *North by Northwest*. The film was successful at the box office, but it is barely remembered today, and in that sense it does not do much justice as the final film of his career.

Despite the success, Grant still yearned to retire during the decade, and he later explained, "Acting became tiresome for me. I had done it. I don't know how much further I might have gone in it. I have no knowledge of that, of course. But I enjoyed going from where I started on to a different world, equally interesting—perhaps more so."

Cary Grant's film career may have been in its twilight phase during the 1960s, but his personal life remained quite active. After divorcing Betsy Drake in 1962, he married Dyan Cannon in 1965, and it was with Cannon that Grant became a father for the first time. In 1966, his daughter Jennifer was born, and even after Cary and his wife divorced in 1968, Grant remained heavily involved in his daughter's life, obsessively archiving every possible aspect of her life. In her memoir, *Good Stuff: A Reminiscence of My Father, Cary Grant*, Jennifer noted, "Until I was about twelve, Dad took painstaking care to ensure that I had an accurate record of my life… He wanted me to have accurate records of my life growing up with him because his own records were burned in the bombings of Bristol in World War II. So he made all of these tapes and Super 8 films, and took slides and photographs. And every note I wrote him, every note he wrote me — and letter — he saved in boxes. And he put them in a fireproof vault in our house to ensure the safety of these archives for me." (10). Jennifer's book suggests that Cary's relationship with his daughter effectively replaced his commitment to his own career. Until he remarried in 1981, Grant's attention was primarily paid to his daughter. Throughout his entire adult life, Cary had eschewed raising a family, but after having a child he proved to be a more than capable father.

Cary Grant in 1973

Even though his life slowed down during his final two decades, Cary Grant's latter years were far from quiet. He drew attention to his private life when it was revealed that he had maintained an affair with 33 year-old Cynthia Bouron during the late 1960s, and he may have had a child with her, but Grant forever denied that this was the case (Eliot). Grant received more positive publicity in 1970 when he was given an Academy Award for Lifetime Achievement.

In 1976, Grant made headlines by introducing Betty Ford at the 1976 Republican Convention, which generated interest only because he had long refused to reveal his political preferences. At a time when Hollywood was full of politically charged tensions, especially during the Red Scare of the 1950s, Grant never discussed politics one way or the other

In addition to raising his daughter, Cary became involved in a series of business ventures, including a position with Western Airlines and another with MGM. 1981 saw Cary get married for the fifth and final time, as he wedded Barbara Harris, a British public relations agent less than half his age. Despite the wide age gap, Grant and Hutton were happily married and remained together through Grant's death. In 1986, they renewed their wedding vows, and that same year, he embarked on a one-man show, *A Conversation with Cary Grant*, in which he screened clips from his films and held question-and-answer sessions with the audience.

While on tour, Cary Grant suffered a cerebral hemorrhage, and he died shortly thereafter on November 29, 1986. In her book about life with her father, Jennifer talked about how Cary wanted to be remembered after his death:

"In my father's later years he asked several times that I remember him the way I knew him. He said that after his death, people would talk. They would say "things" about him and he wouldn't be there to defend himself. He beseechingly requested that I stick to what I knew to be true, because I truly knew him. I promised him I would. I've easily kept that oath. Although many books about him have been published, I've read none. Not out of a lack of interest. I'm sure there are some wonderful things I could learn about my father, but most likely more misconceptions than are worth weeding through. To me, he was like a marvelous painting. All the art historians wish to break down the motives, and the scheme, and so on. I would rather know, as I do, his essence. I believe that at the heart of a person lies passion. For the last twenty years of his life, I was given the extraordinary privilege to experience the full, vital passion of his heart. Dad used the expression "good stuff" to declare happiness or, as one of his friends put it, he said it when pleased with the nature of things. He said it a lot. He had a happy way of life. His life was 'good stuff'…

Why didn't Dad write his own book? One archived audio cassette recorded in 1962 is a self- hypnosis session made for Dad. He was being instructed to exercise, gently, daily, and to write his autobiography. Presumably these are activities he wished to pursue, and he'd hired someone to help him with autosuggestion. The woman soothingly advised that he complete his autobiography with tremendous compassion for his subjects and not to worry, not to criticize the work, just to do it. Also, to exercise a bit each day. This was four years prior to my birth. Was Dad examining his life before having a child? Why didn't Dad finish his book? Did he consider revealing his history, his childhood, to the world? He never spoke of the endeavor, but he saved the tape for me. What turned him around? With so much misinformation out there, did he want to address and correct it? Is this why he stayed up at night? Was he too distressed about involving others' lives? Of course, his was the definitive voice. His parents were already gone. Any writing would have served Dad and Dad alone. Dad's parents weren't famous, he was. He knew his story. Anyone reading his story would have done so to learn about him. His motives were therefore the central theme. My guess is he came to terms with his past, and with anyone who wished to write about it. Let them examine their own motives. In my case, ultimately it's the same matter. Dad is gone; I write about him for me."

Though he never wrote an autobiography, one of Cary Grant's quotes is telling in this regard: "I used to hide behind the façade that was Cary Grant … I didn't know if I were Archie Leach, or Cary Grant, and I wasn't taking any chances. … Another thing I had to cure myself of was the desire for adulation, and the approbation of my fellow man. It started when I was a small boy and played football at school. If I did well they cheered me. If I fumbled I was booed. It became very important to me to be liked. It's the same in the theater, the applause and the laughter give you courage and the excitement to go on. I thought it was absolutely necessary in order to be happy. Now I know how it can change, just like that. They can be applauding you one moment, and booing you the next. The thing to know is that you have done a good job, then it doesn't hurt to be criticized. My press agent was very indignant over something written about me not too long ago. 'Look,' I told him. 'I've known this character for many years, and the faults he sees in me are really the faults in himself that he hates.'"

Cary Grant's career is marked by its consistency, manifesting not only through the types of roles he appeared in but also the stability of his reputation. It is telling that no matter the director or plot, every Grant film - even his ones with Alfred Hitchcock - bears traces of the screwball comedy. Over the course of his career, he acted in a diverse array of films, and it is a testament to the power of his stardom that he was able to unify them by virtue of his star identity. To some degree, Cary Grant's image became so ubiquitous that some critics claimed he was simply playing the same character in every movie: himself. To that, Grant himself responded, "Well, who else could I portray? I can't portray Bing Crosby; I'm Cary Grant. I'm myself in a role. The most difficult thing is to be yourself—especially when you know it's going to be seen immediately by 300 million people…I don't care what people say. I don't take into consideration anything anyone says, including the critics. There's no point. You've made the film, it's done and if they want to criticize it, that's up to them. I don't pay attention to what anybody says —except perhaps the director, the producer and my fellow actors. "

Grant's fourth wife, Dyan Cannon, captured exactly what made her husband so captivating when she said, "The word 'icon' has been hopelessly devalued over the years, but Cary Grant was exactly that and more. More than an actor, really. Cary Grant was glamour. Cary Grant was charm. Cary Grant was class, intelligence, refinement. Women hardly dared to fantasize that such a combination of warmth, wit, and dash would walk into their lives. Men who took a page from his playbook came to believe in the power of being a gentleman. Cary Grant made manners, civility, and style as thrilling as Humphrey Bogart made a good pistol-whipping."

As Richard Dyer notes of both Grant and Bette Davis, "Apart from growing older, the image of

Cary Grant or Bette Davis has not really 'deepened' since the period in which they were established as stars" (110). Dyer made this claim several decades ago, and yet his point still holds true. It is safe to assume that Grant will still be admired as the paragon of male elegance well into the future.

Bibliography

Benshoff, Harry M., and Sean Griffin. *America on Film: Representing Race, Class, Gender, and Sexuality at the Movies*. West Sussex: John Wiley & Sons, 2011. Print.

Britton, Andrew. *Britton on Film: The Complete Film Criticism of Andrew Britton*. Detroit: Wayne State University Press, 2009. Print.

Cannon, Dyan. *Dear Cary: My Life with Cary Grant*. New York: HarperCollins, 2011. E-book.

Cavell, Stanley. *Pursuits of Happiness: The Hollywood Comedy of Remarriage*. Cambridge: Harvard University Press, 1981. Print.

Dyer, Richard. *Stars*. London: BFI, 1986. Print.

Eliot, Marc. *Cary Grant: A Biography*. New York: Random House, 2004. Print.

Grant, Jennifer. *Good Stuff: A Reminiscence of My Father, Cary Grant*. New York: Alfred A. Knopf, 2011. Print.

Hitchcock, Alfred, and Francois Truffaut. *Hitchcock*. New York: Routledge, 1985. Print.

McCann, Graham. *Cary Grant: A World Apart*. New York: Columbia University Press, 1996. Print.

Modleski, Tania. *The Women Who Knew Too Much: Hitchcock and Feminist Film Theory*. London: Routledge, 2005. Print.

Schickel, Richard. *Cary Grant: A Celebration*. New York: Hachette Book Group, 1983. E-book.

Willett, Cynthia. "Hollywood Comedy and Aristotelian Ethics: Reconciling Differences." *Sexual Politics and Popular Culture*. Ed. Diane Christine Raymond. Bowling Green: Bowling Green State University Popular Press, 1990. 15-24.

Wood, Robin. *Hitchcock's Films Revisited*. New York: Columbia University Press, 1989. Print.

Jimmy Stewart

Chapter 1: Hard Work and Hardware

"John Ford always said that the best things that have ever happened in film, in American film, have happened by accident." – Jimmy Stewart

Throughout his life, Jimmy Stewart remained firm in his convictions, and this tendency was inherited by his parents, Elizabeth Ruth and Alexander Maitland Stewart. Both Alex and Elizabeth descended from families with rich lineages in the United States, as their ancestors had arrived in the 18th century, and this established a fierce patriotism that would be passed down to subsequent generations. The Stewarts arrived in America in 1784, and Alex's father received a college education (at Westminster College in Pennsylvania) and enlisted in the service (Eliot). After returning from duty, he invested in the hardware store Sutton, Marshall, and Stewart, which opened in 1848. He and his wife had four sons, two of whom died before reaching adulthood.

During his youth, Jimmy's father Alex gained a reputation for being reckless, but he maintained a studious side as well and enrolled at Princeton to study chemistry (Eliot). However, before graduating he enlisted in the Spanish-American War, and upon his return, he purchased the family hardware store and assumed complete operation over it (Eliot). It would not be until 1906 that Alex would marry Jimmy's mother, Bessie. She too was born into a longtime American family, one with even more storied ties to American past. Indeed, her family, the Jacksons, had first arrived in the country in 1773 and fought in the Revolutionary War. As with the Stewarts, the family resided in Pennsylvania, and her father, Samuel Jackson, served as Brigadier General in the Civil War and earned great renown for his accomplishments at the Battle of Gettysburg defending Little Round Top on the second day of the battle (Eliot). After the conclusion of the war, he moved the family to Indiana, Pennsylvania, a town roughly 55 miles east of Pittsburgh and the one in which Jimmy would later be raised. Bessie's father parlayed his military success into a position as President of the Apollo Trust Company, a position that allowed him to facilitate the rebuilding of the P.H. Kaufman Steel Company (Eliot). Bessie did not possess the dashing looks of her future husband, but she was nevertheless popular, largely due to her talents as an organ player. By the time she married Alex, Bessie was past the age at which most young women married, but the marriage was a natural fit given the similarly privileged backgrounds of the two.

Alex may have been somewhat unruly during his younger years, but that side had all but disappeared by the time Jimmy was born on May 20, 1908. The family led a strict Presbyterian lifestyle, and Alex even disapproved of referring to his son as "Jimmy," preferring instead the more masculine (from his perspective) title "Jimbo." This nickname also developed out of the fact that Jimmy was chubby as a young child, a fact his father resented; it would not be until puberty that he would lose his baby fat. Alex ruled the household with a strict sense of discipline, and despite his wife's musical background, he forbade all manner of musical activity that was not directly related to the Church, even though he personally spent the vast majority of his time at his hardware store. While he acquired a reputation for his sternness, Alex's religious values also led him to express great generosity; for example, in cases in which patrons were unable to cover the expense of an item, he would generously allow them to pay based on credit or even the exchange of other items. This latter tendency would later prove instrumental in nurturing Jimmy's musical interests.

With a father who was busy at work and a mother who was more fun-loving and musically-inclined, it would be easy to jump to the conclusion that young Jimmy Stewart was far closer to his mother than his father, but this was not actually the case. He certainly spent more time with Bessie, but from an early age Alex became his idol and the two were quite close. Jimmy's father maintained a tough façade, but he was eager to please his son and held firm to the belief that Jimmy needed a committed father.

Even so, Jimmy did not receive as much attention from Alex as he would have liked, and the birth of his two sisters - the first in 1912 and the second in 1914 - led to him becoming increasingly independent (Eliot). He spent much of his time building model airplanes, and in a hobby he inherited from his father, Jimmy also designed chemistry experiments. From the time his sisters were born, he also became a role model to his sisters, a position that would elevate in importance over the next decade.

During these early years, there was every expectation that he would follow in his father's footsteps and assume operation over the store. For this reason, at the age of 10, Jimmy was called upon to serve as an apprentice and worked at the store after school and on weekends. This responsibility represented a significant time commitment, but the store was a meeting-place within the town and Jimmy was exposed to the social happenings of the town.

Despite his mother's talents, Alex's strict religious sensibility prevented Jimmy from pursuing music at a young age, but in one of the more transformative events of Jimmy's childhood, his father took him to a production staged by a traveling vaudeville act. Following the show, the troupe paid a visit to the hardware store, after which one of the players was unable to pay for an item in full. In lieu of monetary payment, he traded Alex his accordion, and since he had no use for the device, Alex gifted the instrument to his son. From that point forward Jimmy would maintain an interest in music, theater, and (later) cinema. While Alex was at work, Bessie and her children performed musical numbers together, with Jimmy on the accordion and the daughters playing the piano. Given that he rarely played musical instruments in his films, it is perhaps difficult to imagine him on the accordion, but it reflects both Jimmy's predilection for performing and the importance he placed on familial interaction.

Aside from the birth of his two sisters, the first decade of Jimmy Stewart's life was relatively unremarkable and unmistakably all-American. In 1918, however, the status quo would be loudly disrupted through a couple of significant developments. First, with a recently-expanded family, Alex made the decision to relocate his family to a new, larger home in the same neighborhood. The most substantial change to accompany the move into the new home was that it corresponded with a shift in schools for Jimmy, as he was then enrolled in the Model School. This institution was more prestigious than his previous school because it was affiliated with the Indiana State Teachers College. Hailing from a family that valued education quite highly, and formerly attending Princeton College himself, Alex held high ambitions for his son's future, and the shift to the more rigorous school was certainly seen as a positive development. For his part, however, Jimmy was far from a committed student and would struggle with his studies until arriving at Princeton more than a decade later. From Jimmy's perspective, the chief benefit of enrolling at the new school was that he met a group of friends with whom he would remain close for the remainder of his life, including Joe Davis, Hall Blair, and Bill Neff. Through interacting with this group of friends, Jimmy slowly began to overcome the shyness of his early years.

Even more significant than the change in residence and school was Alex's decision to enter the armed services. With the United States still fiercely involved overseas in World War I, and still firmly clutching onto the patriotism that had been instilled in him, Alex made the difficult choice to leave his family while his children were still in their formative years, but before his departure, he famously entrusted his son with authority over the family. In 21st century America, this decision appears entirely absurd, given that Bessie was more than capable of running the family, but Alex subscribed to a paternalistic ethos that was still popular during the early decades of the 20th century. Jimmy did not operate the family business, but he was relied upon to help raise his sisters, and perhaps most importantly, he was denied a masculine presence while his father was gone. This period was understandably difficult for him, but there are areas in which Alex's absence was productive. For example, Jimmy was able to indulge his penchant for theater, which included staging plays about World War I in the family basement (Eliot). It is only natural that Jimmy would have preferred his father's presence during this time, but the heightened independence was instrumental in building independence and fostering his own sense of individuality.

Ultimately, Alex's time in the army proved short-lived because World War I ended less than two years after America actually joined the war. As a result, Alex was back roughly one year after enlisting. However, there was a distinct change in his personality; he had lost much of his outspoken character, became far more withdrawn, and absolutely refused to discuss any of the events he had experienced while he was enlisted (Eliot). What did not change, however, was his ambition for Jimmy. Alex intended for his son to excel in school and support the family business as well, and feeling the need to satisfy his father created a difficult dynamic that would envelop Jimmy for the remainder of his upbringing and into early adulthood. Jimmy faced the challenge of satisfying his father's highly conventional standards for masculinity while also pursuing his personal interests in music and theater, a conflict that would not have an easy resolution. Even though Jimmy maintained an amicable relationship with Alex, a sense of tension continued to exist.

Jimmy also experienced dramatic physical changes during his upbringing, growing to a height of 6'3 by his early teenage years. At the same time, he weighed just over 140 pounds, making him considerably underweight at the time, and he struggled to even maintain that weight. Ever the nurturing mother, Bessie forced her son to eat copious amounts of strength-building cuisine, but Jimmy's rapid metabolism resulted in his maintaining the lanky physique that would later become his signature. Perhaps not surprisingly, Alex was less than pleased by his son's physical maturation, as Jimmy was unable to build muscle and fell well short of the physical standards he envisioned for a Stewart male.

For all of the control that Alex exerted over Jimmy, he was entirely absent when it came to instructing his son about how to behave around girls. This posed a problem for Jimmy, who was called upon to help raise his sisters yet continued to be nervous around girls. During his adolescence, Jimmy had no idea how to engage with and date women. While this is not unusual with teenagers, it is relevant to any discussion of Jimmy Stewart because his befuddled conduct toward women would later constitute a foundational element of his star persona. In any event, Jimmy did not have a girlfriend during his teenage years and would not become comfortable around women until entering Princeton.

As Jimmy entered his teenage years, the film industry became increasingly popular and institutionalized across America, and given his interest in theater and music, it was only natural that the adolescent Jimmy would become absorbed in the still relatively new art form. He accepted a part-time job as a projectionist, and the complicated process of handling the reels of film came naturally to Stewart, who drew from the fine technical skills he had perfected while designing chemistry experiments and building model airplanes. Jimmy's interest in movies incurred much scorn from his father, but Alex acquiesced and allowed for his son to indulge his new interest.

Although Alex allowed Jimmy to work as a weekend projectionist at the local Strand, he still held onto his long-term aspirations for his son, which included attending Princeton and subsequently operating the family business. Recognizing that Jimmy's performance at school was unlikely to earn admission to the Ivy League institution, Alex realized that his son would need to attend a preparatory academy in order to accelerate his progress. At the same time, Jimmy's lack of academic success prevented him from gaining admission to any of the more prestigious institutions, despite the family's affluence. In fact, it was only through Alex's personal intervention that Jimmy gained acceptance to Mercersburg Academy, a prep school roughly 100 miles from Indiana, Pennsylvania. Jimmy matriculated in fall of 1923 and would attend the institution throughout his high school years.

As any biography of Jimmy Stewart makes clear, the first 15 years of his life were defined in large part by the actions of his father, which alternated between benevolence and something close to disregard. Alex cared deeply for his son, yet he exhibited a clear insensitivity toward the fact that Jimmy had interests that deviated sharply from his own. Much of Stewart's childhood can be filtered through the division between activities that Alex approved of - designing chemistry experiments, building model airplanes, and helping out in the store - and those that were seen as unproductive, non-masculine, or both, like acting and music. For all the harshness that Alex displayed toward Jimmy, however, it is important to avoid labeling Stewart's childhood as abusive or troubled. There were challenges, but Alex believed he was acting in his son's best interest, and there was a strong reciprocal love between father and son. It is no exaggeration to assert that Jimmy's relationship with his father was the most challenging of his life, but it's only fair to recognize all of its complexity.

Chapter 2: Independence at Mercersburg and Princeton

"I was going to be an architect. I graduated with a degree in architecture and I had a scholarship to go back to Princeton and get my Masters in architecture. I'd done theatricals in college, but I'd done them because it was fun." – Jimmy Stewart

Attending Mercersburg Academy was a major transition for Jimmy, but in some respects it furthered the status quo, because the school was Presbyterian and maintained the strictness that had been present in his family household. Like Jimmy, many of the students had been underachieving students themselves, their parents covering the substantial tuition with the intention that they would receive a rigorous academic experience that would prepare them for an Ivy League acceptance. A significant difference in attending Mercersburg, at least for Stewart, was that his new peers were predominantly wealthy. Most of the students at his school back home were affluent, but not to the level of those at the prep school (Eliot).

Stewart ended up attending Mercersburg for five years, a year longer than traditionally expected, because during his senior year he fell ill just months before graduation was scheduled, forcing him to repeat his year. This experience notwithstanding, his time at Mercersburg was largely positive, as he received a strong education and began investing himself more deeply into extracurricular activities, most notably the debate team and literary society. Stewart tried out for the football team, but his frail physique prevented him from receiving any playing time and he quit the team shortly after joining. Jimmy remained shy and never had a girlfriend for any substantial amount of time, but he maintained a steady social life. He returned to his home town of Indiana each summer, working either menial jobs designed to build strength (including a stint as a bricklayer), or as an entertainer (working the summer before graduating as an assistant for his good friend Bill Neff, who had begun working as a magician). And even though he no longer worked at the movie theater, Stewart remained a fervent fan of cinema throughout his time at Mercersburg.

As Stewart's high school years drew to a close, his fate remained ambiguous. From an early age, it had been clear that Alex had every intention of watching his son follow in his footsteps and attend Princeton, but Stewart's grades were not stellar and he lacked the athletic or theatrical prowess that might help him overcome his academic shortcomings. He applied to Princeton during his final year at Mercersburg, but he was slow to receive a decision from the admissions committee and upon graduation, he still had yet to be notified. He found employment working as a bricklayer, a profession that Alex had endorsed during Jimmy's high school years but was quick to disapprove of following his graduation. Finally, in the summer of 1928, he was notified of his acceptance and enrolled in fall of the same year.

By the time Jimmy Stewart arrived at Princeton, he was still far from a stellar student, but he had begun to commit himself more deeply to his studies. It is commonly stated that he majored in architecture, yet this was impossible as there was no architecture major offered; instead, he majored in electrical engineering, all the while maintaining an interest in architecture (Eliot). One of the curiosities of his time at Princeton is that his experience there was divided between his formal studies in engineering and his extracurricular interest in theater, which developed quite rapidly. With a gaunt frame, he was still woefully incapable of making the football team, so naturally he found theater and the choir more suitable. During his sophomore year, he tried out for the Glee Club (choir), serving as a second tenor, but even more influential than the choir was the Triangle Club, a theatrical organization spearheaded by Josh Logan, who would later go on to serve as a premier director in Hollywood. Logan and Stewart formed an unlikely but intense friendship, and the gregarious Logan brought out Stewart's outgoing personality, which had long been submerged beneath his bashful façade. It should also be noted that Logan, a homosexual, was almost certainly physically attracted to Stewart, which was perhaps the biggest reason for his surprising decisions to cast the inexperienced Stewart in high-profile performances on stage at Princeton (Eliot). Even with no formal training as an actor, Jimmy excelled in his performances and quickly became a major attraction in the collegiate productions. He later joked, "I always stayed for the first curtain call and people always said, 'Who's that?' But this got me started in acting."

Logan

Stewart thrived with his new acting hobby, and he similarly flourished in his studies, demonstrating an academic ability that had never quite surfaced prior to college. He displayed a sharp mind as an engineer and fully intended to parlay his talents into an eventual position working for his father's store. He was accepted into the graduate program in architecture, and Stewart very nearly committed himself to a life as an engineer and hardware store owner. However, the balance between math and theater that Jimmy had always maintained grew untenable; roughly two weeks before graduating, Logan recruited Jimmy to serve as his star actor in the University Players, a summer stock company based in Cape Cod. Believing that his duties with the troupe would only span through the summer, he accepted the position, but after entering the company, he would never again set foot in the classroom. By this time, Logan had already graduated from Princeton, and recruiting Stewart must certainly be seen as an attempt to build his own name as a burgeoning theater director. The University Players were an ambitious group that was set to gain decent exposure, and Logan had recruited a superlative roster of actors, several of whom would eventually find great success in Hollywood. Among the talents were Henry Fonda and Margaret Sullavan, each of whom had served in the University Players during past seasons. From 1931 to 1932, Fonda and Sullavan had been married, and Stewart made their acquaintance through his connection to Logan. Sullavan was a stunningly beautiful actress, and it is undeniable that Stewart's decision to join the University Players was in large part due to his infatuation with Sullavan.

Fonda and Sullavan

Perhaps sensing that his son would never resume his studies, Alex was vehemently opposed to Jimmy entering the University Players, and Stewart only joined after Logan personally pleaded with Alex. Even though joining the theater troupe was intended to be just a form of summer employment, it was one of the more significant decisions of his life, if only because it represented the first significant time Jimmy had defied his father's wishes. Had the opportunity to join surfaced several years earlier, it's very likely Jimmy would have declined and worked for his father's store during the summer. Until this point in his life, Jimmy had revered his father and lived his life in what could be characterized as a state of loving fear. Whether joining the University Players signified that Logan had usurped Alex, or whether his theatrical pursuits simply reflected the independence that accompanies adulthood, the importance of entering the University Players cannot be overstated.

Chapter 3: From Starving Actor to Success in Hollywood

"It was Margaret Sullavan who made James Stewart a star, and she did, too." – Edward Griffith

With a cast full of people who would go on to enjoy success in Hollywood in acting and scriptwriting, it should come as no surprise that the University Players were quite successful in the summer of 1932. Stewart was drawn to Sullavan, but he and Fonda quickly became great friends, and they would remain so even after their film careers ended decades later. As the summer stock season drew to a close, Stewart made the decision not to begin his graduate studies at Princeton, opting instead to move to New York City to continue acting. He shared an apartment with Fonda, Logan, and Myron McCormick, maintaining the camaraderie that had existed over the summer. Stewart's friendship with the others in the University Players is made all the more noteworthy by the fact Stewart seemed to be an unlikely fit within the circle. After all, Stewart's firm conservative background stood in stark contrast with the extreme liberal mentality of his cohorts, particularly Fonda. In many ways, both physical and mental, Stewart had moved away from his father by his early 20s, yet he never broke away from his father's political beliefs, and even as Stewart transitioned into the Hollywood scene, the conservative ethos that had been instilled in him during his upbringing never left him. With the emergence of the Popular Front in full swing, Hollywood in the 1930s and 1940s was even more liberal than it is today, which made Stewart something of an outlier. It's a testament to Jimmy that he was able to maintain amicable relations with colleagues regardless of their political preference; a friend later Stewart saying about Fonda, "Our views never interfered with our feelings for each other, we just didn't talk about certain things. I can't remember ever having an argument with him."

Unfortunately, at the beginning Stewart did not have any sustainable reputation within the industry. Fonda and Logan were better known, if only because Fonda was married to a big star in Sullavan, but even they were unable to rely on getting significant parts. Nevertheless, Stewart began to make progress, beginning in earnest with his Broadway debut in *Goodbye Again* (1932), though a critic for *The New Yorker* noted of his role, "Mr. James Stewart's chauffeur... comes on for three minutes and walks off to a round of spontaneous applause." Later that fall, he was cast in a more substantial performance in the Broadway production of *Carry Nation* (1932), but the play lasted for just 17 performances. By the end of the decade, he and Fonda would become among the leading actors in Hollywood, but from 1932-1934, there was little hint of progress as they struggled to gain momentum on the New York theater circuit. Stewart would later recall, "From 1932 through 1934, I'd only worked three months. Every play I got into folded."

In fairness, the adversity Jimmy experienced after moving to New York had less to do with his own acting abilities and more to do with the nation's economic state. The onset of the Great Depression hit theater particularly hard—much harder than the motion picture industry—and there simply were not enough acting opportunities. In a desperate state, he accepted a position as a stage manager for a production in Boston of *Camille*, but he was fired shortly thereafter (Eliot). Subsequently, he was able to find parts in a long line of plays but fared no better.

It was not until 1934 that Stewart began to find more attractive roles, garnering strong reviews for *Page Miss Glory* (1934) and then *Yellow Jack* (1934), both of which solidified his status as a capable leading actor. Ultimately, a major change occurred when Fonda was noticed by a talent agent, after which he relocated to Hollywood. Shortly thereafter, Stewart's performance in

Divided by Three caught the attention of MGM talent scout Bill Grady, and after meeting with Grady, Stewart was offered the opportunity to perform in a screen test for MGM. His test was successful, and in April 1935, Stewart was signed to a contract of $350 per week, renewable for up to seven years.

After arriving in Hollywood, Stewart was relegated to the characteristically unglamorous roles given to every new actor. At first, he was tasked with acting alongside actresses auditioning for their screen tests, and when that was completed, he was finally permitted to appear in movies, acting in one during 1935 and eight the following year. In many of these, he did not receive a screen credit, but he kept busy.

Part of the problem was that MGM was a strange fit for Stewart. By the mid-1930s, MGM was considered the premier studio in Hollywood, but it was recognized for its musicals and screwball comedies, neither of which suited Stewart's more bashful disposition. His films with MGM are hardly jarring, but it is unlikely that he would have ever risen to fame had he remained with the studio. At the same time, even if Jimmy's tenure with MGM is now largely forgotten, it was with MGM that he received his first major break when he was cast in *After the Thin Man* (1935). As the title suggests, the film was a sequel to the MGM hit *The Thin Man* (1934). Although it was by far the most important role of his career to that point, the murder mystery plot was not only a strange match for the young actor but also the rare suspense film produced by the studio. Even more strange is the fact that Stewart was cast as the killer, a role that was entirely at odds with his performances later in the decade but foreshadowed some of his later films. Still, even though *After the Thin Man* bears similarities with Stewart's more mature films, it reflects just how much MGM had misread the acting style of its young actor. For his part, Stewart didn't question MGM's decision-making, and he even complimented MGM, saying, "You hear so much about the old movie moguls and the impersonal factories where there is no freedom. MGM was a wonderful place where decisions were made on my behalf by my superiors. What's wrong with that?"

Stewart in *After the Thin Man*

Stewart's next major film brought him outside the confines of MGM, and it was at this point that his connections with Margaret Sullavan proved invaluable. Sullavan jockeyed hard for Jimmy to be cast alongside her in *Next Time We Love* (1936), which was made by Universal and thereby required MGM's permission in order to cast Stewart. MGM agreed, and the film was a major turning point in his career, not so much for the success of the film but because of Sullavan's profound influence on his craft. She helped him gain presence before the camera, with a more assured command over his body and speaking voice. Even when director Eddie Griffith complained that Stewart was "wet behind the ears" and would make a "mess" of things, Sullavan would not relent. By the time Sullavan was done working with Stewart, one MGM worker noted, "That boy came back from Universal so changed I hardly recognized him."

Building on the success of the film, Stewart and Sullavan appeared in three additional films together, including one in 1938 and two in 1940. The notorious Louis B. Mayer took note of their work, commenting "Why, they´re red-hot when they get in front of a camera. I don't know what the hell it is, but it sure jumps off the screen." One co-star may have had the answer; Walter Pidgeon, who acted alongside Stewart and Sullavan in *The Shopworn Angel*, explained, "I really felt like the odd-man-out in that one. It was really all Jimmy and Maggie...It was so obvious he was in love with her."

Sullavan and Stewart in *The Shopworn Angel*

Chapter 4: Frank Capra

"I've always been skeptical of people who say they lose themselves in a part. Someone once came up to Spencer Tracy and asked, 'Aren't you tired of always playing Tracy?' Tracy replied, 'What am I supposed to do, play Bogart?' You have to develop a style that suits you and pursue it, not just develop a bag of tricks." – Jimmy Stewart

In addition to Sullavan, the other major connection Stewart made during the decade was with director Frank Capra, who remains famous even in the 21st century. During the late 1930s, Capra was well-regarded in Hollywood, as he had directed Clark Gable in *It Happened One Night* (1934). There may be no director who better encapsulated the spirit of the 1930s, as Capra's all-American, moralistic films offered great hope to the American public during the nation's economic crisis. In his major study on sentimentality in film and literature, James Chandler likens Capra to Charles Dickens, as both exhibited a similar level of compassion toward the disenfranchised: "the Capraesque incarnation of the sentimental mode increasingly opens on to Dickens and the literary tradition behind him" (96). Years later, the similarities between Capra and Victorian literature would result in Capra losing favor, particularly with academic audiences, but Capra has since regained acclaim, especially for his collaborations with Stewart. It's easy to see why Capra's characteristics as a director matched Stewart's own brand of wholesome masculinity, and he and Capra collaborated on two of the most significant films of the decade.

Frank Capra

The Stewart and Capra pairing was an obvious match, but working together once again required the permission of MGM, as Capra was under contract with Columbia. Fortunately, MGM still did not consider Stewart to be one of their premium actors, so they gave permission to Columbia. It has already been noted that Stewart and MGM were an unlikely fit from the start, and W.S. Van Dyke, who was employed by the studio, is actually not entirely inaccurate in his assessment of the young Stewart as "unusually usual" (Thomas 7). What Van Dyke failed to realize was that it was Stewart's "usualness" that could be used to full effect, because American audiences felt as though they were watching one of their own.

The first of the Capra-Stewart films, *You Can't Take it With You*, was released in 1938, and the romantic comedy plot features Stewart and Jean Arthur as an unlikely couple who are attracted to one another against the best wishes of their families. Stewart's parents are wealthy capitalists, while Arthur's are similarly wealthy yet more charitable toward the poor. The plot served as a thinly-veiled plea for the wealthy to assist the poor, yet for all of its sentimentality, its many exchanges of playful banter and physical screwball comedy keep the film from becoming overbearing. In a fun bit of production trivia, Stewart even put his chemistry background to good use by assisting in the staging of the chemistry experiments that take place in the film (Quirk). In an age in which Cary Grant was the premier actor in Hollywood, Stewart began to chip away at Grant's popularity, winning over the American public with his everyman star persona. The film was arguably the best-regarded one of the year, earning seven Academy Award nominations and winning the Oscar for Best Picture and Best Director.

Stewart in *You Can't Take it With You*

With the success of *You Can't Take it With You*, Stewart had not only found a director who could bring out his best talents but also gained widespread popularity. This status also moved him into the uppermost social strata of Hollywood, and he was constantly featured in newspapers for his dating exploits. During the late 1930s, he dated many of Hollywood's most famous actresses, including Ginger Rogers and Norma Shearer. Obviously, it was hardly unusual for a major actor to maintain a prolific dating life, but it was also somewhat surprising that he resisted marriage. In 1938, he turned 30, and while men were not pressured to marry young quite like women were, remaining single was antithetical to Stewart's conservative beliefs and another manner in which he defied the values instilled in him by his father. It would be another decade before he finally got married.

Building on the success of *You Can't Take It With You*, Stewart and Capra reunited to collaborate on the even more famous *Mr. Smith Goes to Washington* (1939). Today, the film is recognized as one of Stewart's greatest achievements, but Columbia originally intended for Gary Cooper to star in the role. The film features much of the same populist ethos as *You Can't Take It With You*, as Stewart is cast in the part of a morally superior Senator who must contend with a bunch of corrupt politicians. The film also includes many of Stewart's most memorable lines, including a famous monologue in which he rebukes Congress for the political corruption pervading the political arena. Despite being cast as a politician, it is clear that Stewart serves as the voice of the American public, a figure who was willing to fight on behalf of American values against politicians who had lost their principles. Indeed, the very last name of Stewart's character signifies his everyman status. Capra said about Stewart's character, "The more uncertain are the people of the world, the more their hard-won freedoms are scattered and lost in the winds of chance, the more they need a ringing statement of America's democratic ideals. The soul of our film would be anchored in Lincoln. Our Jefferson Smith would be a young Abe Lincoln, tailored to the rail-splitter's simplicity, compassion, ideals, humor, and unswerving moral courage under pressure." Stewart called his performance "entertaining and slick and smooth".

At the same time, Capra understood the controversial nature of the movie, as it came against the backdrop of the start of World War II. He later said about the movie, "Japan was slicing up the colossus of China piece by piece. Nazi panzers had rolled into Austria and Czechoslovakia; their thunder echoed over Europe. England and France shuddered. The Russian bear growled ominously in the Kremlin. The black cloud of war hung over the chancelleries of the world. Official Washington from the President down, was in the process of making hard, torturing decisions. And here was I, in the process of making a satire about government officials...Wasn't this the most untimely time for me to make a film about Washington?" Nevertheless, the film received even more acclaim than Stewart's earlier film with Capra, and he was nominated for an Academy Award for Best Actor.

Stewart and Jean Arthur in *Mr. Smith Goes to Washington*

While *Mr. Smith Goes to Washington* was the most significant film in which Stewart appeared during 1939, another film that warrants mention is *Destry Rides Again*, which featured Stewart in a somewhat unlikely pairing with the sultry Marlene Dietrich. By the end of the 1930s, Dietrich had solidified her iconic status in Hollywood, but she had begun to lose popularity. Starring her with Jimmy represented a clever attempt to gain publicity, and the film is clearly constructed around both stars. Stewart is the male lead, but Dietrich also commands long stretches of the film herself, including a famous musical number in which she performs "See What the Boys in the Back Room Will Have." Part-Western, part musical, the film stands as another example that no film exists in just one genre, and it received favorable reviews. The film is also notable for the fact that Stewart and Dietrich dated during its production.

Stewart and Dietrich

Chapter 5: A Flurry of Honors

"Hollywood dishes out too much praise for small things I won't let it get me, but too much praise can turn a fellow's head if he doesn't watch his step." – Jimmy Stewart

By 1940, Stewart had already acted in nearly two dozen films, but he had yet to appear in a major film with MGM, the studio that had first signed him. This changed in 1940 when he starred in *The Philadelphia Story* (1940), the only role for which he would win an Academy Award. The movie reprises Stewart's everyman image, but it features an unlikely pairing between Jimmy and Katharine Hepburn and also reflected the rivalry in Hollywood between Stewart and Cary Grant. An adaptation of the stage hit of the same title, *The Philadelphia Story* casts Katharine Hepburn in the headlining role of Tracy Lord, a socialite whose snobbish ways prevent her from ever meeting a man who meets her standards. In true screwball tradition, the script follows the comedy of remarriage format in which a couple are divorced at the start of the film, only to get back together over the course of the narrative and marry at the conclusion. Tracy begins the film divorced from C.K. Dexter Haven (Cary Grant) and is set to marry a similarly rich man. Eventually, she realizes that she does not love her fiancée and nearly marries Stewart's character instead. However, at the end of the film, Tracy and Dexter are reunited and marry.

Stewart and Hepburn in *The Philadelphia Story*

It should be clear from the plot description that all of the elements of the Stewart persona were firmly in place in *The Philadelphia Story*. As in the Capra films, Stewart is cast as a counterpoint to rich characters who have less-than-stellar moral compasses, making him the surrogate for the average American viewer and someone who viewers could attach themselves to while feeling as though they were morally superior to the rich (albeit far worse off financially). Even though it was Cary Grant's character who eventually wins Hepburn's hand in marriage, the blue-collar personality of Stewart's character resonated more strongly with audiences, and he was awarded with the Academy Award for Best Actor. As film critic Bosley Crowther famously put it, the film "has just about everything that a blue-chip comedy should have—a witty, romantic script derived by Donald Ogden Stewart out of Philip Barry's successful play; the flavor of high-society elegance, in which the patrons invariably luxuriate, and a splendid cast of performers headed by Katharine Hepburn, James Stewart and Cary Grant. If it doesn't play out this year and well along into next they should turn the Music Hall into a shooting gallery....Metro and Director George Cukor have graciously made it apparent, in the words of a character, that one of 'the prettiest sights in this pretty world is the privileged classes enjoying their privileges.' And so, in this instance, will you, too."

That said, it would be a mistake to claim that Hepburn and Grant's characters were portrayed in an entirely unsympathetic light, as the script was largely predicated around improving Hepburn's standing in Hollywood. By the end of the decade, she had gained a reputation for being arrogant, the result of her haughty demeanor and privileged background, and in 1938 the Independent Theatre Owners of America famously declared her "Box Office Poison" (Berg). MGM realized that she needed to star with a male actor who could humanize her, and Stewart fit the bill perfectly. Even if Hepburn and Stewart did not end the film together, the warm rapport between them showed American viewers that Hepburn could appear in a sympathetic light, and the film was instrumental in resurrecting her career. In fact, she was awarded an Oscar for her performance as well.

In 1940, Stewart also appeared in two films with Margaret Sullavan for MGM. The first, and more famous, was *The Shop Around the Corner*, directed by Ernst Lubitsch. Lubitsch was a master at directing romantic comedies, while Stewart and Sullavan were a natural pairing. The 1930s had aligned Stewart with the romantic comedy genre, and it would only be after World War II that he would diversify his image.

The Lubitsch film is the best-known of Stewart's 1940 films with Sullavan, but it was his second film with her that was more relevant. The film, *The Mortal Storm*, was released at the time in which World War II was becoming a bigger issue in America, and though the nation had not yet joined the war, the film is somewhat propagandistic in its endorsement of the Allies. Stewart stars as a German who befriends Sullavan's character, a German Jew who is engaged to marry a member of the Nazi party. Realizing the political affiliations of her fiancée, she attempts to break free from him and begin a relationship with Stewart's character, but she is eventually shot and killed by the Nazis. The plot is unusual on several levels. First, it displays an over political commitment that has rarely been seen in Hollywood, either before or after the film, and it is remarkably unusual for the leading female character to die at the conclusion of a film. The death of Sullavan's character reflects the film's mission to arouse American sentiment for the war effort.

Months before Pearl Harbor, Stewart enlisted in the Army in March 1941, even after a previous attempt was rejected because he was underweight by five pounds. In fact, it's unclear whether Stewart ever met the weight requirements for the service, which required him to weigh 148 pounds, but he was accepted in 1941. By this time, he was already an experienced pilot; in 1935, he had obtained his Private Pilot certificate, and in 1938 he acquired his Commercial Pilot certificate. Stewart became the first major film actor to wear an army uniform, but as was the custom with actors, Stewart was given undemanding roles at first. He assisted in a March of Dimes rally and was then appointed to a position instructing pilots. However, he grew restless for more demanding opportunities, which eventually led to him being promoted to Captain, after which he was promoted to Major. Stewart flew in many missions and ultimately earned the rank of Major General. By the end of the war, he received the Air Force Distinguished Service Medal with three oak leaf clusters, as well as the French *Croix de Guerre* with Palm. Even after the war, he served in the Air Force Reserve. While it is true that much of his adult life had involved a shift away from his father, Stewart held firm to the commitment of serving the country and carrying on the family's military legacy.

Stewart as a bomber pilot in 1943

Stewart Receiving the French *Croix de Guerre* with Palm in 1944

Chapter 6: Career Maturation

"Remember no man is a failure who has friends." – *It's a Wonderful Life*

Jimmy Stewart returned from World War II during the autumn of 1945 with his career very much at a crossroads. Stewart had not appeared in any films since 1941, but more importantly, his personality changed profoundly during his time in the service. The bashful youthfulness that had defined his star image during his earlier years had virtually disappeared, and even though he maintained his wholesome, approachable nature, Stewart was very much a hardened man. Years later, his son noted that Jimmy refused to divulge any significant details surrounding his war experience, just like his father Alex: "My father's experiences during World War II affected him more deeply and permanently than anything else in his life. Yet his children knew almost nothing about those years. Dad never talked about the war. My siblings and I knew only that he had been a pilot, and that he had won some medals, but that he didn't see himself as a hero. He saw only that he had done his duty." (Starr 12).

This description reveals much about Stewart's post-war career persona. His modesty is on full display, but the refusal to discuss the experience reflects the turn toward expressing a darker, arguably more mature sensibility in his post-war films. This personality shift is also illuminating because it reveals a similar trajectory to that of his father, as Alex was similarly transformed by his time in the service. All of the films that Stewart appeared in following World War II reveal to some degree the struggle to maintain a genial disposition in the face of the horrors he experienced in combat.

Given that Jimmy had not acted in nearly five years, deciding on a comeback film was a delicate endeavor. He later explained, "When I got back from the war in 1946 people didn't want the Mr. Smith kind of movie any more, and I refused to make war pictures." Stewart opted against re-signing with MGM, a decision that had probably been a long time coming, but instead of signing with a different studio, he chose to sign with the MCA talent agency, with which his agent, Leland Hayward, was affiliated. Considering that two of Stewart's most lauded performances were for director Frank Capra, it should come as no surprise that his first film after returning was a Capra film: *It's a Wonderful Life* (1946). In an interview, Stewart recounted how Capra approached him for the film, "He said, 'It starts in heaven and you're down here on earth and you're going to commit suicide, because you think you're a failure. And you get out on a bridge and you're going to jump off the bridge, and then your guardian angel, he comes down.' He said, 'Jesus, this just sounds awful, doesn't it?' And I said, 'Frank, if you want to make a picture that starts in heaven with a guardian angel, I'm all for it.' And it went from there." On another occasion, he described the pitch in a similar way, "Frank called me one day and said, 'I have an idea for a movie, why don't you come over and I'll tell you?' So I went over and we sat down and he said, 'This picture starts in heaven'. That shook me."

The film has since gone on to achieve iconic status within American culture, and the plot is familiar to anyone who has even a passing familiarity with the canon of classical Hollywood movies. Stewart stars as George Bailey, a family man who is driven to contemplate suicide after he is held responsible for the misplacing of a substantial bank loan. His guardian angel intervenes, the town raises money for him to pay off the money he owes from the loan, and the film ends with Bailey, his family, and his fellow townspeople rejoicing. *It's a Wonderful Life* is likely the most famous movie of Stewart's career, and Lawrence Quirk's description expresses the common view toward the film: "The Stewart persona was on magnificently irresistible display here, as a decent man in a small town who undergoes a great trial of soul. *Mr. Smith* may have called for more resources of passion and *Vertigo* may have demanded a display of his darker, more complex aspects, but he is as affectingly human and charismatically forceful in *It's a Wonderful Life* as he would ever be." (155).

   This explanation is not incorrect, but it is clearly a retroactive look at the film that is highly dissimilar from the way in which it was received by post-war viewers. Indeed, the film is so well-known that it is difficult to view the film from the lens of post-war America, but it is important to understand that the film had a very different way with contemporary audiences than it would have decades later. Viewers struggled to embrace the darker aspects of the film, especially the near-suicide, because it was a significant departure from the more happy-go-lucky roles Stewart played early in his career. It was only after the film was released on video and screened on television that it acquired its mythic status. The passage of time has also obfuscated the biographical subtext that was especially potent at the time of the film's release, as Stewart's professional image was very much at risk. To this end, Charles Wolfe argues, "The figure of James Stewart [in the film] thus stands in not only for 'George Bailey', but also for the anxious veteran" (104). Focusing on the film's tidy narrative resolution and the image of Stewart's character surrounded by his family at the close of the film, Wolfe notes how the film's happy ending doubles as an attempt to point toward a happy late career for Stewart the actor. This astute reading of the film illuminates the commercial imperatives that undergird so many classical Hollywood films. Moreover, the film largely failed in its commercial goals, as it was hardly a success and did not resurrect Stewart's career. For the next several years, he would struggle to establish himself in Hollywood (Lawrence).

Stewart with Donna Reed and Karolyn Grimes in *It's a Wonderful Life*

During the late 1940s, Stewart not only went about rebuilding his career but also settled into domestic life. In 1949, he married Gloria McLean, a former fashion model, and he also adopted McLean's two sons, Michael and Ronald). Gloria then gave birth to twins Judy and Kelly on May 7, 1951. While Stewart's decision to postpone marriage until his early 40s went against the conservative values of his parents, his marriage was highly traditional. He would remain wedded to McLean until her death in 1974, and he never remarried after she passed away. The turn from playboy before the war to family man after it not only reflected his maturation but also established a clear correspondence between his onscreen and off-screen lives.

Jimmy and Gloria on their wedding day.

For the second half of the 1940s into the beginning of the 1950s, Stewart had little success, and his achievements during the period were more esoteric. One of his films, *Rope* (1948), established his relationship with Alfred Hitchcock and is now viewed as a cult classic for its innovative, extended long-take camera technique. The film also went a step beyond the dark side of Stewart that had appeared in *It's a Wonderful Life*, gesturing toward the performances Stewart gave during the following decade.

Jimmy's first collaboration with director Anthony Mann took place in 1950, when he appeared in *Winchester '73*. In 1950, Stewart remained busy producing films independently, but his interest in regaining his popularity led him to seek out Mann (Gomery). In *Winchester '73*, Stewart displays a psychological dimension that was largely absent early in his career and constitutes arguably the defining component of his late career. He plays a skilled marksman who wins a rifle in a shooting contest, only to have it stolen, launching him on a mission to exact revenge. The film was a massive hit, as viewers were far more amenable to the 'psychological Jimmy Stewart' than they had been with *It's a Wonderful Life*, and it was clear that the Stewart-

Mann pairing was a successful one. Jeanine Basinger locates the collaboration as foundational to Stewart's transition into the ranks of Hollywood legend: "Mann's westerns starring Jimmy Stewart secured the actor's future as a legendary star. The films showcased him as a more age-appropriate hero, more violent and disillusioned, yet still likeable, an idea that was embraced by Stewart" (80). In the 21st century, it is common to associate the young Stewart with Capra and the more mature Stewart with Hitchcock, but Basinger explains that the role of Mann was instrumental in facilitating the shift toward the Hitchcock performances: "There was the Capra Stewart and the Hitchcock Stewart as well as the Mann Stewart, and the three bear a direct linear relationship (Capra to Mann to Hitchcock). But the use of Stewart as an icon was never better than in the Anthony Mann westerns, in which an inherent and inexplicable psychosis seemed to dominate and motivate his characters" (83). In Anthony Mann, Stewart located the director who could bring out the psychological unrest that defines his post-war performances.

Anthony Mann

From 1950-1955, Jimmy appeared in seven films directed by Anthony Mann that featured him playing roles with varying degrees of psychological complexity. In *The Naked Spur* (1954), for example, Stewart plays an almost pathological Western antihero; the blue eyes that helped supplied his boy-next-door charm from his earlier films were rechanneled in Mann's film and magnified in full Technicolor glory to portray madness. It would be a mistake, however, to simply declare Stewart's performances with Anthony Mann one-dimensional exhibits in psychopathology. Rather, the Anthony Mann westerns convey a complex, Freudian unrest that remains powerful to this day, and the films mark a paradigmatic shift toward the psychological within the western genre.

Stewart in *The Naked Spur*

In addition to his psychological westerns, the 1950s also marked the height of Jimmy Stewart's collaborations with Alfred Hitchcock, as he acted in three major films with Hitchcock from 1954-1958. The first of these was *Rear Window* (1954), which is both a favorite among the general public and also a staple in academic curricula. It is not difficult to understand why the film holds such broad appeal, because the tale of an immobilized photographer who endeavors to solve a murder mystery from his apartment appeals to the voyeurism of the cinematic spectator. Meanwhile, the photographer's camera constitutes a clever metaphor for the film camera itself, making the film a popular favorite among film school audiences. To this day, Stewart's performance in *Rear Window* is recognized as one of his very best. Elaborating on his performance, James Naremore contends that "the film is as much a *tour de force* for the star as for the director, heightening the cleverness of Stewart's performance by severely constraining him" (241). This tendency to handicap his characters, either physically, mentally, or both, not only surfaces in Stewart's late-career performances but also allows for deeply affecting portrayals of psychological conflict.

Jimmy Stewart in *Rear Window*

Although not as well-known as *Rear Window* or *Vertigo*, *The Man Who Knew Too Much* (1955) is arguably the most suspenseful film in Hitchcock's arsenal. A loose remake of Hitchcock's 1934 film of the same title, the film features Stewart as a father who takes his family to Morocco only to have his son kidnapped. Even though the plot lacks the feeling of everyday reality like in *Rear Window*, the kidnapping plot is gripping, and Stewart was not the only A-list star to headline the film because Doris Day stars as his character's wife. Her performance of "Que Sera, Sera" won an Academy Award for Best Song, and the film's immense success at the box office can be attributed to its ability to appeal to both Stewart and Day's respective fan bases.

If *Rear Window* and *The Man Who Knew Too Much* successfully developed the relationship between Hitchcock and Jimmy Stewart, it is in *Vertigo* that the pairing reaches its peak. Robin Wood, one of the first major champions of the film, described the film, "*Vertigo* seems to me of all Hitchcock's films the one nearest to perfection. Indeed, its profundity is inseparable from the perfection of form: it is a perfect organism, each character, each sequence, each image, illuminating every other. Form and technique here become the perfect expression of concerns both deep and universal…Together with its deeply disturbing attitude to life goes a strong feeling for the value of human relationships…Hitchcock is concerned with impulses that lie deeper than individual psychology, that are inherent in the human condition." (129).

In this description, one can see many of the principles that began to come out during the Anthony Mann films, particularly the attention to psychology, the dark side of human nature, and a "disturbing attitude to life." In the role of a man obsessed with capturing the woman of his dreams, the film allowed Stewart to fully expose the tormented psychology that he displayed in his films from earlier in the decade. Where the film is perhaps superior to the Mann westerns is in its use of suspense and the virtuoso formal technique that accompanies most any film directed by Hitchcock. *Vertigo* is filled with virtuoso scenes like the surrealistic dream sequence, that show off Hitchcock's talents and also feature Stewart at his most inspired.

Stewart and Kim Novak in *Vertigo*

It is important to acknowledge that, similar to *It's a Wonderful Life*, the popularity that *Vertigo* now enjoys stands in stark contrast with the reception it received upon release. If Jimmy Stewart is now praised for his performance as a tormented detective, the psychological unrest he displays in the film (and in the Mann ones as well) caused many viewers to disparage the film. For those who fell in love with the 1930s Jimmy Stewart, it was impossible to accept his 1950s films, to the extent Andrew Britton argues that for contemporary viewers, "his performances, for Mann and Hitchcock, as obsession neurotics and 'action-heroes' trembling on the brink of psychosis, simply do not exist" (14). While 21st century viewers see in these characters exemplary deconstructions of American masculinity, many 1950s viewers were unwilling to accept that Stewart could deviate so sharply from the performances of his youth. Accordingly, it was not until decades after its release that *Vertigo* truly entered the pantheon of acclaimed American films, and this is likely the primary reason Stewart was not awarded an Oscar for his efforts during the decade.

Stewart acted in one additional film of great significance during the decade, starring in Otto

Preminger's *Anatomy of a Murder* (1959). A German expatriate, by 1959 Preminger had cultivated a reputation within Hollywood for exploring risqué, often subversive subject matter, and *Anatomy of a Murder* was no different. Stewart stars as district attorney Paul Biegler, who defends a man against charges of murder. In the process of successfully defending his client, he exposes that one of the more prominent citizens in the local town has an illegitimate child. The film was particularly risqué for its frank treatment of rape and illicit sexual intercourse, but Stewart's character is perhaps less frenzied than in his roles from earlier in the decade (though he displays his full temper on select occasions). The film is in some respects a balance between his pre-war films and his most recent ones; by portraying a lawyer with a conscience, his character recalls his title role from *Mr. Smith Goes to Washington*. On the other hand, his character expresses a volatility that would never have been seen in his earlier performances.

Stewart in *Anatomy of a Murder*

Chapter 7: Late Career and Retirement

"If I had my career over again? Maybe I'd say to myself, speed it up a little." – Jimmy Stewart

As Stewart shifted into middle age, his film career began to slow down and he explored new ventures. His film productivity waned during the 1960s, as he appeared in just 12 films over the decade, down from 23 during the 1950s. Stewart's most significant film of the decade was probably *The Man Who Shot Liberty Valence*, a John Ford film from 1962. The film is remarkable for a number of reasons. It returned Stewart to the western genre and offered him the chance to work with John Ford, with whom he had also collaborated on *Two Rode Together* (1961). Ford was a director symbolically associated with the western, and Stewart was even paired with the genre's biggest icon, John Wayne. The opportunity to witness Stewart and John Wayne together is reason enough to view the film, but as with many of Ford's films, the movie also functions as a meditation on the importance of maintaining law and order in civilization. Stewart gives an inspired performance in the role of a Senator determined to uphold the law, and similar to *Anatomy of a Murder*, the film gestures toward his earlier moralistic movies.

Many of Stewart's other late films were also westerns, a truly remarkable development considering that he had built his reputation acting in the sentimental films of Frank Capra. None of the films Jimmy acted in after *The Man Who Shot Liberty Valence* are especially famous, but this does not mean they are not worthy of interest. In 1964, he worked with John Ford once again, this time starring as Wyatt Earp in *Cheyenne Autumn*, and in a return to his pre-Hollywood days, Stewart and Henry Fonda worked together again, starring in the westerns *Firecreek* (1969) and *The Cheyenne Social Club* (1970). The latter film is a comedy-western released at a time in which the genre had begun to veer toward self-parody. Many of his final films also featured him in films with other aging stars. In *The Shootist* (1976), he and John Wayne appear together once more in another western. The following year, he joined an A-list cast in *Airport '77* (1977), and 1978 saw the release of Stewart's final onscreen role in *The Magic of Lassie*.

In addition to film, Stewart also acted in a television program for NBC during the early 1970s called *The Jimmy Stewart Show* (1971-72). The sitcom starred Jimmy as Anthropology Professor James K. Howard, but reviews were highly critical and it was canceled after just one season. The show is now best remembered for being the only instance in which Stewart was actually credited as "Jimmy Stewart." In 1973, he starred in *Hawkins*, in which he played a small-town lawyer in a role not unlike that of *Anatomy of a Murder*. The series was short-lived, however, even though Stewart won the Golden Globe Award for Best Actor. Over the next 10 years, he would make several television appearances, but he remained in a state of semi-retirement.

In old age, Jimmy Stewart's personal life remained relatively uneventful. He lived a domestic married life with his wife and did not attempt any significant career comebacks. By far, the most drastic event was the death of his adopted son Ronald, who was killed in Vietnam, but Ronald's death did not shake Stewart's support for the nation's involvement in the Vietnam War. Throughout his later years, he continued to support the Republican Party, campaigning for Richard M. Nixon and Ronald Reagan.

After retiring from film and television, he stayed busy through his philanthropy efforts, and he remained in good health through much of the 1990s. However, once his wife died, he clearly had less will to go on, and instead of replacing his pacemaker in 1996, he chose not to continue with it. Eventually, his heart condition grew particularly severe, and Jimmy Stewart died on July 2, 1997, with the cause of death listed as a blood clot on his lung.

It's safe to say that the scope of Jimmy Stewart's career is rivaled by very few actors or actresses. The many films he appeared in with Alfred Hitchcock and Frank Capra alone were enough to ensure his legacy, not to mention his inspired collaborations with Anthony Mann, Otto Preminger, and others. At the same time, analyzing his career illuminates the way in which it had two vastly different halves. There were the pre-World War II films, in which he appeared in happy-go-lucky, typically sentimental movies based on his earnest charm, while his films after the war displayed his more overtly psychological dimensions. It is futile to attempt to declare one "version" of Jimmy Stewart's career as superior to the other, since it depends purely on a viewer's personal tastes, but acknowledging the differences between Stewart's early and late performances not only sheds light on the way in which he aged before the public eye but also how he was able to sustain his career as he advanced through middle age.

In addition to recognizing the distinction between the two halves of Stewart's career, it's important to remember the stark differences between the way in which Stewart's films were received at the time in which they were made and how they are remembered and beloved today. This gulf is most stark with *Vertigo* and *It's a Wonderful Life*, but several of Jimmy's movies were significantly less valued among contemporaries than they are today. Only after his career ended and the films continued to circulate among home viewers, festivals, and academic audiences did Stewart's most cherished films truly soar in popularity. Paradoxically enough, it is not incorrect to state that Stewart's career itself also gained importance after it ended. As a star, Stewart derived his appeal from a wholesome, all-American earnestness that is certainly captivating but also seems safe and timeless, but the rising popularity of Jimmy Stewart in the 21st century bears testament to the fundamental mutability of any actor's career, which is far from timeless and perpetually shaped by audiences of the past, present, and future.

Bibliography

"AFI's 100 Years, 100 Stars." *American Film Institute*. 1999. Web., 30 Oct. 2013.

Basinger, Jeanine. *Anthony Mann*. Middletown: Wesleyan University Press, 1997. Print.

Bordwell, David, Kristin Thompson, and Janet Staiger. *The Classical Hollywood Cinema: Film Style & Mode of Production to 1960*. London: Routledge, 1988. Print.

Britton, Andrew. *Katherine Hepburn: Star as Feminist*. New York: Columbia University Press, 2003. Print.

Chandler, James. *An Archaeology of Sympathy: The Sentimental Mode in Literature and Cinema*. Chicago: The University of Chicago Press, 2013. Print.

Eliot, Marc. *Jimmy Stewart: A Biography*. New York: Random House, 2006. Print.

Gomery, Douglas. *Movie History: A Survey: Second Edition*. New York: Routledge, 2011. Print.

Lawrence, Amy. "American Shame: *Rope*, James Stewart, and the Postwar Crisis in American Masculinity. *Hitchcock's America*. Eds. Jonathan Freedman and Richard Millington. New York: Oxford University Press, 1999. Print.

Naremore, James. *Acting in the Cinema*. Berkeley: University of California Press, 1988. Print.

Quirk, Lawrence J. *Behind the Scenes of a Wonderful Life*. New York: Applause Books, 1997. Print.

Smith, Starr. *Jimmy Stewart: Bomber Pilot*. St. Paul: Zenith Press, 2005. Print.

Thomas, Tony. *A Wonderful Life: The Films and Career of James Stewart*. New York: Citadel Press, 2000. Print.

Wolfe, Charles. "The Return of Jimmy Stewart: The Publicity Photograph as Text." *Stardom: Industry of Desire*. Ed. Christine Gledhill. New York and London: Routledge, 1991. 92-106. Print.

Wood, Robin. *Hitchcock's Films Revisited*. New York: Columbia University Press, 1989. Print.

Marlon Brando

Chapter 1: Early Years

"An actor's a guy who, if you ain't talking about him, ain't listening." - Marlon Brando

The story of Marlon Brando begins in a city as complex and unexpected as the artist himself:

Omaha, Nebraska. Although its position in the heart of the Midwest lends the impression of tranquility and tolerance, the Omaha, Nebraska, of the early 20th century was riddled with civil unrest, primarily stemming from fierce labor conflicts. Its population, newly comprised of immigrants who developed individual ethnic enclaves, was growing faster than the city could absorb, and the lack of decent working conditions brought about riots, disorder, resentment and chaos. Strikes were rampant, and because of the practice by companies of hiring minority or ethnic strikebreakers, racial tensions soared.

In response to the civil strife, however, a rich artistic community was born, nurturing the talents of such noted artists as feminist writer Tillie Olsen, trumpeter Lloyd Hunter and singer Anna Mae Winburn. Omaha also had some of the earliest roots in the civil rights movement, dating back to 1912 when the city became home to the first chapter of the NAACP (the National Association for the Advancement of Colored People) founded west of the Mississippi River.

The youngest of three children, Marlon Brando was born amidst this tumultuous, evolving Omaha on April 3, 1924, to Marlon Brando, Sr., a pesticide and chemical feed manufacturer, and his wife, Dorothy Julia Pennebaker. He soon moved with his parents to Evanston, Illinois, living there until their separation in 1935. His mother took her three children, Jocelyn, Frances and Marlon, to live with her mother in Santa Ana, California, but two years later Brando's parents reconciled and moved together to Libertyville, Illinois, a suburb north of Chicago.

Brando's background reflected German, Dutch, English, and Irish ancestry. In fact, his father's family traced its American roots to the 1600s, when Johann Wilhelm Brandau immigrated to New York City from his native Germany. Sadly, the actor's background also reflected multigenerational alcoholism. His father's mother, Marie Holloway, abandoned her family when her son was five years old, using the child support her husband Eugene sent her to indulge her gambling and alcohol addictions and leaving her son to fare for himself from an early age.

In the face of all this adversity, both of Brando's parents exhibited a proclivity for the arts. Marlon Brando, Sr., was an amateur photographer of considerable accomplishments despite his own acute drinking, and his wife Dorothy, known as Dodie, was unconventional and talented, having been a local actress in her youth. She smoked, wore trousers (much like Katherine Hepburn and Marlene Dietrich in later years), and drove cars, all of which were unconventional for women at the time; however, she, too, was an alcoholic, a condition supposedly made worse by her husband's lack of support for her acting career. Her illness reached such depths that one of Marlon's most vivid childhood memories was retrieving her from a neighborhood bar, drunk and naked among strangers. She eventually sought and received help from a local Chicago Alcoholics Anonymous chapter, after which she returned to acting and became an administrator at an Omaha community theatre.

During this tenure, Dodie mentored many Midwestern actors (including a young Henry Fonda) and encouraged her son Marlon's interest in the stage. However, due to Dodie's theatrical involvement and maternal shortcomings, Brando was semi-raised by his maternal grandmother, Bessie Gahan Pennebaker Meyers. A young widow, Bessie Meyers worked as a secretary and later as a Christian Science practitioner, passing the religion on to her grandson. Bessie's father, Myles Gahan, was a physician from Ireland; her mother, Julia Watts, was from England.

While a student at Libertyville High School, Brando's teenage-inspired insolence flourished, foreshadowing his eventual iconic defiance on film. He was held back a year in school and was later expelled for riding his motorcycle through the corridors. Marlon later recalled, "I hated authority and did everything I could to defeat it by resisting it, subverting it, tricking it and outmaneuvering it. I would do anything to avoid being treated like a cipher." In spite of the rebellion, or perhaps partly because of it, Brando was popular in school. Students recalled his insatiable curiosity about nature, his self-taught skill on drums, and his love of body-building, all of which helped in developing the physical charisma that defined his early career.

Naturally, Marlon's parents were less amused with his antics. His father, exasperated at this point, sent him to Shattuck Military Academy, his own alma mater. Brando excelled at theatre and did well in the school, but his insubordinate nature still caused problems. In his final year, he was put on probation for pranks and a declining academic record. More shenanigans followed until the faculty finally voted to expel him, though he was supported by the students who thought punishment was too harsh. He was invited back for the following year, but he decided instead to drop out of high school altogether.

Suggesting his future reputation for uncanny mimicry, Brando was able to imitate characteristics and mannerisms from early age. It was soon apparent that he was drawn towards performing, as it was both a means of artistic expression and a way to get the attention he so desperately sought. His sister Jocelyn was actually the first Brando to pursue an acting career, enrolling at the American Academy of Dramatic Art and appearing on Broadway, as well as in movies and on television. Brando's other sister Frances left college in California to study art in New York. Both sisters gave young Marlon the motivation to follow his siblings after dropping out of school, arriving in New York himself in 1943, where he dug ditches and worked as both a department store elevator boy and a factory night watchman to support himself. His father, eventually acknowledging that acting was what truly motivated his son, offered to help support him so that he could pursue his vocation.

Chapter 2: A Start in Acting

Portrait of Brando in 1948

"To grasp the full significance of life is the actor's duty, to interpret it is his problem, and to express it his dedication." - Marlon Brando

Brando eventually enrolled at the American Theatre Wing Professional School, the Dramatic Workshop of The New School for Social Research (with classmates including Harry Belafonte, Shelley Winters and Rod Steiger), and at the Actors Studio. The Actors Studio had its roots in the Group Theatre (1931-1941), whose work was inspired by the discoveries of the great Russian actor and director Constantin Stanislavski and his best student, Eugene Vakhtangov, as revealed in the legendary productions that the Moscow Art Theatre brought to America in 1923. In fact Stanislavski's dedication in his famous 1924 book, *My Life in Art,* reads: "I dedicate this book in gratitude to hospitable America as a token and a remembrance from the Moscow Art Theatre which she took so kindly to her heart." When the Moscow Art Theatre ended the American tour, several members of the theatre stayed behind and trained artists, including Lee Strasberg, Harold Clurman and Stella Adler, who would go on to form the Group Theatre along with other artists such as Elia Kazan, Sanford Meisner and Robert Lewis.

Stanislavski

These artists studied, explored, developed and improved the work of the inspiring Russians with extraordinary results, paving the way for a new kind of acting. Often called "The Method," or Method Acting, the approach was, and is, a combined variety of techniques used by actors to immerse themselves the thoughts and emotions of their characters in order to develop lifelike, realistically powerful performances. The "method" in Method Acting usually refers to the practice created by Lee Strasberg in which actors draw upon personal emotions and memories to inform their performance, especially where physical and emotional details from a situation similar to those of their characters are available. While classical acting instruction focused on developing external expression, movement and mannerisms to develop a character, Method actors did the opposite, focusing on deep, internal components based in the sensory, psychological, and emotional arsenal of the human psyche. (Even today, one might see these opposing schools of technique when, for example, comparing contemporary American actors – primarily champions of The Method – to their British counterparts, who still tend to emphasize the predominantly external-based, classical approach.)

Despite being commonly regarded as a Method actor, Brando saw himself as anything but. He claimed to have abhorred Lee Strasberg's teachings: "After I had some success, Lee Strasberg tried to take credit for teaching me how to act. He never taught me anything. He would have claimed credit for the sun and the moon if he believed he could get away with it. He was an ambitious, selfish man who exploited the people who attended the Actors Studio and tried to project himself as an acting oracle and guru. Some people worshipped him, but I never knew why ... Strasberg never taught me acting."

Strasberg in 1978

Instead, Brando was an avid student and proponent of Stella Adler, who taught the young actor the techniques of the Stanislavski System. Adler came from a distinguished family of Yiddish actors and lived by the mantra, "Don't act. Behave." Unlike Strasberg, her version of the Method is based on the idea that actors should evoke emotion not through personal memories but by using a scene's specific circumstances. Adler often taught that drawing on personal experience alone was too limited, and therefore urged her students to draw on their imaginations in order to utilize emotional memory to the fullest.

Stella Adler

There is a story in which Adler spoke about teaching Brando, saying that she had instructed the class to act like chickens, then added that a nuclear bomb was about to fall on them. While others flailed about, Brando sat still and pretended to lay an egg. Asked by Adler why he had chosen to react this way, he said, "I'm a chicken. What do I know from a bomb?"

Where he refused to credit Strasberg, Brando considered Stella Adler an important influence and mentor. "What Stella taught her students was how to discover the nature of their own emotional mechanics and therefore those of others," Brando once wrote. "She taught me to be real." She also helped turn him from an unsophisticated Midwestern boy into a knowledgeable and cosmopolitan artist who one day would socialize with presidents.

Chapter 3: The Big Break

I said to Tennessee, "This is becoming The Marlon Brando Show." - Elia Kazan

After only a year in New York, Brando was hired to play the teenage son Nels in John van Druten's play *I Remember Mama*. The production, as well as his performance, was a major hit, and it was followed by his role in 1946 as a troubled veteran in Maxwell Anderson's *Truckline*

Café, directed by Elia Kazan. It was during this run that the power of Brando became evident. Kazan was challenged as a director to keep the actor's magnetism confined and was forced to re-block scenes in order for the audience to even notice the rest of the cast. New York theater critics voted Brando Broadway's Most Promising Actor for this performance in spite of the play's lack of commercial success; the boy from Omaha was beginning to make his mark, and people took notice.

Kazan

Kazan, known for his work at the Group Theatre, was slated to direct Tennessee Williams' classic *A Streetcar Named Desire* on Broadway, and after *Truckline Café*, he was intent on the young actor playing the role of Stanley Kowalski, the brutish, outwardly sexual brother-in-law of the main character, Blanche DuBois, the fragile, alcoholic, guilt-ridden Southern belle that the playwright based on himself. Producer Irene Selznick was set to cast John Garfield or Burt Lancaster in the role of Stanley, but Brando personally campaigned for the role, resulting in Kazan giving him carfare to Provincetown, Massachusetts to audition for Williams. It was an impressive reading, and the playwright was convinced that the production had found its Stanley. Kazan convinced Selznick to cast Brando, while Jessica Tandy, after her role in Williams' one act *Portrait of a Madonna,* was cast as Blanche.

Tennessee Williams

A Streetcar Named Desire is the story of an aging vestige of the gentility of the Old South. Blanche DuBois is a repressed yet delusional woman who is trapped by her own desperate attempts to cling to her youth, physical attractiveness and sexuality. The play intends to follow her descent into madness, partially due to her callous, cruel and ultimately violent treatment by Stanley. But soon after rehearsals began, it became more than apparent that a shift had occurred, and the focus of the play surrendered to the power of Brando's interpretation of Stanley. A force of nature himself, Brando basically wrestled the focus of the play from the hands of Tandy, making it Stanley's story, not Blanche's. It was, in the words of the director, "becoming The Marlon Brando Show." Still, Kazan was credited with helping Brando get past his fear of memorization – a problem that plagued him throughout his career – and teaching him the advantage of props, a technique he used in performances for years to come.

Streetcar opened in 1947, and Brando's performance was hailed as a landmark theatrical event. His Kowalski was unprecedented as a man of irresistible sexuality and frightening violence, one who simultaneously used his animal appeal to conquer and manipulate his wife Stella and terrorize his sister-in-law Blanche. Opening night earned a 30 minute standing ovation. Making the performance perhaps all the more remarkable, Brando once wrote that he was "the antithesis of Stanley Kowalski. I was sensitive by nature and he was coarse, a man with unerring animal instincts and intuitions."

During the two-year Broadway run, Brando and Jessica Tandy consistently clashed. Tandy was classically trained, and didn't understand the visceral, naturalistic approach to which Brando subscribed. She found his soon-to-be trademark mumbling speech pattern a distraction, to the point that it caused her to miss her verbal cues onstage, regularly knocking her performance out of sync. Never one to take things sitting down, Brando found himself retaliating with a series of juvenile backstage pranks which further exacerbated the tension between the lead stars. But the play was a breakthrough in establishing the Brando persona – raw, uncompromising and mysteriously magnetic, but able to inspire fear and intimidation, even though the actor barely stood at five feet ten inches and possessed an almost angelic, feminine face with soft, full features. And just as Kazan had noticed the Brando appeal on the stage, it was now Hollywood's turn to tap the talents of this uniquely compelling young star.

Brando in *Streetcar*. Photo by Carl Van Vechten

Chapter 4: Hurray for Hollywood?

"Never confuse the size of your paycheck with the size of your talent." - Marlon Brando

On the heels of his immense stage success in **Streetcar**, Hollywood quickly beckoned, and after refusing many offers Brando finally made his motion picture debut in 1950 as a paraplegic World War II veteran in Stanley Kramer's independent film, **The Men.** To prepare for the role, the actor spent a month in bed at the Birmingham Army Hospital in Van Nuys. By his own account, this role may have also been instrumental in changing his own draft status from 4-F to

1-A. While at Shattuck, a teenaged Brando had suffered an injured knee which required a surgery; however, it did not exclude him from the draft. When he reported to the induction center, he answered a questionnaire by saying his race was "human," his color was "seasonal-oyster white to beige," and then proceeded to tell an Army doctor that he was psycho-neurotic. When the draft board referred him to a psychiatrist, Brando told him how he had been expelled from military school and that he had severe problems with authority. Coincidentally, the psychiatrist knew a doctor friend of Brando, and Brando was able to avoid military service during the Korean War.

The Men featured another arresting performance by Brando, but due to the timing of its release and its unpopular subject matter (the plight of crippled war veterans), it met with a tepid response from its target audience. This fueled Brando's already healthy mistrust of and disregard for the Hollywood machine; nonetheless, he followed *The Men* by reprising his role of Stanley Kowalski in the film version of *Streetcar* in 1951. Although sanitized to accommodate the Hays Code restrictions, the film set Hollywood on fire, earning four Academy Awards and bringing the motion picture industry the first of Brando's many iconic performances. Naturally, it also shot Brando's career into the stratosphere. Jessica Tandy's Blanche was replaced by Vivien Leigh, the exquisitely beautiful English actress and wife of Sir Laurence Olivier. Brando was thrilled by the casting, as he always thought that Tandy was shrill, an attribute which encouraged the audience to side with Stanley. He thought Leigh was ideal, as she was not only a great beauty but she, like Blanche, was a troubled soul in her real life, battling ongoing mental illness. Her performance came much closer than Tandy's to his own in its depth, indelibility and complexity. Earning a Best Actor nomination, Brando lost to Humphrey Bogart's sentimental win for *The African Queen*, further strengthening his lack of respect for the film community.

Vivien Leigh in *Streetcar*

1952 brought *Viva Zapata!*, Brando's next film with a script by John Steinbeck. *Viva Zapata!* traced the meteoric rise of Emiliano Zapata from peasant to revolutionary to the president of Mexico and underlined Brando's masculine presence. He followed this role with that of Mark Anthony in *Julius Caesar* (1953), and then Johnny in *The Wild One* (1954), another iconic role in which he played a motorcycle-gang leader (with Brando riding his own Triumph Thunderbird 6T bike) with a systemic sense of rebellion. In one scene Brando's character is asked, "What are you rebelling against?" Johnny replies, "What have ya got?" *The Wild One* quickly became a cult classic, influencing music, attitudes and even fashion, inspiring other 1950s icons such as James Dean, Steve McQueen and Elvis Presley.

Brando as Zapata

As a break from what he considered Hollywood's toxicity, Brando made a brief return to the stage in 1953, starring in Lee Falk's production of George Bernard Shaw's *Arms and the Man* in

Boston. Falk was proud to tell people that Marlon Brando turned down an offer of $10,000 per week on Broadway in favor of working on Falk's play in Boston, a contract that had Brando earning less than $500 per week. It was, however, the last time he ever acted in a stage play.

That play aside, Brando continued to dominate the world of film during the 1950s. Capped by his performance as Terry Malloy in *On the Waterfront* in 1954, which finally earned him his Oscar for Best Actor, Brando's first five films firmly established him as a star for the ages. He was also awarded BAFTA awards for Best Actor in a Leading Role for three consecutive years (1951 through 1953).

Brando in *On The Waterfront*

On the Waterfront's Terry Malloy, like *Streetcar*'s Stanley Kowalski, is one of the roles most closely associated with Brando. As the down-and-out boxer-turned-longshoreman fighting New York's union corruption, Brando delivered a performance rife with poignancy. Once again directed by Elia Kazan, his famous "I coulda been a contender" speech is considered one of the great moments on film. Legend has it that Brando was not convinced by the scene's original lines written by screenwriter Budd Schulberg and ultimately improvised the final take with Rod Steiger, his former New School classmate. About that famous scene and its impact, Brando later stated:

"In a movie that I was in, called *On the Waterfront*, there was a scene in a taxicab, where I turn to my brother, who's come to turn me over to the gangsters, and I lament to him that he never looked after me, he never gave me a chance, that I could have been a contender, I coulda been somebody, instead of a bum ... 'You should of looked out after me, Charley.' It was very moving. And people often spoke about that, 'Oh, my God, what a wonderful scene, Marlon, blah blah blah blah blah.' It wasn't wonderful at all. The situation was wonderful. Everybody feels like he could have been a contender, he could have been somebody, everybody feels as though he's partly bum, some part of him. He is not fulfilled and he could have done better, he could have been better. Everybody feels a sense of loss about something. So that was what touched people. It wasn't the scene itself. There are other scenes where you'll find actors being expert, but since the audience can't clearly identify with them, they just pass unnoticed. Wonderful scenes never get mentioned, only those scenes that affect people."

For the remainder of the decade, Brando's screen roles were nothing if not eclectic: Napoleon Bonaparte in *Désirée* (1954); Sky Masterson in *Guys and Dolls* (1955); Sakini, a Japanese interpreter for the U.S. Army in postwar Japan in *The Teahouse of the August Moon* (1956); United States Air Force officer Lloyd Gruver in *Sayonara* (1957); and Nazi officer Christian Diestl in *The Young Lions* (1958). The role of Sky Masterson was especially surprising, as he was elevated to the romantic lead in an adapted Broadway musical, requiring him to both sing and dance. This incredibly versatile body of work caused movie exhibitors to vote him one of the Top Ten box office draws from 1955 to 1958.

Chapter 5: Fall From Grace

"The only thing an actor owes his public is not to bore them." - Marlon Brando

Not all of Brando's films in the 1950s were financial or critical successes, but they were certainly marketed to be, and he was averse to participating in the endless Hollywood publicity initiative, and grew more and more tired of commercial products. As a result, he began looking for more independent and unusual projects, taking on the role of the wandering musician in Sidney Lumet's *The Fugitive Kind* (1959), an adaptation of Tennessee Williams' play *Orpheus Descending,* and the anti-hero in *One-Eyed Jacks* (1961). Although he didn't lack work, the 1960s ushered in a career decline for the eminent star.

Stanley Kubrick was originally slated to direct *One-Eyed Jacks,* but he grew increasingly frustrated with Brando's concept for the film and instead went off to direct *Spartacus* with Kirk Douglas. *One-Eyed Jacks'* budget, originally set at $2 million, zoomed to $6 million when Brando took over directorial duties and began championing improvisational acting techniques, even among cast extras. The end result was a five-hour-long film. When the studio cut it, an angry Brando succumbed to his excesses and began one of his famous eating binges. It was then that Brando started to attract the label of "bad boy", with Los Angeles magazine aptly putting it, "Brando was rock and roll before anybody knew what rock and roll was."

MGM's 1962 remake of *Mutiny on the Bounty*, a film with an enormous budget but not enough ticket sales, proved to be another disaster. Brando portrayed an overly-effete Fletcher Christian, the role Clark Gable played in the 1935 original, and his growing self-indulgence reached new heights on the set. Criticized for tantrums, demands and script control, he also had numerous affairs as he distanced himself from the cast and crew. His contract included the stipulation of an extra $5,000 for every day the film went over its original schedule. By the end of the film, he had made $1.25 million, and the increasingly eccentric actor loved Tahiti so much during the work that he purchased a 12-island atoll, Tetiaroa, and had a hotel built on it.

After the *Mutiny* debacle, Brando became more drawn towards social activism and began his longest commercial slump by choosing a series of films that were important for casting a critical eye on American socio-political mores. He played a diplomat in *The Ugly American* (1963); a sheriff in a town of Southern vipers in *The Chase* (1966); a square politician in the Charlie Chaplin-directed *A Countess of Hong Kong* (1967); a repressed gay Army officer in *Reflections in a Golden Eye* (1967); and a sex guru in *Candy* (1968). In Italian director Gillo Pontecorvo's anti-colonial film *Burn!* (1969), Brando portrayed Sir William Walker, a British agent provocateur sent to a fictional Portuguese colony in Antilles. Walker's mission is to organize an uprising of black slaves to overthrow the Portuguese regime so that Great Britain could take economic control of the sugar-producing island. He considered the role the apex of his career up to that point, as it reflected his acting inclinations as well as his activism. Still, it was another failure.

Brando and James Baldwin at the Civil Rights March on Washington D.C., 1963

Dealing with film and personal woes, Brando grew increasingly depressed and began another eating binge. His career slowed down by the end of the decade as he gained a reputation for being difficult to work with. He retreated to Tahiti, which he had discovered as a peaceful escape while filming *Mutiny*, and bought an entire private island in 1967 for $270,000.

NEW TRIUMPHS

"If you want something from an audience, you give blood to their fantasies. It's the ultimate hustle." - Marlon Brando

1972 brought Brando a third role of a lifetime and perhaps his most iconic in the character of Vito Corleone in Francis Ford Coppola's masterpiece, ***The Godfather***. Book and screenwriter Mario Puzo had sent him the script because he had written the character with Brando in mind, and Brando was so intrigued by the story of family set against the backdrop of corporate greed and violence that he replied favorably. As he explored the role with Coppola, he submitted to a make-up test to try out physical looks for the patriarch. Doing his own make-up and stuffing his jowls with cotton balls to puff up aging cheeks, he dazzled the director and many of the producers involved.

There was still one more hurdle. Due to Brando's reputation for being indulgent and problematic, the Paramount brass was hesitant to cast him, wanting to cast Danny Thomas instead. Thomas had no interest in the role, instead urging the studio to cast Brando at the request of those who had witnessed the screen test.

Danny Thomas

A true cinematic triumph, Brando's performance was partially inspired by organized-crime figure Frank Costello. He mimicked Costello's thin voice from Costello's testimony during a 1950s Senate hearing led by Estes Kefauver (D-Tenn.) and met with other underworld heads to copy their styles and mannerisms. True to his Adler training, he was also quite inventive on camera, adding many memorable improvisations, most notably placing the slice of orange in his mouth to amuse his grandson just before his death in the tomato garden.

At the same time, the role went beyond just acting tricks and conceits. Brando was able to capture an immensely complex character – one who embodied loyalty and compassion but also ruthless violence. "I had a great deal of respect for Don Corleone" he said. "I saw him as a man of substance, tradition, dignity, refinement, a man of unerring instinct who just happened to live in a violent world and who had to protect himself and his family in this environment. I saw him as a decent person regardless of what he had to do, as a man who believed in family values and was shaped by events just like the rest of us."

Don Vito Corleone brought Brando another Oscar for Best Actor, but he refused to accept it.

Sacheen Littlefeather represented him at the ceremony. Appearing in full Apache clothing, she announced that owing to the "poor treatment of Native Americans in the film industry," Brando would not accept the award. There was no starker way for Brando to voice his objections to Hollywood's depictions of the Native American community.

Brando followed *The Godfather* with Bernardo Bertolucci's controversial 1973 film *Last Tango in Paris*, playing Paul, an American expat who has a fatal fling with a young Frenchwoman. Although the film earned an X rating for its sexual content, Brando's performance revitalized his career and secured his reputation as one of film's greatest actors. For his role, Brando dug into himself at the encouragement of his director, finding the rage - against himself and against the women he famously seduced and abandoned - that lies just beneath the surface in so many of his performances.

Respected film critic Pauline Kael wrote that director Bertolucci and Brando "have altered the face of an art form," calling the film revolutionary. And despite his refusal of his statue the year prior, the Academy once again nominated him for Best Actor. Brando, however, did not share the enthusiasm: "*Last Tango in Paris* required a lot of emotional arm wrestling with myself, and when it was finished, I decided that I wasn't ever again going to destroy myself emotionally to make a movie. I felt I had violated my innermost self and didn't want to suffer like that anymore."

Chapter 6: Another Downward Slide

"The only reason I'm in Hollywood is that I don't have the moral courage to refuse the money." - Marlon Brando

After his second professional surge in the early 1970s, Brando admitted he made many of his later films for the money. He reportedly made $3.7 million for 12 days of work on *Superman*, portraying Jor-El, the superhero's father. Other demands included that he didn't have to read the script, and that his lines would basically be fed to him from off-screen. Still, even in this and other seemingly inane roles, like the cross-dressing hit man in *The Missouri Breaks* (1976) or the harmless Mafia don in *The Freshman* (1960), his charisma remained intact. Critic Hal Hinson, writing about *The Freshman* in *The Washington Post*, said, "Brando is never less than a miraculously magnetic camera subject; just to have him in front of the lens is, in most cases, enough."

1979's *Apocalypse Now* reunited Brando with *Godfather* director Francis Ford Coppola. Inspired by Joseph Conrad's novella *Heart of Darkness,* the film explored the Vietnam War, with Brando playing Colonel Walter E. Kurtz, a decorated American Army Special Forces who goes renegade. Running his own operations based in Cambodia, Kurtz is feared by both the U.S. military and the Vietnamese alike. The actor delivered a creepily compelling performance while earning a million dollars a week. "It's been said I sold out," Brando was once quoted as saying. "Maybe that's true, but I knew what I was doing. I've never had any respect for Hollywood. It stands for greed, avarice, phoniness, crassness – but when you act in a movie, you act for three months and then you can do what you want for the rest of the year."

Despite announcing his retirement from acting in 1980, Brando subsequently gave supporting performances in movies such as *A Dry White Season* (for which he was nominated for a Best Supporting Actor Oscar in 1989) and *Don Juan DeMarco* in 1995 with upcoming film legend, Johnny Depp. In his last film, *The Score* (2001), he starred with Robert De Niro, who played the young Vito Corleone in *The Godfather: Part II.* Other performances, such as the title role in *The Island of Dr. Moreau* (1996), earned Brando some of the most uncomplimentary reviews of his career, adding to his depression, reclusiveness and binging. By now morbidly obese and despondent after the deaths of family and friends, he spent the last decade more as a symbol of media curiosity than as an actor looking for the next challenge.

In 2004, Brando signed with Tunisian film director Ridha Behion and began pre-production on a project to be titled *Brando and Brando.* Shortly before his death, he was working on the script in anticipation of a July/August 2004 start date, but production was suspended in July 2004 following his passing. Behion stated that he would continue the film as an homage to Brando, with a new title, *Citizen Brando.*

Chapter 7: Social Activism

"If we are not our brother's keeper, at least let us not be his executioner." - Marlon Brando

Marlon Brando's involvement in civil rights and activism was a part of him for nearly all of his adult life. Perhaps because his own tumultuous youth among raging alcoholic parents was so riddled with emotional strife, he had an understanding of and compassion for the downtrodden, a commitment he was known for until the end of his life. Brando also had an extremely difficult time reconciling his own wealth and success with the state of the world's tribulations. He donated much of his money to worthy social causes, and always found his profession to be a frivolous blip on the radar of the human condition.

In 1946, Brando showed his dedication to the idea of a Jewish homeland by performing in Ben Hecht's play *A Flag is Born*. His involvement had an impact on three of the most divisive issues of the early post-war period: the fight to establish a Jewish state, the smuggling of Holocaust survivors to Israel, and the battle against racial segregation in the United States. At the same time, Brando would make head-turning comments about Jews later in his life that led to charges of anti-Semitism, claiming in an interview with Larry King, "Hollywood is run by Jews; it is owned by Jews, and they should have a greater sensitivity about the issue of—of people who are suffering."

A supporter of John F. Kennedy's run for the Presidency, he was an active fundraiser for JFK's campaign. In August 1963, he participated in the March on Washington along with fellow celebrities Harry Belafonte, James Garner, Charlton Heston, Burt Lancaster, and Sidney Poitier. Brando also, along with Paul Newman, participated in the freedom rides.

Brando with Charlton Heston and James Baldwin in Washington

After the 1968 assassination of Dr. Martin Luther King Jr., Brando made one of his strongest commitments to furthering King's tenet of nonviolent resistance. Shortly after King's death, he announced that he was exiting a major film (*The Arrangement*) which was about to begin production in order to devote himself to the civil rights movement. As a guest on the then popular late night talk show, *The Joey Bishop Show,* he told Bishop, "I felt I'd better go find out where it is; what it is to be black in this country; what this rage is all about."

While that made headlines, Brando's participation in the African-American civil rights movement actually began well before King's death. In the early 1960s, he contributed thousands of dollars to both the Southern Christian Leadership Conference (SCLC) and to a scholarship fund established for the children of slain Mississippi NAACP leader Medgar Evers. The actor also tried to seek out projects that reflected messages of human rights, such as *Sayonara,* which addressed interracial romance, and *The Ugly American,* which depicted the conduct of U.S. officials abroad and its harmful effect on the citizens of foreign countries. For a time, he was also donating money to the Black Panther Party and considered himself a friend of founder Bobby Seale; however, he broke ties with the group over what he perceived as its increasing radicalization and Eldridge Cleaver's support of indiscriminate violence.

On a more local stage, Brando appeared before the California Assembly in support of a fair housing law and joined picket lines protesting discrimination in the state's housing developments.

Chapter 8: Family Life (Or Lack of It)

"I come from a long line of Irish drunks." - Marlon Brando

Brando's excesses – eating, drinking, and sex – may very well have manifested from a childhood filled with loneliness. His father traveled extensively on his job, and when he was home, was usually drunk. His mother, too, was an alcoholic, and until she became sober with the help of Alcoholics Anonymous, she was an absent and reticent parent. His best acting performances – Stanley Kowalski, Terry Malloy – are roles that required him to show a confined yet evident rage and angst, and it's no wonder that he had the emotional ammunition to do so with skill and excellence. *Time* magazine reported, "Brando had a stern, cold father and a dream-disheveled mother – both alcoholics, both sexually promiscuous – and he encompassed both their natures without resolving the conflict." Brando himself wrote in his autobiography, "If my father were alive today, I don't know what I would do. After he died, I used to think, 'God, just give him to me alive for eight seconds because I want to break his jaw.'"

Brando's relationships with women were just as angst-ridden and controversial. The actor himself once noted, "With women, I've got a long bamboo pole with a leather loop on the end. I slip the loop around their necks so they can't get away or come too close. Like catching snakes." Although Brando rarely if ever spoke in detail about his many relationships, it is known that he married three times to three ex-actresses.

Brando's first married actress Anna Kashfi in 1957, who raised eyebrows with her book, *Brando for Breakfast,* in which she discusses controversies surrounding her race and ethnicity in detail. Brando and Kashfi had a son, Christian Brando, on May 11, 1958, but they divorced shortly after in 1959.

In 1960 Brando married Movita Castaneda, a Mexican-American actress who had appeared in the first *Mutiny on the Bounty* film in 1935, 27 years before the 1962 remake with Brando playing Fletcher Christian. This marriage was also short-lived, with the two divorcing in 1962, but they had two children together: Miko Castaneda Brando (b. 1961) and Rebecca Brando (b.1966).

Movita Castaneda in *Mutiny on the Bounty*

Ironically, while filming the later adaptation of ***Mutiny on the Bounty***, Brando met and fell in love with Tahitian actress Tarita Teriipia, who also happened to be playing his love interest in the movie. At just 20 years of age, she was considerably younger than the 38 year old Brando, but he attempted to make it work, to the extent that he became fluent in her native French. Teriipia gave birth to two more of his children: Simon Teihotu Brando (b. 1963) and Tarita Cheyenne Brando (b. 1970). Brando also subsequently adopted Teriipia's daughters, Maimiti Brando (b. 1977) and Raiatua Brando (b. 1982), despite the fact they had divorced in July 1972.

Brando also had a running relationship with his housekeeper, Maria Christina Ruiz, who bore him three more children: Ninna Priscilla Brando (b. 1989), Myles Jonathan Brando (b. 1992), and Timothy Gahan Brando (b. 1994). And he had four more children whose mothers were never identified: Stephen Blackehart (b. 1967), Michael Gilman (b. 1967), Dylan Brando (b. 1968), and Angelique Brando.

Brando hinted at the struggles he had with establishing and living some semblance of a normal family life: "This is a false world. It's been a struggle to try to preserve my sanity and sense of reality taken away by success. I have to fight hard to preserve that sense of reality so as to bring up my children."

In May 1990, Brando faced what was the beginning of perhaps his most profound family tragedy. Dag Drollet, the Tahitian lover of Brando's daughter Cheyenne, died of a gunshot wound after a confrontation with Cheyenne's half-brother Christian at the family home in Beverly Hills. Christian claimed the shooting was accidental and a result of his being drunk, but rumors spread that he had actually retaliated because Dag was physically abusing Cheyenne, who was pregnant at the time. Brando happened to be in the house when the shooting took place and called 911 while trying in vein to resuscitate Drollet.

Given Marlon Brando's stature, the pre-trial proceedings were heavily publicized. Christian pleaded guilty to charges of voluntary manslaughter and using a gun, but the proceedings were made more newsworthy by Brando's own testimony. When Brando took the stand, he was full of anguish and delivered a self-castigating courtroom plea in which he said he and his former wife had failed Christian: "I tried to be a good father. I did the best I could." He also told Drollet's family, "I'm sorry…If I could trade places with Dag, I would. I'm prepared for the consequences." Drollet's family was unmoved by the display, and Dag's father Jacques later accused Brando of acting to help his son get away with murder.

The tragedy continued to impact the family. Cheyenne had a history of drug abuse and was in and out of rehabilitation centers and mental hospitals for much of her life. *People* magazine reported in 1990 that Cheyenne said of Brando, "I have come to despise my father for the way he ignored me as a child." After Drollet's death, Cheyenne became even more reclusive and depressed; a judge ruled that she was too depressed to raise her child and gave custody of the boy to her mother, Tarita. Cheyenne took a leave from a mental hospital on Easter Sunday in 1995 to visit her family, and while at her mother's home that day, Cheyenne, who had attempted suicide before, hanged herself.

Christian Brando died of pneumonia at age 49 on January 26, 2008.

Chapter 9: The Final Decline

"An actor is at most a poet and at least an entertainer." - Marlon Brando

Brando's notoriety, his troubled family life, and his morbid obesity eventually began to attract more attention than his acting career. By the 1990s, he had ballooned to over 300 pounds and suffered from diabetes. Like other luminaries such as Orson Welles or Elvis Presley, he had a history of weight fluctuations through his career, stemming from his years of stress-related overeating followed by crash dieting. Nevertheless, he continued busying himself with pursuits that piqued his interest. He had several patents issued in his name from the U.S. Patent and

Trademark Office, all of which involve a method of tensioning drum heads, from June 2002 – November 2004, and he reportedly returned to his childhood fondness for mimicry, communicating to faceless strangers in disguised voices on his collection of ham-radios.

A longtime close friend of entertainer Michael Jackson, Brando paid regular visits to his Neverland Ranch in his later years, resting there for weeks at a time. He also participated in the singer's two-day solo career 30th-anniversary celebration concerts in 2001, and starred in his 13-minute-long music video, "You Rock My World." in the same year. On Jackson's final 30th anniversary concert, Brando gave a speech to the audience on humanitarian work that received a poor reaction from the audience and went unaired. Brando's son Mike noted, "The last time my father left his house to go anywhere, to spend any kind of time... was with Michael Jackson. He loved it... He had a 24-hour chef, 24-hour security, 24-hour help, 24-hour kitchen, 24-hour maid service."

In a documentary accompanying the DVD of *A Streetcar Named Desire,* Karl Malden, Brando's friend and fellow actor in *A Streetcar Named Desire, On The Waterfront*, and *One-Eyed Jacks* (the only film directed by Brando), discussed a call he received from Brando shortly before his death. Brando told Malden that he had been suffering from frequent falls, but when Malden offered to go to Brando's home, the star resisted, questioning the need or rationale behind it. Three weeks later, Marlon Brando was dead of respiratory failure from pulmonary fibrosis with congestive heart failure at the UCLA Medical Center on July 1, 2004. Shortly before his death, he had apparently refused the insertion of oxygen tubes into his lungs, which doctors told him was the only way to extend his life.

Brando was cremated, and his ashes were combined with those of his close childhood friend, actor Wally Cox. Brando had once said of his friend, "If Wally had been born a woman, I would have married him and we'd be living happily ever after." His ashes were also combined with another longtime friend, Sam Gilman, and they were then scattered partly in Tahiti and partly in Death Valley.

Chapter 10: Brando's Legacy

"Regret is useless in life. It's in the past. All we have is now." - Marlon Brando

It was clear from Brando's cinema debut as a paraplegic war veteran in *The Men* (1950) and his explosive work as Stanley Kowalski in A Streetcar Named Desire (1951) that he was a new breed of actor, able to convey a passion-fueled, emotional nakedness in each and every performance. One critic noted that in *The Men*, Brando "comes like a blood transfusion into cinema acting," and later writers confirmed his legacy: "With his pinup good looks and incomparable versatility, he dominated film acting."

One of his greatest legacies as an actor was to identify the deepest thoughts of his characters and convey their motivations with the precision and accuracy of a surgeon. His was a lifetime of emotional distress, and he used it to his artistic advantage. His mimicry and his own intuition brought multiple psychological dimensions to all his performances. Although his leading men were capable of rape and violence, he was praised for making those actions appear almost poetic and tragic, lending an unprecedented depth to his art.

Brando also hugely impacted the cultural landscape. The young actor personified the muscular, defiant leather-jacketed masculinity that emerged and was popularized during the 1950s. He was known to wear jeans to formal parties (his influence on style continues to this day, i.e. via the fashions of elite designers such as Dolce and Gabbana), he regularly insulted influential industry columnists, and wore his disdain for social conventions on his sleeve for all to see. In short, he fought anything that the Hollywood system utilized to control his public image.

But it was his acting that made him special, his artistry that transcended everything else. Critic Stanley Crouch wrote, "Brando's main achievement was to portray the taciturn but stoic gloom of those pulverized by circumstances," while Newsweek's Jack Kroll wrote in 1994 that "Brando's legacy whether he likes it or not – is that he is the stunning actor who embodied a poetry of anxiety that touched the deepest dynamics of his time and place." Perhaps actor David Thewlis, Brando's co-star in *The Island of Dr. Moreau*, said it best: "When he walks into a room, you know he's around."

Actors' Quotes About Brando

Would people applaud me if I were a good plumber? - Marlon Brando

"I'll never forget the wonderful experience working with Marlon filming On The Waterfront. Playing those scenes with him was something I shall always treasure. He was one of the most generous and talented actors." - *Eva Marie Saint*

"People always ask me who was the most influential guy to us young guys back then. Anyone who doesn't tell you Brando was the man, they're lying. He influenced more young actors of my generation than any actor. Anyone who denies it never understood what it was all about. I loved him." - *James Caan*

"Actors such as him should be immortal. He was a wonderful work companion, a person of great education, a great professional." - *Sophia Loren*

"Actors such as him should be immortal. He was a wonderful work companion, a person of great education, a great professional. When Marlon dies, everybody moves up one. We are all Brando's children. He gave us our freedom." - *Jack Nicholson*

"I'm angry at Marlon because he does everything so easily. I have to break my ass to do what he can do with his eyes closed." - *Paul Newman*

"It was incomprehensible how good Brando was. He was just a phenomenon. I was acting before I ever saw a Brando picture. I'm very proud to be able to say that but I'll be imitating him until the day I die." - *Al Pacino*

"He acted with an empathy and an instinctual understanding that not even the greatest technical performers could possibly match." - *Sir Laurence Olivier*

"I admire Marlon's talent, but I don't envy the pain that created it." - *Anthony Quinn*

Career Retrospective

Awards and Honors

Theatre World Promising Personalities Award, 1945;

Academy Award nomination, Best Actor, 1951, for ***A Streetcar Named Desire;***

British Academy Award, Best Foreign Actor, British Academy of Film and Television Arts, Cannes International Film Festival Award, Best Actor, and Academy Award nomination, Best Actor, all 1952, for ***Viva Zapata!;***

British Academy Award, Best Foreign Actor, and Academy Award nomination, Best Actor, both 1953, for ***Julius Caesar;***

Academy Award, Best Actor, 1954, British Academy Award, Best Foreign Actor, 1954, and Golden Globe Award, Best Actor, Hollywood Foreign Press Association, 1955, all for ***On The Waterfront;***

Golden Globe Award, World Film Favorite, 1956, 1973, and 1974;

Academy Award nomination, Best Actor, 1957, for ***Sayonara;***

Academy Award, Best Actor, 1972, and Golden Globe Award, Best Actor, 1973, both for ***The Godfather;***

Academy Award nomination, Best Actor, 1973, for *Last Tango in Paris;*

Emmy Award, Outstanding Supporting Actor in a Miniseries, 1979, for *Roots: The Next Generations;*

Tokyo International Film Festival Award, Best Actor, and Academy Award nomination, Best Supporting Actor, both 1989, for *A Dry White Season.*

Filmography

(Debut) Ken Wilozek, *The Men* (also known as *Battle Stripe*),United Artists, 1950

Stanley Kowalski, *A Streetcar Named Desire*, Warner Bros./TwentiethCentury-Fox, 1951

Emiliano Zapata, *Viva Zapata!,* Twentieth Century-Fox, 1952

Marc Antony, *Julius Caesar* (also known as *William Shakespeare's Julius Caesar*), Metro-Goldwyn-Mayer, 1953

Johnny, *The Wild One*, Columbia, 1953

Napoleon Bonaparte, *Desiree,* Twentieth Century-Fox, 1954

Terry Malloy, *On The Waterfront*, Columbia, 1954

Guy Masterson, *Guys and Dolls*, Metro-Goldwyn-Mayer, 1955

Sakini, *The Teahouse of the August Moon*, Metro-Goldwyn- Mayer, 1956

Major Lloyd Gruver, *Sayonara*, Warner Bros., 1957

Christian Diestl, *The Young Lions*, Twentieth Century-Fox, 1958

Val "Snakeskin" Xavier, *The Fugitive Kind*, United Artists, 1960

Rio, *One-Eyed Jacks*, Paramount, 1961

Fletcher Christian, *Mutiny on the Bounty,* Metro-Goldwyn-Mayer, 1962

Harrison Carter MacWhite, *The Ugly American*, Universal, 1963

Freddy Benson, *Bedtime Story*, Universal, 1964

Robert Crain, *Morituri* (also known as *Code Name Morituri* and *The Saboteur*), Twentieth Century-Fox, 1965

Matt Fletcher, *The Appaloosa* (also known as *Southwest to Sonora*), Universal, 1966

Sheriff Calder, *The Chase*, Columbia, 1966

Meet Marlon Brando (documentary), Maysles Films, 1966

Ogden Mears, *A Countess from Hong Kong*, Universal, 1967

Major Weldon Pendelton, *Reflections in a Golden Eye*, Warner Bros.,1967

Grindl, *Candy* (also known as *Candy e il Suo Pazzo Mondo*), Cinerama, 1968

Bud the chauffeur, *The Night of the Following Day,* United Artists, 1969

Sir William Walker, *Burn!* (also known as *Queimada!* and *Quemada!*), United Artists, 1970

Peter Quint, *The Nightcomers,* Avco Embassy, 1971

Don Vito Corleone, *The Godfather* (also known as *Mario Puzo's The Godfather*), Paramount, 1972

Paul, *Last Tango in Paris* (also known as *Le Dernier Tango a Paris* and *Ultimo Tango a Parigi*), United Artists, 1973

Robert E. Lee Clayton, *The Missouri Breaks*, United Artists, 1976

Jor-El, *Superman* (also known as *Superman: The Movie*), WarnerBros., 1978

Colonel Walter E. Kurtz, *Apocalypse Now*, United Artists, 1979

Narrator, *Raoni: The Fight for the Amazon*, Interama, Inc., 1979

Adam Steiffel, *The Formula*, Metro-Goldwyn-Mayer, 1980

Ian McKenzie, *A Dry White Season*, Metro-Goldwyn-Mayer, 1989

Carmine Sabatini, *The Freshman,* TriStar, 1990

Hearts of Darkness: A Filmmaker's Apocalypse, Paramount, 1991

Tomas de Torquemada, *Christopher Columbus: The Discovery*, Warner Bros., 1992

Dr. Jack Luchsinger, *Don Juan DeMarco* (also known as *Don Juan and the Centerfold* and *Don Juan DeMarco and the Centerfold*), New Line Cinema, 1995

Title role, *The Island of Dr. Moreau*, New Line Cinema, 1996

McCarthy, *The Brave*, Acappella Pictures/Brave Pictures/Majestic Films, 1997

Film Director

One-Eyed Jacks, Paramount, 1961

Television Appearances

Episodic

"I'm No Hero," *Actor's Studio,* CBS, 1949

Larry King Live, syndicated, 1994

Specials

Person to Person, CBS, 1955

"Miracle on 44th Street: A Portrait of the Actors Studio," *American Masters,* PBS, 1991

Other Television Appearances

George Lincoln Rockwell, *Roots: The Next Generations* (miniseries),CBS, 1979

*Jericho,*1992

Sven the Swede, *Free Money* (movie), Starz!, 1999

Television Director

(With others) *Roots: The Next Generations,* CBS, 1979

Major Stage Appearances

Bobino, Adelphi Theatre, New York City, 1944

Nels, *I Remember Mama,* Music Box Theatre, New York City, 1944

Truckline Cafe, New York City, 1946

Candida, New York City, 1946

A Flag Is Born, New York City, 1947

Stanley Kowalski, *A Streetcar Named Desire,* Ethel Barrymore Theatre, New York City, 1947

Writings

(Author of introduction) Christopher Davis, *North American Indian,* Hamlyn Feltham, 1969

(Author of foreword) Stella Adler, *The Technique of Acting,* Bantam (New York City), 1989

(Author of epilogue) Tennessee Williams, *Five O'Clock Angel: Letters of Tennessee Williams to Maria St. Just, 1948-1982* with commentary by Maria St. Just and preface by Elia Kazan, Penguin (New York City),1991

(With Robert Lindsey) *Brando: Songs My Mother Taught Me* (autobiography), Random House (New York City), 1994

Fred Astaire

Chapter 1: From Omaha to New York City

"Old is like everything else. To make a success of it, you've got to start young." – Fred Astaire

Frederick Austerlitz II was born on May 10, 1899, with a name that could not seem more different than the one he would come to be known by. In fact, the difference between Fred's real last name and the name he was given in Hollywood is significant, because Astaire intentionally evoked a French etymology, whereas his birth name reflected Prussian heritage. The young boy's name was an homage to his father, Frederic "Fritz" Austerlitz (the only difference being that his father had no "k" at the end of his first name). Meanwhile, Astaire's mother was Johanna "Ann" Geilus. Fred had an older sister, Adele, who was two-and-a-half years his senior.

Fred's parents came from very different backgrounds. His father, Fritz, was born in Austria and was raised in a traditional Prussian family. The pedigree of his family is still not entirely clear, but it is believed that his family was Jewish before converting to Catholicism, and Fritz was raised Catholic. Born in 1868, it was not until he was an adult that he moved to the United States. In fact, throughout his adolescence Fritz had no clear aspirations of relocating across the Atlantic; it was only after he was punished by the Austro-Hungarian Army in 1892 that he decided to move (Epstein). The circumstances surrounding his punishment are possibly apocryphal, as they were retold frequently over the years, but it was said that Fritz was an officer in the Austro-Hungarian Army alongside his two brothers, Otto and Ernst. Since Ernst was his superior, Fritz was required to salute his elder brother, and when he failed to do so, his brother (who was very bureaucratic in nature) orchestrated his imprisonment (Levinson). While staying in prison, Fritz realized that he did not intend to spend his adult life in the army, so he made the decision to immigrate to the United States (Epstein).

When Fritz arrived at Ellis Island in 1892, he had aspirations of achieving great wealth, but naturally there weren't many lucrative employment opportunities for newly arriving immigrants, and he was relegated to pursuing menial jobs. After a short while, he and a small group of Austrian friends moved to Omaha, where they intended to start a business publishing studio photographs. Even though Fritz was not skilled in operating a camera, his jovial disposition was well-suited for interacting with the public, making him a good fit for the position of company salesman. Unfortunately for Fritz and his colleagues, the economic Panic of '93 ruined the company, which went bankrupt shortly after they set it up in Omaha. (Levinson). In the bad economy, opportunities were scarce, and Fritz eventually accepted a job working as a salesman in a brewery.

In contrast with Fritz, Fred's mother, Johanna, came from a more subdued background. While Fritz was gregarious and a natural salesman, Johanna was shy and worked as a schoolteacher. The two met shortly after Fritz's arrival in Omaha, and their relationship was expedited when Johanna got pregnant. It was socially frowned-upon to raise a family prior to getting married, and it is quite possible that Fritz and Johanna would have never gotten married if not for the unplanned pregnancy.

Even though no one could deny Fritz's charm, his in-laws had legitimate reasons to worry about their daughter marrying Fritz. Johanna was just 17 years old when she got pregnant, an especially young age to give birth to a child, and she was eight years younger than Fritz as well. Moreover, Fritz had done nothing to prove that he could sustain employment, and while the failure of the photography studio was not his fault, the fact remained that he had yet to demonstrate that he could provide for Johanna and their child. Nevertheless, Fritz and Johanna got married ahead of the baby's birth, only to lose the baby anyway. (Epstein). It would not be until two years later that Johanna would give birth to their first child, Adele, and Fred followed in 1899.

Over the course of Fred Astaire's life, he would benefit from good fortune on many occasions, which was ironic considering that clearly was not the case for his father. Fritz would continue to be a failed businessman, despite having ambition and a strong work ethic, and he and Johanna settled into a lower-middle class environment in Omaha, with Fritz continuing to work at the brewery while Johanna tended to the children. Still, for all of the differences between Fred's parents, they were each highly ambitious, with Johanna yearning to escape Omaha and Fritz wanting his children to succeed.

Like many young boys, Fred was fascinated by trains and enjoyed the many trains that passed through the Omaha landscape, but his upbringing was hardly a normal one, because it quickly became evident that Fred and his sister exhibited precocious talent as singers and dancers. When Fred was two years of age, Adele was enrolled in the Chambers Dancing Academy in Omaha, and after she demonstrated her innate talents as a dancer, Fred began taking classes himself. Since Adele began dancing training before her brother, it's evident that Fred's career owes a great debt to his sister, since he followed in her lead throughout his childhood. Not only did Adele possess great physical talent, but it was immediately clear from a young age that she was a great beauty (Epstein). Her dazzling appearance stands in stark contrast to Fred's unremarkable appearance as an adult, but it was Fred who was the outlier; both of Fred's parents were very attractive, and Adele inherited her mother's soft eyes and dark hair.

Fred and Adele performing vaudeville circa 1906

The siblings performed together even as young children, but their success rose as Fritz's professional fortunes diminished. By 1902, he had worked for the Omaha Brewers Association since arriving in the city nine years earlier, but that year the company was bought out by Storz Brewery. Fritz was not forced to relinquish his job altogether, but he had to take a pay cut. Around this time, he also began drinking heavily and (allegedly) having affairs, though Fred would later adamantly claim that his family environment as a young child was peaceful (Levinson). Still, Fritz's lack of success meant that the Astaires were in no way beholden to the Omaha region; Johanna's parents lived there, but she had long yearned to move away herself. If anything, it seemed the talents of their children might be the way in which the entire family could get out.

Thus, even though Fritz and Johanna did not possess any talents that would facilitate their relocation to another city, they could rationalize the family's departure due to the fact their children, particularly Adele, were too talented to receive sufficient dancing instruction in the Midwest. Moreover, due to her husband's behavior, Adele was not bothered by the possibility of living apart from her husband, so long as he provided for the family as best he could. As a result, Fred's parents began looking into the possibilities of moving even before Fred entered the first grade.

Ultimately, it was decided that Fred, Adele, and Johanna would relocate to New York City, and they moved there in 1905. Although Fred and his sister would eventually achieve great fame, the move was entirely motivated by naiveté; Johanna improbably believed that her daughter (and possibly her son, if lucky) could quickly gain training as top-flight dancers and begin supporting the family. While they received their training, Fritz was to send money and subsidize their schooling at the dance school. What Fred did not realize at the time (only to eventually disclose in his autobiography) was that he and his sister had not even gained acceptance at the dancing institution before the move:

> "As I learned years later, this trip was really a stab in the dark. We were going to New York without so much as a letter of introduction to somebody's aunt. My mother had never been there, and she knew no one, theatrical or otherwise. She had not even written ahead to enroll us in a dancing school. So none of the Astaires could have known what was in store for them." (Astaire 14)

Astaire's description suggests a bit of Midwestern innocence, as though no one in his family could have known what was in store for them in the big city. However, this is perhaps unfair, because Fritz had lived in New York City after arriving to Ellis Island. While his stay had been more than a decade earlier, it is still surprising that he had not warned Johanna and his children of the improbability of achieving any success in such an immense, competitive environment. The fact Fritz supported the move reflects his idealism, the same idealism that led him to expect to earn great riches after emigrating from Europe to America years earlier.

Chapter 2: Growing Up in New York and On the Road

Astaire would later note in his autobiography that upon getting off the train, he looked around and remarked to his sister, "This is a big city." She tartly replied, "This is only the depot." Of course, New York was the big city at the time, and when Fred, his mother, and his sister arrived there in 1905, they stayed at the Herald Square Hotel. As with many hotels of the time period, the hotel acted as a boarding residence of sorts, with guests remaining for extended visits (Levinson).

After securing residence, Johanna enrolled her children in dancing school. Even though they had not yet been admitted, she, Fritz, and her children's dancing instructor at Omaha identified the Claude Alvienne Dance School, located at Grand Opera House Building, as a suitable institution. Shortly after arriving in New York City, the Astaires began their dancing instruction at the dance school, attending classes during the day, and after returning to their residence at the hotel, Johanna taught them more traditionally academic subjects, a task for which she was well-suited given her experience working as a school teacher in Omaha. Astaire later remembered, "I simply did not get the idea that dancing was for me. However, I took it as a matter of course. It seemed natural enough to go with Adele and do what she did."

The Claude Alvienne Dance School was not an educational institution in the traditional sense, as students were not expected attend for years on end. Rather, it served a vocational purpose, offering intense instruction with the expectation that students would quickly gain the skills needed to succeed in the dancing profession. That children were placed in such an explicitly vocational setting may seem tantamount to child abuse, but Fred would later look back on his time at the dance school with fondness, claiming that the exercises were not disagreeable and that the instructors were nurturing and gentle (Astaire). Noting that the instructor would never scold students but would tell them if they did something wrong by hitting a chair with a stick, Astaire wrote, "I still had no urge to dance, but I loved that stick."

Shortly after enrolling in the school, the benevolent Claude Alvienne (founder of the school) would prove instrumental in securing roles for Fred and his sister. Before they performed professionally, however, Alvienne advised the Astaires that in order to achieve success they would need to change their name. "Austerlitz" was difficult to pronounce and sounded too foreign, while "Astaire" was far more marketable. Around the same time, Johanna also changed her own name by shortening it to "Anna" (Epstein). By this time, the siblings were perfecting dancing acts together, some of which had them playing bride and groom, and as their vaudeville picture from 1906 indicates, Fred and Adele appeared very comfortable before the camera. There is no trace of self-consciousness, and any trace of the children's Omaha background seemed to have already vanished. Not only does Fred don a stylish outfit that predates the top-hats that he would later make his signature, but Adele appears in an ornate, florid outfit that connotes an upper-class upbringing. From an early age, Fred and Adele had the ability to give off a sense of elegance and class that was not traced to their family heritage.

Alvienne was able to use his connections in order to schedule bookings for Fred and Adele to perform, but the Astaire children were also assisted by their father. Despite spending the majority of his time in Omaha, Fritz made frequent trips to New York City, and when he could be there, he parlayed his salesman charm to good effect, establishing strong connections with theater managers and other influential figures within the industry. Through the assistance of Fritz and Claude Alvienne, Fred and Adele remained busy and earned a moderate income for the family performing all throughout the East Coast (Levinson). There is some disagreement over the site of their first professional performance, but it's believed to have been either in Newport, Rhode Island or Keyport, New Jersey (Levinson). Astaire later joked, "The Keyport newspaper proclaimed, 'The Astaires are the greatest child act in vaudeville.' I think if two words had been added, 'in Keyport', this might have been more accurate."

In their first years performing together, the Astaires performed most often in New Jersey and Pennsylvania. In New Jersey, they made stops in Atlantic City, Perth Amboy, Passaic, Paterson, Newark, and Union Hill; Pennsylvania trips included Philadelphia, Pottsdown, and Lancaster. Traveling along the East Coast gave the Astaire children valuable experience, but their first major break came when they were signed to a high-profile contract to perform along the Orpheum Circuit, a vaudeville circuit that would eventually become subsumed by the RKO film studio. Performing along the Orpheum Circuit led to Fred and Adele traveling to more distant locales, including Pennsylvania, Iowa, Colorado, Washington, D.C., California, Utah, Nebraska, Minnesota, and Wisconsin (Levinson). It is important to remember that the vaudeville circuit effectively served as the predecessor to cinema; years later, films would be exhibited throughout the country, but during the early years of the motion picture medium, the American public enjoyed vaudeville and other popular forms of entertainment (baseball being a notable example) instead.

As Fred and Adele grew older, Adele's physical growth threatened the success of their act. As she neared her teenage years, it became increasingly unconvincing for both siblings to play young children. Due to her stunning beauty, it would not necessarily have been difficult for Adele to secure appearances on the vaudeville circuit, but the children's act that she and Fred had perfected over the previous several years became untenable. Making matters worse, as they became better-known throughout the Orpheum Circuit, the Astaire siblings faced the scrutiny of the Gerry Agency, and they were forced to lie about their ages in order to comply with child labor laws. It was illegal for children to work to the extent that Fred and Adele were, and while Fred would later give no indication that he was displeased with the heavy performance schedule, it was clear that it would be impossible to continue the routine as it had operated.

One aspect of Fred and Adele's success that is easily overlooked is the role played by their mother. Johanna possessed a shrewd business sense and understood that it would pay dividends over time for her children to take a hiatus from acting (Levinson). Not only would this appease the Gerry Agency, but Fred and Adele could resume their careers after Fred caught up with his sister physically. Moreover, they could use their "sabbatical" to good effect by rehearsing new material and transforming their act from one involving little children to one featuring more age-appropriate material.

During their two-year break from performing, which took place in 1909 and 1910, Fred and Adele relocated with their mother to Weehawken, New Jersey, a working-class neighborhood. At this time, Fritz remained in Omaha, and the marriage between him and Johanna suffered from the effects of their estrangement. Johanna learned that Fritz lived with another woman in their Omaha house, and Fritz continued to drink heavily — Fred would indeed grow up to be an entirely different person from his father. Meanwhile, in New Jersey, Fred enrolled in the 5th grade, his first exposure to formal education. In 1911, the teenagers enrolled in the Ned Wayburn's school in New York City, where the Astaires resumed their training in the dramatic arts. Even though they had achieved great success for their age, they were still relatively untrained in areas such as dance, ballet, and singing, but at the Ned Wayburn's school, they received valuable instruction in these areas. In yet another shrewd move, Johanna also paid Wayburn $1,000 to devise a new routine for her children, an investment that would pay dividends over the next several years.

Immediately after returning to performing, Fred and Adele experienced adversity and negative reviews. Their return to the stage occurred in February of 1912, where they performed at the Proctor's Fifth Avenue Vaudeville Theatre, but they were poorly received and the engagement was not sustainable. The following year proved to be no better, as Fred began suffering from worrying bouts of anxiety, a surprising problem in light of the ultra-confident aura he would project in his later film roles. However, Astaire would in fact suffer from anxiety during his entire career, a tendency that would actually prove productive because it led to a tireless perfectionism. In contrast, Adele was far less driven than her brother and felt less of a need to rehearse and perfect the routines and rapport between the two siblings. The two were also polar opposites; Fred was socially conservative and became an Episcopalian in 1912 (remaining devoutly religious for the rest of his life), while Adele was a free spirit who was unafraid to cuss or flaunt her sexuality (Levinson).

Unsurprisingly, the difference in their personalities and approaches led to a shift in the talent dynamic between the Fred and his sister. For the first decade or so of their career, Adele was deemed by far the more talented of the two, but over time there was a gradual shift that led to Fred being considered by far the more adept. Indeed, Epstein notes, "Without Adele as his dancing partner at the beginning of his career, Fred Astaire might have ended up as a suburban husband, selling swank high-line cars (for which he had a lifelong taste). In their early years as a dance team, Adele supplied the main excitement. But the commitment to perfection was not in her in a way that it was in her brother." (10). While Adele may well have been more gifted than her brother and assisted in giving her brother his first exposure to the world of professional entertainment, Fred's unmatched work ethic separated him from her and played an instrumental role in his later success. Actress and dancer Nanette Fabray later said about Fred, "He was a dictator who made me work harder and longer than anyone."

After weathering the adversity that initially greeted their return to performing, the Astaires achieved more success than ever before in 1914. Around that time, they enlisted the services of Aurelia Coccia, who taught Fred how to tap dance. Over the past year, it had become clear that Fred needed a new skill in order to remain successful, and tap dancing offered a niche that separated him from others in the industry. They began securing more bookings, appearing first throughout New England and then expanding their demographic. Fred and Adele earned $350 per week, more than double what they had made years earlier on the Orpheum circuit. Over time their price continued to escalate, and in 1917 they made their debut on Broadway with the show *Over the Top*. Their price rose, and they soon began commanding $550 per week.

In 1918, the siblings appeared in the Broadway show *Apple Blossoms*, which endured a long run that would last until 1920. During this period, the Astaires were also hired by the Brothers Shubert to appear in *The Passing Show of 1918*, and critic Heywood Broun wrote of their performance, "In an evening in which there was an abundance of good dancing, Fred Astaire stood out ... He and his partner, Adele Astaire, made the show pause early in the evening with a beautiful loose-limbed dance." That performance also brought them into contact with performers such as Al Jolson, Fanny Brice, and Charlie Ruggles (Epstein). Fred and his sister had not only rebounded from the disappointment of 1912 and 1913 but soared to greater heights than they had achieved during their early years performing together. By 1920, the Astaires found themselves in the upper strata of society, mingling with the wealthy elite of New York and Philadelphia, and as they began earning more money, they began to adopt a more liberal (though not reckless) attitude with their money, staying in high-end hotels and spending more freely. Performing in Atlantic City, Fred took an interest in craps and poker, and he began to make room for leisure in his crowded routine (Levinson). In addition, they began performing abroad in London, where they were exposed to British culture, which would have a profound influence on Fred and his sister.

Chapter 3: Stage and Screen

"He is a truly complex fellow, not unlike the Michelangelos and da Vincis of the Renaissance period. He's a supreme artist but he is constantly filled with doubts and self-anger about his work--and that is what makes him so good. He is a perfectionist who is never sure he is attaining perfection." - Rouben Mamoulian

One of the great formative experiences of Astaire's entire career was his first trip to London, which not only exposed him to a foreign culture for the first time but one that would form the foundation for his star persona. Epstein elaborates, "On his first trip to England, Fred Astaire turned from a young man who was well-groomed and carefully dressed into someone close to what used to be called a fashion plate. He became mid-Atlantic in his taste in clothes; his speech, with its splendidly clear diction, seemed a touch mid-Atlantic, too. He found himself admiring the clothes of the British aristocracy." (36)

Of course, working as a performer meant that spending money on clothes was not only a personal hobby but also a business investment. Through effecting a well-heeled fashion style, Astaire only strengthened his stage persona, and it was during this period that the Fred Astaire identity was formulated. He was not born into wealth or knowledge of fashion but quickly learned how to present himself with an air of sophistication that made it seem as though he had been born into royalty.

Adele in 1919

Fred in 1920

By 1920, Fred and Adele commanded $750 per week, and as they began earning greater sums of money, they were introduced to prominent cultural figures. The Astaires counted Tallulah Bankhead, Gertrude Lawrence, and Noel Coward among their friends, and they moved into the Carlton Hotel in Manhattan. The 1920s were a period of great financial and cultural triumph for Fred and Adele, and they proved that it was possible to progress from childhood success to adult triumph. In 1924, they appeared in George and Ira Gershwin's *Lady Be Good* (1924), which was performed on Broadway, and three years later, they would appear in another Gershwin production, *Funny Face*, that also included runs on Broadway and in London. By this time, it was clear that even though Adele was an adept dancer in her own right, Fred possessed the generational talent, and his work ethic ensured his talent continued growing. One of the benefits of residing in New York City was that the city not only provided a diverse array of performing venues but also allowed Astaire to learn from the artistic customs of different cultures. He frequently visited Harlem, learning from and appropriating the tap dancing talents of popular performers there during the late 1920s (Levinson).

The Astaires remained in high demand throughout the decade, but the contrasting personalities of the two siblings eventually created an impasse. Where Fred was ambitious and dynamic, Adele was more passive and ultimately disinterested in furthering her career. After all, by the start of the 1930s, Fred was widely considered the top dancer in the world, a designation that Adele could not hope to equal (Mueller). As American writer Robert Benchley put it in 1930, "I don't think that I will plunge the nation into war by stating that Fred is the greatest tap-dancer in the world." Despite the fact that they had risen to fame through the success of their teamwork, Astaire was driven in a way that his sister was not, and their final show together occurred in 1931. Titled *The Band Wagon*, the show first ran in June of 1931 and lasted for 261 performances.

Fred and Adele performing in 1921

After *The Band Wagon*, Adele retired and married Lord Charles Arthur Francis Cavendish, the Son of the Duke of Devonshire. The marriage was a tumultuous one, fraught with conflicts resulting from Cavendish's addiction to alcohol. He would eventually pass away in 1944 and remained married to Adele through the end of his life. At the time of Adele's courtship to Lord Charles, Fred began taking an interest in women for the first time. Naturally much shier than his sister, he was bashful around women and had difficulty talking with them. However, beginning in 1931, Astaire began a relationship with Phyllis Potter, a wealthy Boston socialite who had not even heard of him at the time they met (Epstein). The relationship was frowned upon by Adele and Astaire's mother, largely due to the fact that Phyllis had already been married to Eliphalet Nott Potter III, but after a brief courtship, they were married in 1933, beginning a long and healthy marriage. Astaire would later frame his married life with Phyllis in idyllic terms: "Phyllis was an extraordinary girl. We were always together other than in my working hours. She seldom came to the studios…At the completion of a film, we would travel abroad or go on shooting and fishing trips here. I usually managed three months off between pictures. Weekends during productions were spent at our Blue Valley Ranch, which she loved so much. We established that in 1950." (6)

Astaire's marriage with Phyllis highlights that even as his career became increasingly more glamorous throughout the 1930s, his personal life remained quiet. Still, while his personal life settled down during the early 1930s, the retirement of his sister left him looking for a new female partner with whom to perform. From 1931-1933, he danced alongside Claire Luce, a talented dancer, but initially, Fred's shyness made their rapport awkward. He eventually grew accustomed to working with her, thanks in part to prodding from Luce, who reminded him he could add more romantic undertones to the performances by saying, "Come on, Fred, I'm not your sister, you know." In 1932, they starred together in *The Gay Divorce*, a production that is remembered for featuring Cole Porter's hit song "Night and Day." The play would be Astaire's final Broadway show, and also enjoyed a run in London. Two years later, after Fred had begun acting in Hollywood, it would later be adapted for the cinema by RKO with Fred reprising his role.

Astaire and Luce in *Gay Divorce* on Broadway in 1932

By 1933, Astaire had just gained a spouse but lost his longtime professional partner in Adele. Adele would later be asked why she didn't perform with her brother in Hollywood, and she replied, "If people would only realize when they ask me why I don't do a picture with him - they ask me that all the time, and were quite keen on it while I was in Hollywood - if they'd only realize that he's gone 'way ahead of me. Why I couldn't begin to keep up with him. I couldn't even reach the steps he throws away."

Even though he and Luce were successful together, his partnership with Luce would prove to be short-lived. Instead of returning to Broadway, Astaire looked to Hollywood for his next career venture. In fact, his foray into cinema was not his first attempt to do so. Several years earlier, he and Adele had explored the possibility of acting on screen, but to no avail. Still, his past failure did not prevent RKO from signing him to a contract, and 1933 is credited as the year that he first broke into the motion picture industry. The man who signed Astaire, David Selznick, wrote at the time, "I am uncertain about the man, but I feel, in spite of his enormous ears and bad chin line, that his charm is so tremendous that it comes through even on this wretched test."

The major difference between Astaire's first attempt to break into Hollywood and his successful entry in 1933 was not that he had grown substantially as a dancer. Rather, the major difference was that by 1933, synchronized sound had come into existence, leading to the rise of the Musical as one of the preeminent genres in Hollywood. Astaire's dancing prowess would still have been a visual attraction during the silent era, but his physicality was significantly more arresting when accompanied by singing and a musical score. In this regard, it is not unreasonable to attribute Astaire's rise to fame in large part to the developments that occurred to the cinematic medium between the late 1920s and early 1930s.

Fred was by no means old when he entered Hollywood, but it is nevertheless important to note that he was no longer a young adult either. The fact that he had so long resisted marriage and had yet to start a family obscures the fact that he was already 34 years old by the time he appeared in his first movie. The relative brevity of his film career should not be held as a criticism of his acting but instead as an indicator of the importance of his stage career. While everyone is aware of Astaire's achievements on screen, it is often forgotten that his career as a stage performer lasted longer than his time as a film actor. For Astaire, screen acting was for the most part a middle-aged pursuit, making his dancing performances on screen all the more remarkable.

Even though Astaire was signed by RKO in 1933, his first film was not with his parent studio but instead with MGM. In a sense, it was fitting that his first film, *Dancing Lady*, should be produced by MGM, because that studio remains the one most closely associated with the musical, and Astaire is the film star still inextricably linked with the musical. At the same time, RKO had a clear rationale for loaning their new actor, because Astaire's role was minor and he appeared as himself. The plot, which involves Joan Crawford's character attempting to leave her job as a stripper and join forces with a stage director (played by Clark Gable), is clearly a vehicle for Crawford and Gable. Nevertheless, the film was an ideal opening film for Astaire, because having him to appear as himself allowed him to ease into the new medium. Writer G. Bruce Boyer wrote over half a century later, "I think I can pinpoint the one moment when the American style of dressing first appeared. It was in an appalling 1933 movie called Dancing Lady during an otherwise forgettable dance number. It also just happened to be Fred Astaire's first on-camera dance. But don't look at the steps. Look at the outfit: Astaire is wearing a single-breasted, soft flannel suit with two-tone spectator shoes and a turtleneck. You wish you could look that stylish! Later that year, in Flying Down to Rio, we get the full Astaire impact. The muted plaid suit is not all that striking, but Fred is wearing it with a soft button-down shirt, a pale woven tie, silk pocket square, bright horizontally striped hose and white bucks. Whoa! Now that's different. This melange of the classic and the sporty was an American innovation. As we approach the impeccable Astaire's 100th birthday on May 10, it's worth remembering that he remains the greatest exemplar of that style."

While *Dancing Lady* was Astaire's first film, his next picture was far more significant because it united him with Ginger Rogers, the actress most associated with Astaire. The film, titled *Flying Down to Rio* (1933), features Fred and Ginger as Fred Ayres and Honey Hale, a band leader and star vocalist for the same orchestra, but the plot is little more than a thinly veiled opportunity to showcase the bravura dancing theatrics of Astaire and Rogers. In a way, the film is not drastically different from *Dancing Lady*, because Astaire might as well have been playing himself in the film, and his character's initials are the same as his own. As *Variety* magazine wrote in a review, "The main point of Flying Down to Rio is the screen promise of Fred Astaire ... He's assuredly a bet after this one, for he's distinctly likable on the screen, the mike is kind to his voice and as a dancer he remains in a class by himself. The latter observation will be no news to the profession, which has long admitted that Astaire starts dancing where the others stop hoofing."

In the film, Astaire and Rogers perform together in four musical numbers, including the title song, "Orchids in Moonlight," and "Music Makes Me." *Flying Down to Rio* was a moderate success, but it grossed nowhere near the sums that the later Astaire-Rogers films would garner. Even so, it was clear that RKO had a winning formula; audiences might have been familiar with Astaire's dancing on stage, but they had never been privy to such dancing on the screen, and RKO simply possessed a commodity that no other studio could match.

Moreover, Astaire and Rogers displayed an intuitive chemistry that made it seem as though they had performed together for years. Of course, the chemistry was the result of plenty of hard work, as Rogers noted, "How do you think those routines were accomplished? With mirrors?... Well, I thought I knew what concentrated work was before I met Fred, but he's the limit. Never satisfied until every detail is right, and he will not compromise. No sir! What's more, if he thinks of something better after you've finished a routine, you do it over."

Astaire and Rogers in *Flying Down to Rio*

The one potential problem facing Astaire in his transition to cinema was that his voice was undeveloped. While it is common to conceive of singing and dancing as intertwined, such that Astaire represents a "song and dance man," in actuality he had never embraced singing. Sound cinema thus posed a significant obstacle for him, as he was forced to sing and did not want to create a jarring contrast between his singing and dancing. Certainly, there is no doubt that Astaire's vocal performances lag behind his physical achievements, but one of Astaire's major accomplishments in Hollywood was that he managed to sing well enough that it did not distract from his dancing. Indeed, by the time he entered Hollywood, dancing was second nature to him (even though he would continue to work tirelessly at it his entire career), but singing was an area of deficiency, and the success of his films can largely be traced to his ability to sing at a passable level.

In 1934, Astaire famously wrote to his agent, "What's all this talk about me being teamed with Ginger Rogers? I will not have it Leland--I did not go into pictures to be teamed with her or anyone else, and if that is the program in mind for me I will not stand for it. I don't mind making another picture with her but as for this teams idea, it's out." But of course, pairing Astaire with Ginger Rogers was obviously a wise decision, as the chemistry between the two is beyond reproach. When conceiving of the tandem, it is common to think of Astaire as the dominant figure, and indeed Astaire was the far more accomplished dancer. At the same time, however, Rogers was significantly more experienced as a film actress, as she had broken into Hollywood in 1929. The same year that she starred with Astaire in *Flying Down to Rio*, she also appeared in the major Warner Brothers musical *42nd Street* (1933), and her star rose fast in Hollywood. For all of Astaire's dancing abilities, one could justifiably argue that Rogers was the more accomplished actress, a claim that is substantiated by the fact that she would act in a broader array of genres throughout her film career and appeared in non-musicals even while she was professionally aligned with Astaire.

There was no way that RKO could possibly supply Astaire with a dance partner who could match his abilities, but Rogers was an ideal fit since she was an adept dancer in her own right and also possessed the acting skills and glamorous physical appearance required of a leading actress. As Katharine Hepburn would later note of Astaire and Rogers, "He gives her class and she gives him sex appeal." Each supplied the other with a necessary missing ingredient for film stardom.

Flying Down to Rio - or more accurately, the professional partnership it inaugurated with Ginger Rogers - was truly the spark that ignited Astaire's career in Hollywood. From 1933-1939, he would appear in nine films with Rogers and just one movie without her. Their second film was *The Gay Divorcee*, a film for which Astaire was well-qualified in light of the fact that he had performed in the Broadway version of the play. Despite sharing its basic plotline, the film was far different from the play, most notably due to the introduction of a series of new musical numbers. One of these, "The Continental," was awarded the Academy Award for Best Song in 1934. Unlike many film musicals, the entire film, not just the musical numbers, was a critical success; it was nominated for an Academy Award for Best Picture and demonstrated the capability for musicals to not only captivate the viewer during the song sequences but also during the narrative proper.

The narrative introduced in *The Gay Divorcee* would continue throughout the remaining Astaire-Rogers films. Late in 1934, the duo's third film, *Roberta* (1935), was shot. The plot features Astaire as a dance instructor who visits Paris with a friend, where he encounters an old love interest (played by Rogers) who has become a Countess. The film is often forgotten within the Astaire-Rogers canon, but it made a substantial profit and included famous musical numbers such as "Smoke Gets in Your Eyes." As with *The Divorcee* (as well as the later Astaire-Rogers movies), one of the most notable aspects of the film is the way in which there is no clear divide separating the musical numbers from the rest of the plot. The romance between the two major stars is directly embedded within the plot, rather than existing outside of it, as was common during the time period. To this end, it is important to note that the major model for the film musical during the first five years of synchronized sound was the style popularized by Busby Berkeley, who was responsible for *Gold Diggers of 1933* (1933), a film that, ironically enough, starred Ginger Rogers. In Berkeley's films, the plot itself is flimsy and essentially accomplishes little other than filling time between the lavish, fantastical musical productions. In fact, on many of his films, Berkeley designed only the musical sequences, with a separate director in charge of the rest of the plot.

Berkeley

In contrast with that style, when watching Astaire's films, viewers do not feel as though the narrative has been paused for the musical numbers. On a formal level, this effect is achieved through the differences in camera technique that separate their films; where Astaire's musical numbers were always conveyed through a single shot, Berkeley deployed kaleidoscopic montages, splicing up the scene into an array of images that occasionally cause an aesthetic overload. Discussing the use of a single shot with a camera later called the "Astaire dolly", producer H.C. Dolley explained, "It was on tiny wheels with a mount for the camera that put the lens about two feet above the ground. On it rode the camera operator and the assistant who changed the focus and that's all. Fred always wanted to keep the camera in as tight as possible, and they used to shoot with a 40 millimeter lens, which doesn't give you too much leeway. So every time Fred and Ginger moved toward us, the camera had to go back, and every time they went back, the camera went in. The head grip who was in charge of pushing this thing was a joy to watch. He would maintain a consistent distance, and when they were in the midst of a hectic dance that's quite a stunt."

Either way, the glamorous sight of Astaire and Rogers dancing provided escapist entertainment during the 1930s, a time in which America was in the throes of the Great Depression and relied upon film as a means through which to forget about the anxieties of the moment, if only for a few hours. At the same time, much of the appeal of films such as *Roberta* is that they feature relatable characters rather than the ornamental figures deployed by Berkeley in his films.

Astaire and Rogers in *Roberta*

Expounding on the differences between Astaire and Berkeley is necessary since the two would remain rivals throughout the decade. Historically, it has been common to argue that Astaire's model for the film musical usurped that of Berkeley, but this was hardly the case. Astaire's films may have been more popular, but Berkeley continued to offer an alternative model for the genre. Andrew Sarris explains the actual dynamic between Astaire and Berkeley that existed during the 1930s: "It is customary for film historians to assume that Busby Berkeley's style of mass choreography and aerial cinematography were completely eclipsed by the relative grace and simplicity of the Fred Astaire-Ginger Rogers musicals. Actually, Berekeley and Astaire overlapped and coexisted as stylistic alternatives for the Hollywood musical to follow." (172) Thus, while it is impossible to deny that Astaire's musical style became the dominant method on film, Berkeley remained in Hollywood even while Astaire eclipsed his popularity, and the differences between the two musical styles demonstrate there were multiple elements of the musical as a genre.

Building on the success of *Roberta*, Astaire and Rogers made arguably their most famous film later that same year. *Top Hat* (1935) is routinely listed among the most successful in the genre, and it included some of the most famous Astaire-Rogers musical numbers. In addition, the success of the film can also be attributed to the allure of the plot, which consists of Astaire as a dancer traveling abroad in London. He falls in love with Rogers, who plays a professional model. The narrative involves a case of mistaken identity that is eventually reconciled, culminating with Astaire and Rogers agreeing to marry. A number of famous musical numbers are included, including Astaire and Roger together in "Cheek to Cheek" and Astaire by himself in "No Strings I'm Fancy Free" and "Top Hat, White Tie, and Tails." The latter number was responsible for establishing the top hat and coat tails that are associated with the Astaire image. The film was truly the ideal vehicle for Astaire, as no other film offered him so many ideal opportunities to showcase his dancing technique.

Astaire and Rogers at the climax of "Cheek to Cheek"

Of course, the success of *Top Hat* not only resulted from Astaire's dancing but also his chemistry with Ginger Rogers and the general appeal of the plot. The dancing sequences are not a narrative digression (in the Busby Berkeley tradition) but instead serve as a form of courtship. In an age in which the Hays Code restricted romantic activity, Astaire's dancing signifies his sexual potency, while Rogers's ability to hang with him during long, complicated sequences suggests that she is capable of satisfying his romantic desires and serving as his wife. The film thus managed to be very romantic (if not sexy) without ever showing its two stars engaged in explicitly sexual activity.

The plot of *Top Hat* is also notable for representing what Rick Altman refers to as the "fairy tale musical," one of three categories that Altman identifies for the musical genre. In the fairy tale musical, the formation of the romantic couple is framed in such a way that the romantic leads appear predestined to fall in love, with their romance forming a private kingdom of sorts (Altman). As Altman clarifies, this subgenre is indebted to opera: "The fairy tale musical, first of the three subgenres to reach maturity in film, did so thanks to massive borrowing from a long tradition of European and American operettas. While the history of the Hollywood fairy tale musical reveals numerous attempts to 'Americanize' the pattern established in nineteenth-century European operetta, it must nevertheless be admitted that the fairy tale musical on film is part of a tradition that begins long before cinema." (131)

Altman's description identifies salient elements associated with Astaire individually and the musical genre as a whole. Specifically, the high-class nature of European opera fed seamlessly into the image that Astaire had first cultivated during his stage career; ever since his first trip to Europe as a dancer alongside Adele, Fred had been enraptured by the high culture elements of European society, and the fairy tale musical was the ideal model through which to project the cultured, high society image he wished to exude. On a broader level, the many Astaire-Rogers fairy tale musicals popularized the subgenre. They were hardly the first examples of the fairy tale musical genre in Hollywood, but the chemistry between Astaire and Rogers brought the form to greater popularity than it had previously enjoyed.

With the success of *Top Hat*, Astaire and Rogers rose to the top of the Hollywood elite, and while most actors relatively new to Hollywood are forced to appear in numerous films per year, Astaire was granted the privilege of appearing in no more than two. This arrangement gave him plenty of time to rehearse for his parts, and he was also given the leeway to alter his parts as he saw fit. Meanwhile, Rogers was far more active, regularly working on pictures for RKO. Rogers would later note, "We were only together for a part of my career, and for every film we did, I did another three on my own. The studio was working me too hard. Fred would rush off for a holiday and call me and say: 'Hey, ready to do another?' And I didn't have the sense to say that I was too tired. Those times were murder for me. Oh, I adored Mr. A but all the hard work...the 5 a.m. calls, the months of non-stop dancing, singing and acting. We just worked it out and had a lot of fun and got very exhausted. And Mr A was quite divine."

Though it would be easy to argue that Astaire's freedom to appear in fewer films than his co-star was sexist (and there may be an element of truth to this), it's only fair to point out Astaire had creative responsibilities that precluded him from appearing in more films. Edward Gallafant explains that Astaire was the chief architect behind his dancing routines: "Within the period of the RKO musicals, the pattern evidently was that while Astaire choreographed and rehearsed the dances for the next film, mostly with Hermes Pan, Rogers was employed by the studio making (usually) more modestly budgeted productions" (10).

Gallafant's description of Astaire's workload reflects the importance of Hermes Pan, an individual who is often forgotten about but who played an instrumental role in choreographing Astaire's famous dance routines. Indeed, from a creative standpoint, the Astaire-Pan relationship was even more important than his storied professional relationship with Ginger Rogers. Despite possessing just an eighth grade education, Pan was an adept choreographer and he and Astaire remained lifelong friends (Franceschina). Even after he and Rogers completed their final film together, Astaire continued to work with Pan in devising his dance routines.

Following *Top Hat*, Astaire-Rogers films continued to do well at the box office. In 1936, they appeared in *Follow the Fleet* and *Swing Time*, the latter of which is regarded as the stronger film. In the Fred-Ginger canon, the film is notable for introducing a more lavish visual style that at times resembles that of Busby Berkeley. In the "Bojangles of Harlem" number, for example, Astaire dons blackface and wears stilts. The sequence is perhaps more vulgar than the musical numbers from *Top Hat*, but Astaire's skill remained intact. Furthermore, however far Astaire and Rogers strayed from the plot elements of *Top Hat*, audiences knew that they could rely on the formation of the romantic couple at the film's conclusion.

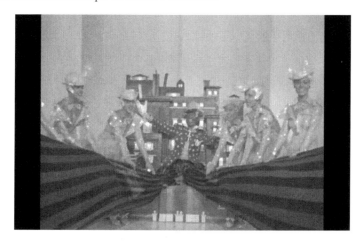

Astaire as Bojangles

The critical and commercial successes Astaire enjoyed in 1936 corresponded with similarly positive changes in his personal life. That same year, Astaire and his wife, Phyllis, had their first child, Fred Jr., who was born on New Year's Day. Six years later, in March of 1942, Phyllis would give birth to a second child, Ava Ashire McKenzie. With two kids, one boy and one girl, the Astaires embodied the American Dream, and for all the high-class trappings associated with his top hat and coat tails, Astaire led a quiet private life in California. During a time in which Hollywood was filled with left-wing political activists, Astaire was a Republican (although not an outspoken one), and it is no exaggeration to state that he was a social conservative as well. Instead of expressing political critiques in his films, the Astaire movies are predicated solely toward showcasing his dazzling dancing techniques.

From 1937-1939, Astaire appeared in four films, three of which were with Ginger Rogers. The first of these, *Shall We Dance* (1937), was the most famous. In a major feat for the studio, RKO was able to secure George and Ira Gershwin to score the film, reuniting Astaire with one of his favorite collaborators from his stage career. The film did not bring the commercial or critical success of the earlier Fred and Ginger pictures, but working with the Gershwins was an example of how fortunate Astaire was to collaborate with musical luminaries. To this end, Epstein astutely contends, "A good measure of the success behind the Astaire-Rogers partnership is also owed to the fact that they came together at a time when an extraordinary clutch of great songwriters were at work" (xviii).

The final films in which Astaire starred with Rogers during the decade were *Carefree* (1938) and *The Story of Vernon and Irene Castle* (1939). As always, the two films benefitted from the skilled performances of the two stars, but as Astaire and Rogers grew in fame, it became increasingly difficult to generate a substantial profit. Not only did Fred and Ginger command a lofty salary for each picture, it cost a great deal of money to secure the talents of the other members of the production team. As a result, even though the two films performed well at the box office, they each lost money for the studio due to the immense production costs.

Chapter 4: After Ginger

"Oh, there's no such thing as my favorite performance. I can't sit here today and look back, and say, *Top Hat* was better than *Easter Parade* or any of the others. I just don't look back, period. When I finish with a project, I say 'all right, that's that. What's next?'" – Fred Astaire

Despite turning 40 in 1939, Astaire remained a box office draw, but the salaries commanded by Fred and Ginger made it unprofitable for them to continue to star alongside one another. Furthermore, Astaire was driven to pursue other opportunities, and he left RKO in 1939, reuniting with Rogers only on *The Barkleys of Broadway* (1949).

For better or worse, the films Astaire appeared in following his break with Ginger Rogers in 1939 are generally not well-remembered. However, even as he progressed into his middle-aged years, he remained active and danced at a high level. The first film he appeared in after leaving RKO was *Broadway Melody of 1940*, which paired him with Eleanor Powell, an actress with more dancing experience than Rogers had possessed at the start of her working relationship with Astaire. Despite being the only film in which Astaire would appear with Powell, the film remains noteworthy for the musical number "Begin the Beguine."

Astaire and Eleanor Powell in *Broadway Melody of 1940*

As the 1940s progressed, Astaire appeared alongside a wide array of co-stars. In 1941 and 1942, he appeared alongside a very young Rita Hayworth, who would become the most glamorous actress of the time period. The first of these films, *You'll Never Get Rich*, played a crucial role in facilitating Hayworth's rise to fame, and she would later state, "I guess the only jewels of my life were the pictures I made with Fred Astaire."

In the film, Astaire portrays a theater manager, making *You'll Never Get Rich* yet another example of the tendency for Astaire to portray characters employed in show business. The rationale behind his typecasting is easy to understand, since it helped the musical numbers fluidly integrate with the rest of the narrative. At the same time, it is worth considering whether Astaire was even capable of portraying other character types. After all, he did not possess a virile physique, and even in an era replete with relatively diminutive male stars like Humphrey Bogart and Spencer Tracy, Astaire's thin, balding appearance fell well short of the masculine model established by those actors.

Publicity image for *You'll Never Get Rich*

One major career development that occurred during the 1940s was that Astaire no longer occupied center stage in all of his films. Beginning with *Holiday Inn* in 1942, he was firmly relegated to the role of "co-star." In *Holiday Inn*, Astaire and Bing Crosby star as musical performers in a plot that charts the romances of Astaire with Virginia Dale and Crosby with Marjorie Reynolds, all set against the backdrop of the holiday season. The film is best remembered not for Astaire's contributions but instead for Bing Crosby's rendition of "White Christmas." Sharing the screen with a male co-star was difficult for Astaire, but he reunited with Crosby on *Blue Skies* (1946), an enormous box office success.

Holiday Inn

Despite the success of *Blue Skies*, Astaire was displeased with the film, and in a surprising decision, he announced his retirement later in 1946. The rationale behind the retirement was so that he could focus on his interests in horse racing, and while that was definitely a radical change, Astaire's slender physique and short height (about 5 foot 7 inches) made him small enough to be a natural jockey (Epstein). In addition, by 1946 he was already 47 years old, and he and Phyllis already had two children. Aside from his off-screen pursuits, the retirement was motivated by Fred's perception that his career was on the decline. For the first time in his career, he faced competition from Bing Crosby and Gene Kelly, both of whom were securing high-profile roles in Hollywood. Astaire thus had justifiable reasons for ending his film career, even if his retirement caught the public by surprise.

Chapter 5: Retirement

"There comes a day when people begin to say, 'Why doesn't that old duffer retire?' I want to get out while they're still saying Astaire is a hell of a dancer." – Fred Astaire

Astaire's retirement was relatively short-lived, as he returned to the screen after two years and starred in *Easter Parade* alongside Judy Garland in 1948. The film was a major success, and the unlikely pairing of Astaire and Garland paid dividends as they combined for numbers such as "The Ragtime Violin" and "Easter Parade." The film also benefitted from the glossy treatment of MGM, with its sumptuous color punctuating the musical sequences. Despite remaining relatively unknown decades later, *Easter Parade* was the highest-grossing film of Astaire's career.

Over the next several years, Astaire continued to find steady acting opportunities with MGM, and the most acclaimed of Astaire's 1950s films was *The Band Wagon* (1953), directed by Vincente Minnelli. The film features Astaire in a semi-autobiographical role as Tony Hunter, an aging musical comedy star. In fact, one of the major motifs of the film consists of watching an aging Astaire growing old before the camera. In an early musical number, "Shine On Your Shoes," Astaire appears weathered and past his prime. However, the narrative revolves around Astaire proving that he can still succeed in the genre of musical comedy. Dana Polan argues that Astaire "changes from the aged Tony Hunter, has-been, into the graceful Fred Astaire whose every dance movement belies the passage of time. We watch Tony become not the artiste everyone wants him to be, but the song-and-dance man he once was" (141).

The film's most prominent musical number, "That's Entertainment," substantiates Polan's claim. Instead of promoting the production of *Oedipus Rex*, Astaire and his cohorts in the film revel in the joys of performing popular entertainment. Considering that Astaire had long projected a genteel aura, it is perhaps surprising to watch Astaire promote popular entertainment, but the film's celebration of performing song-and-dance routines correctly applies to Astaire's own life. Even though *The Band Wagon* was not a commercial success, it was nominated for a series of Academy Awards, including Best Music, and is routinely listed among Astaire's finest films.

(Image from *The Band Wagon*)

Astaire's productivity waned during the 1950s, a development due not only to his aging but also the death of his wife in 1954. Her death occurred suddenly, and Fred was unprepared for it; at the time of her death, he was busy acting in *Daddy Long Legs* (1955). After her death, he considered relinquishing his role on the film but then changed his mind. Unlike his earlier films from the decade, the film was not produced by MGM but instead by 20th Century Fox, as Astaire had been released from his studio contract two years earlier. The emergence of television was in the process of rendering cinema less profitable than it had been during the previous decade, but the musical remained relatively unscathed when compared with less glamorous genres.

Astaire in *Daddy Long Legs*

Daddy Long Legs was a significant film in Astaire's career for several reasons. First, it represented the first film in which he appeared that was produced in Cinemascope. The wide composition of the image afforded him with an expansive showcase for performing his dancing feats, and he captivates the screen in his role as a wealthy benefactor who becomes romantically involved with a French orphan. In addition to performing in Cinemascope for the first time, the film also marked the first of three Astaire films that were set in France. Two years later, he appeared in *Funny Face* (1957) with Audrey Hepburn. As with *Daddy Long Legs*, the film was one of the few in Astaire's career in which he did not play the role of a show business performer. Instead, he plays a fashion photographer who becomes enamored with Audrey Hepburn's character. The film, produced by Paramount, had an enormous budget, especially because Audrey Hepburn was perhaps the leading actress in Hollywood and famous fashion photographer Richard Avedon was hired to assist with the production. The film was a musical, and Astaire and Hepburn do dance together in the film, but the musical numbers were not integrated as tightly within the narrative as Astaire's earlier films with Ginger Rogers.

Astaire's final film, set in Paris, was *Silk Stockings* (1957), released in the same year as *Funny Face*. The film was a loose remake of Lubitsch's famous *Ninotchka* (1939) and would be Fred's final musical of the 1950s. He played an American film producer, and apart from watching the 5 foot 7-inch Astaire dance alongside Cyd Charisse, the film remains noteworthy for "The Ritz of Rock and Roll," a musical number that spoofed rock and roll. Charisse would later speak at length about Astaire's dancing and compare it to Gene Kelly's, another prominent dancer who she performed with: "If I was black and blue, it was Gene. If I didn't have a scratch it was Fred." On another occasion, she expounded at length:

"As one of the handful of girls who worked with both of those dance geniuses, I think I can give an honest comparison. In my opinion, Kelly is the more inventive choreographer of the two. Astaire, with Hermes Pan's help, creates fabulous numbers - for himself and his partner. But Kelly can create an entire number for somebody else... I think, however, that Astaire's coordination is better than Kelly's... his sense of rhythm is uncanny. Kelly, on the other hand, is the stronger of the two. When he lifts you, he lifts you!... To sum it up, I'd say they were the two greatest dancing personalities who were ever on screen. But it's like comparing apples and oranges. They're both delicious."

Astaire and Charisse in *The Bandwagon*

After *Silk Stockings*, Astaire did not retire, but his career went in new directions. First, he explored television for the first time, appearing in four television programs in which he performs dance routines. Indirectly, the television series returned Astaire to his early, pre-cinema stage career, where his dancing was no longer tied to a cinematic narrative but was the sole attraction. His dancing remained impressive even as he turned 60, and the program won Emmy Awards for Best Performance by an Actor and Most Outstanding Single Program of the Year. Over the next couple of years, he appeared in other television programs, including a role in *It Takes a Thief* in 1968 and a number of made-for-television films.

One of the more surprising developments in Astaire's career was his decision at the end of the 1950s to begin appearing in films other than musicals. In 1959, he acted in *On the Beach*, a nuclear war film with an all-star cast that included not only Astaire but also Gregory Peck, Ava Gardner, and Anthony Perkins. The film led to other non-musical performances, including *The Pleasure of His Company* (1961) and *The Notorious Landlady* (1962). Astaire did return to the musical genre in 1968, appearing in Francis Ford Coppolla's *Finian's Rainbow*, but his final film was *Ghost Story* (1981), a horror film starring a long roster of aging stars, including John Houseman, Melvyn Douglas, and Douglas Fairbanks, Jr. The same year that *Ghost Story* was released, Astaire was awarded a Lifetime Achievement Award from the American Film Institute.

Astaire (right) in *On the Beach*

That Astaire's acting career continued well into old age reflects his excellent physical condition. Even when he was no longer able to dance on screen, he continued to act on a regular basis; *Ghost Story* was released when he was already in his 80s. His personal life also remained active well into old age. In 1980, Astaire married Robyn Smith, a horse jockey 45 years younger than himself. He and Smith had met through a mutual horse racing connection in 1973, and their marriage came after a long courtship. Fred continued to live in Beverley Hills and remained in strong health through his 80s until falling ill from pneumonia in 1989. He would die from the illness on June 22, having just turned 90 years old.

Fred Astaire's career spanned from 1905 through 1981, and the sheer length of it makes it possible to chart the developments that occurred in musical entertainment during the first three-quarters of the 20th century. Perhaps the most remarkable aspect of his career is that he managed to receive virtually unanimous acclaim. Referring to the reactions of cinematographers to the Astaire and Rogers movies, Annette Kuhn notes that Astaire and Rogers "are the only stars mentioned so often and…with such unanimous appreciation" (169). It is near impossible to encounter anyone who doesn't appreciate the films of Fred Astaire, and he managed to perform the seemingly impossible act of staying both critically acclaimed and beloved the entire time.

As unusual as Astaire's talent was, one of the more surprising aspects of his persona is the contrast between the extraordinary dancing feats he performed on screen and his relatively unremarkable physical appearance and personality off the movie set. A casual supporter of the Republican Party, Astaire preferred to distance himself from politics, and while many of his acting colleagues were embattled during the Red Scare, Astaire offered a comforting image of all-American conservatism. Similarly, during the Great Depression, Astaire enabled Americans to bask in the spectacle of his dancing feats with Ginger Rogers.

In the end, Astaire's overriding legacy can be found not so much in his films as the joy and entertainment he provided to America, and he continues to offer an idyllic model of entertainment divorced from the political agendas of celebrities of later generations. Not everyone is familiar with Astaire's films so many years later, but he will continue to hold a unique place in American pop culture, and the image of the top hat and coat tails stand as enduring reminders of the power of song and dance to comfort the viewer and lighten even the darkest of moods.

Testimonials to Fred Astaire and His Dancing

"The fact that Fred and I were in no way similar - nor were we the best male dancers around never occurred to the public or the journalists who wrote about us...Fred and I got the cream of the publicity and naturally we were compared. And while I personally was proud of the comparison, because there was no-one to touch Fred when it came to 'popular' dance, we felt that people, especially film critics at the time, should have made an attempt to differentiate between our two styles. Fred and I both got a bit edgy after our names were mentioned in the same breath. I was the Marlon Brando of dancers, and he the Cary Grant. My approach was completely different from his, and we wanted the world to realize this, and not lump us together like peas in a pod. If there was any resentment on our behalf, it certainly wasn't with each other, but with people who talked about two highly individual dancers as if they were one person. For a start, the sort of wardrobe I wore - blue jeans, sweatshirt, sneakers - Fred wouldn't have been caught dead in. Fred always looked immaculate in rehearsals, I was always in an old shirt. Fred's steps were small, neat, graceful and intimate - mine were ballet-oriented and very athletic. The two of us couldn't have been more different, yet the public insisted on thinking of us as rivals...I persuaded him to put on his dancing shoes again, and replace me in Easter Parade after I'd broken my ankle. If we'd been rivals, I certainly wouldn't have encouraged him to make a comeback." – Gene Kelly

"Fred taught me a step because I said I can't let this experience be over without my learning something. He taught me the most wonderful Fred Astaire-like step, with an umbrella. It was a complete throwaway; it was almost invisible. It was in the way he walked. As he moved along, he bounced the umbrella on the floor to the beat and then he grabbed it. It was effortless and invisible. As a matter of fact, a few years later I was photographing Gene Kelly and told him that Fred Astaire had taught me this trick with an umbrella. And Kelly said, 'Oh I'll teach you one,' and he did, and the two tricks with the umbrella in some way define the difference between Fred Astaire and Gene Kelly, and, in my view, demonstrate who is the greater of the two artists. With Gene Kelly, he threw the umbrella way up into the air, and then he moved to catch it, very slowly, grabbing it behind his back. It was a big, grandstand play, about nothing." - Richard Avedon

"The major difference between Astaire and Kelly is a difference, not of talent or technique, but of levels of sophistication. On the face of it, Kelly looks the more sophisticated. Where Kelly has ideas, Astaire has dance steps. Where Kelly has smartly tailored, dramatically apt Comden and Green scripts, Astaire in the Thirties made do with formulas derived from nineteenth-century French Farce. But the Kelly film is no longer a dance film. It's a story film with dances, as distinguished from a dance film with a story. When Fred and Ginger go into their dance, you see it as a distinct formal entity, even if it's been elaborately built up to in the script. In a Kelly film, the plot action and the musical set pieces preserve a smooth community of high spirits, so that the pressure in a dance number will often seem too low, the dance itself plebeian or folksy in order to "match up" with the rest of the picture." - Arlene Croce

"I suspect it is this Camelot view that leads Miss Croce to be rather unfair to Gene Kelly...I should say the difference starts with their bodies. If you compare Kelly to Astaire, accepting Astaire's debonair style as perfection then, of course, Kelly looks bad. But in popular dance forms, in which movement is not rigidly codified, as it is in ballet, perfection is a romantic myth or a figure of speech, nothing more. Kelly isn't a winged dancer; he's a hoofer and more earthbound. But he has warmth and range as an actor...Astaire's grasshopper lightness was his limitation as an actor - confining him to perennial gosh-oh-gee adolescence;; he was always and only a light comedian and could function only in fairytale vehicles." - Pauline Kael

"I can watch Astaire anytime. I don't think he ever made a wrong move. He was a perfectionist. He would work on a few bars for hours until it was just the way he wanted it. Gene was the same way. They both wanted perfection, even though they were completely different personalities." - Cyd Charisse

"There never was a greater perfectionist, there never was, and never will be, a better dancer, and I never knew anybody more kind, more considerate, or more completely a gentleman...I love Fred, John, and I admire and respect him. I guess it's because he's so many things I'd like to be and I'm not." – Bing Crosby

"At its most basic, Mr. Astaire's technique has three elements - tap, ballet and ballroom dancing. The ballet training, by his account, was brief but came at a crucial, early age. He has sometimes been classed as a tap dancer, but he was never the hoofer he has jokingly called himself. Much of the choreographic outline of his dancing with his ladies—be it Miss Rogers or Miss Hayworth—is ballroom. But of course, no ballroom dancer could dance like this." - Dance critic Anna Kisselgoff

"Mr. Astaire is the nearest approach we are ever likely to have to a human Mickey Mouse; he might have been drawn by Mr. Walt Disney, with his quick physical wit, his incredible agility. He belongs to a fantasy world almost as free as Mickey's from the law of Gravity." – Graham Greene, movie critic.

"But when you're in a picture with Astaire, you've got rocks in your head if you do much dancing. He's so quick-footed and so light that it's impossible not to look like a hay-digger compared with him." - Bing Crosby

"I work bigger. Fred's style is intimate. I'm very jealous of that when I see him on the small screen. Fred looks so great on TV. I'd love to put on white tie and tails and look as thin as him and glide as smoothly. But I'm built like a blocking tackle." - Gene Kelly

"Just to see him walk down the street ... to me is worth the price of admission." - Sammy Davis Jr.

Bibliography

Altman, Rick. *The American Musical*. Bloomington: Indiana University Press, 1987.

Astaire, Fred. *Steps in Time: An Autobiography*. New York: Harper, 2008.

Croce, Arlene. *The Fred Astaire and Ginger Rogers Book*. London: W.H. Allen, 1972.

Epstein, Joseph. *Fred Astaire*. New Have: Yale University Press, 2008.

Franceschina, John. *Hermes Pan: The Man Who Danced with Fred Astaire*. New York: Oxford University Press, 2012.

Gallafant, Edward. *Astaire and Rogers*. New York: Cameron Books, 2000.

Kuhn, Annette. *An Everyday Magic: Cinema and Cultural Memory*. New York: I.B. Tauris, 2002.

Levinson, Peter. *Puttin' On the Ritz: Fred Astaire and the Fine Art of Panache*. New York: St. Martin's, 2009.

Mueller, John E. *Astaire Dancing: The Musical Films*. New York: Alfred A. Knopf, 1985.

Polan, Dana. "It Could Be Oedipus Rex: Denial and Difference in *The Band Wagon*; or, The American Musical as American Gothic." *Vincente Minnelli: The Art of Entertainment*. Ed. Joe McElhaney. Detroit: Wayne State University Press, 2009. 130-153.

Sarris, Andrew. *The American Cinema: Directors and Directions*. Chicago: Da Capo Press, 1996.

Henry Fonda

Chapter 1: Biscuits and a Baby Boy

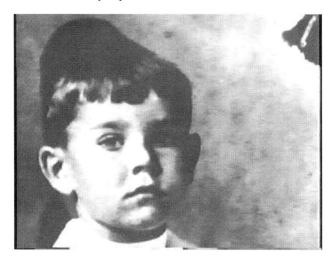

Henry Fonda as a child

"My whole damn family was nice. I don't think I've imagined it. It's true. Maybe it has to do with being brought up as Christian Scientists. Half of my relatives were Readers or Practitioners in the church." - Henry Fonda

Henry Fonda would grow up to be one of Hollywood's greatest icons, and he definitely had one of the greatest birth announcements welcoming him into the world: "Dr. Roeder reports Uneeda Biscuits for sale at any old price from salesman William Brace Fonda this morning, a bright baby boy having arrived at the home of Mr. and Mrs. Fonda on West Division Street yesterday." Henry was born on May 16, 1905 to William and Herberta Fonda, who welcomed their first child into a small house rented to them by a local banker in Grand Island, Nebraska, but when their little boy was just a few months old, the young couple moved back to Omaha, where William found a job working as a printer.

Little Henry, known to his family as Hank, was soon joined by his sisters Harriet in 1907 and Herberta Jayne in 1909, and as he was growing up, his family prospered. William bought a large home for them in Dundee, a suburb of Omaha, and he was soon doing well enough to purchase his own print shop. That is how Henry Fonda came to grow up along the delightfully named thoroughfare of "Happy Hollow Boulevard." Not only did William's print shop provide his family with a comfortable living, it also provided Henry with a valuable source of entertainment. That's because the print shop was located just across from the local nickelodeon, where young Henry wiled away Saturday afternoons watching short subjects starring William Hart and Charlie

Chaplin. If he had seen the movie before, he could just as well stroll down the street to the Orpheum Theater, where he might be able to catch Harry Houdini touring with his magic show or a young Fred Astaire gliding across the stage with his sister Adele.

Unlike many fathers of his era, William Fonda was very involved in his children's lives, building four-year-old Henry a kite and later, when the boy was older, an amateur radio set. Like most children, Henry took his father's love for granted, but when he was a man and a father with troubled children himself, he would later recall, "Only when I grew up and moved away did I realize exactly how much I loved him, how much he meant to me and what an unusual man he was." Indeed, the idyllic family life young Henry enjoyed also helped ensure that his childhood was mostly uneventful. His father's family had been Christian Scientists for several generations, and that is how the Fonda children were raised, despite the fact Herberta was an Episcopalian and insisted that her son be baptized at St. Stephen's Episcopal Church in Grand Island. Since their faith put such emphasis on healthy living and avoiding traditional medicine, the Fonda's worked very hard to maintain both their bodies and their souls, but in spite of his early religious upbringing, Henry would later lose his faith and become a self-described agnostic in adulthood.

As a child, Henry was shy and quiet, especially around girls, and though he had no problem interacting with his sisters, he was likely to find somewhere else to be when they entertained their girlfriends. The athletic youngster enjoyed playing at the nearby lake, swimming in the summer and ice skating in the winter, and like many boys in his neighborhood, he was a member of the Boy Scouts of America and eventually reached Eagle Scout. When no outdoor activities were available, Henry liked to curl up with paper and a pencil, drawing animals and items that he saw around him.

When Henry was old enough, William put his son to work in his print shop, and it was there, from the plant window, that Henry witnessed an event that would be the one black stain on his idyllic youth. When he was about 14, a young black man living in the community was accused of raping a white woman, and as was too often the case in World War I era America, the case never made it to trial because the young man was lynched from a tree just outside the print plant window. Henry Fonda would never forget what he saw that day, and for the rest of his life he would be a determined supporter of racial equality.

Working hard for his father, and later at the local phone company, made Henry a healthy, strong young man. By the time he graduated from high school, he was over 6 feet tall, though he was still shy around members of the opposite sex. After high school, he went off to the University of Minnesota, but that was in keeping more with his family's status and ambition for his future than his own. He studied journalism, but his heart was not in it, and after receiving mediocre grades, he soon dropped out.

Finding himself back home in Omaha in 1925, Henry needed to find something to do. At first, he worked odd jobs that included delivering ice, fixing cars, and even decorating the windows of the local dress shops. However, the only thing in his life at that time that really caught his interest was his work at the Omaha Community Playhouse. At first, it was the backstage aspect of the Playhouse that interested him; he enjoyed set construction and didn't mind sweeping up after the audience left. Still shy as a young adult, he could not picture of himself actually being on stage, but all that changed when a woman named Dodie Brando, a friend of his mother's, suggested that he try out for a small part in the play *You and I*. She shared with Henry that her son, Marlon Brando, had found acting to be an excellent way to overcome his own tongue-tied shyness. Despite assuming that he would never get the part, Henry agreed to audition, and when he was cast as Ricky, he was both amazed and frightened. He would later recall of this first time on stage, "It was a nightmare. I didn't dare look up. I was the kind of guy who thinks everybody is looking at him."

While Henry was interested in the stage, his parents were decidedly less interested in that line of work. William and Herberta were nice, middle-class people living in a nice town in Middle America, and even if acting no longer carried the immoral stigma that it had 50 years earlier, it was still not considered a real job for a grown man. Thus, in hopes of luring his son away from his interest in the stage and back to reality, William used his influence to get Henry an entry-level position with the Retail Credit Company of Omaha.

By this time, however, it was too late. When Henry was cast for the lead in *Merton of the Movies*, he had truly caught the acting bug, and in the spring of 1926, he was hired by Lincoln impersonator George Billings to accompany him on a speaking tour. In addition to translating Lincoln's most famous speeches into scripts, Fonda also played Lincoln's aide, Maj. John Hay. Together, the tour played one little theater after another across the Midwest, and the act, called *The Dramatic Life of Abraham Lincoln*, was well-received by audiences starved for new shows. Billings would prove to be an important influence on Fonda's future acting style, and both men prided themselves on "disappearing into each role" they played.

It was during this trip that one of the most charming stories of Fonda's life occurred. One friend he was traveling with, a young man who was also from Omaha, arranged for the two to go on a double date with sisters named Bobby and Bette one night. As was so often the case in that era, the two couples ended up parking behind the Princeton Stadium. Still shy, but heady with the excitement of being in a new city, young Fonda reached over and gave his date, the 17-year-old Bette, a quick kiss. However, any happiness lingering from the night before quickly disappeared when Bette called him the next morning to him that her mother insisted that the two marry. Fonda quickly left town and returned to Omaha, believing he had put the incident behind him forever, but he was destined to run into Bette Davis again about a dozen years later, by which time she had won her first Oscar and been cast opposite of him in *That Certain Woman*. Fonda would later joke, "I've been close to Bette Davis for thirty-eight years - and I have the cigarette burns to prove it."

Bette Davis in *Jezebel*, which Fonda would co-star in.

By the time he returned to Omaha, Fonda knew he had found his life's work. He spent another year working at the Community Playhouse as the assistant director and starring in as many plays as his schedule would permit. As is often the case with small local theaters, the quality of the productions was mixed. They ranged from the popular *The School For Scandal* to *Rip Van Winkle* to Eugene O'Neill's famous *Beyond The Horizon*. By the end of 1928, Fonda was convinced that he had what it took to make it big, so he quit his job and headed back east to chase fame and fortune.

Chapter 2: The Cape and the Continent

"The only actor of the era with whom I identified was Henry Fonda. I was not alone. A black friend of mine, after seeing Henry Fonda in The Grapes Of Wrath, swore that Fonda had colored blood. You could tell, he said, by the way Fonda walked down the road at the end of the film: white men don't walk like that! And he indicated Fonda's stubborn, patient, wide-legged hike away from the camera." - James Baldwin

Fonda landed his first East Coast role at the Cape Playhouse in Dennis, Massachusetts, and much to his surprise, he won the lead in *The Barker*, a Broadway hit that had made its way north from Broadway over the past year. After a successful run in Dennis, Fonda moved south to Falmouth, Massachusetts, where he joined the University Players Guild. Again, his skills were recognized, and he was given sizable parts in plays performed by the Guild, but the theatres along the Massachusetts coast were only open during the summer months, when tourists visiting the area provided sufficient audiences. Thus, after an ideal summer of eating, sleeping and living the theatrical life, Fonda quickly found himself unemployed.

Fonda spent the next two winters in Washington DC, where he worked for the National Junior Theater performing for children, and he returned to the University Players in the summer of 1929, but in 1930 he moved back to Omaha, where he once more worked for the Community Playhouse, this time playing the lead in their production of *A Kiss for Cinderella*. By this time, Fonda had met Margaret Sullavan, and they dated off and on. Some of Fonda's most memorable quotes were about Sullavan. One time, he described her as "cream and sugar on a dish of hot ashes", and another time, he expounded on that by explaining, "She was not an easy woman to categorize or to explain. If I've ever known anyone in my life, man or woman, who was unique, it was she. There was nobody like her before or since. Never will be. In every way. In talent, in looks, in character, in temperament. Everything. There sure wasn't anybody who didn't fall under her spell."

Margaret Sullavan

The two would marry on Christmas Day in 1931, but they lived together as man and wife for only a few months before separating. They divorced in 1933, but just like with Bette Davis, Margaret Sullavan would turn up in Fonda's life again. 13 years later, the two would find themselves living in the same neighborhood, hauling their own children back and forth to the same parties and sporting events. They would even star in a film together in 1936.

In spite of his youthful optimism, Fonda was initially devastated by the divorce, and he would later remember, "My thinking was scrambled when Sullavan and I separated. Something happened to me that had never happened before. I couldn't cope. It was heartbreak time. I thought it was the end of the world." Not long after his divorce was final, Fonda moved to New York City to try his luck on Broadway, and accompanying him was another young actor that he had met while in Massachusetts: James Stewart. Like most struggling young thespians during the Great Depression, The two worked off and on for the next year, until Fonda finally got his big break. It happened while he was starring in *New Faces* during the summer of 1934; unlike many of his previous roles, Fonda danced and sang his way across the stage in this musical, which eventually attracted the attention of Leland Hayward, a talent scout for the famous Myron Selznick. He assured the young actor that if he would just fly out to Hollywood, Selznick could get him a movie contract with a big company for $750 per week.

Jimmy Stewart in the trailer for *After the Thin Man* (1936)

Leland Hayward

Though he must have by this time has been tired of playing one new show after another every few months, Fonda hesitated at first, explaining, "It wasn't my ambition to be in the movies." In the end, however, curiosity won out over fear, and Fonda found himself standing under a Hollywood palm tree in August 1934, being introduced to a producer named Walter Wanger. Fonda would later recall the deal he was offered: "I could go back to my beloved theater in the winter and come out the next summer to do two pictures for $1000 a week. I turned to [Hayward] and said, 'There's something fishy.' I just couldn't believe it. And he laughed and laughed."

In the end, Fonda took the offer, opening on Broadway on October 30, 1934, in *The Farmer Takes a Wife*. His portrayal of farmer Dan Harrow proved to be his best performance yet, leading one critic to praise his "manly, modest performance in a style of captivating simplicity." Another critic, upon hearing that Fonda would be returning to Hollywood in the spring, predicted that he "will be transferred to the movie colony in geographic time to become the newest of the leading men for Norma Shearer, Constance Bennett or Miriam Hopkins." Director Victor Fleming agreed with the critics and cast Fonda as Dan Harrow in the screen version of *The Farmer Takes a Wife*. While filming this, his first movie role, Fonda quickly learned the differences between stage acting and creating a character on film. Perhaps the most significant change that he had to make was how he projected his voice. After years of speaking loudly and distinctly enough for the audience in the back row to hear, Fonda had to learn to modulate his tones in order not to damage the microphone into which he was speaking.

Another thing that Fonda had to adjust to in Hollywood was the almost incestuous nature of the relationships between successful actors of the 1930s. For instance, he spent his first few months in the city and the company of his ex-wife, Margaret Sullavan; who by this time was the ex-wife of director William Weiler, who would direct Fonda in Jezebel. Leland Hayward represented them both, and he would soon be Margaret Sullavan's third husband. It wasn't so much that Hollywood was a deliberately closed society but more to do with the fact that most actors of that era got their starts on the stages of Broadway and other small playhouses. Therefore, it was inevitable that they would once more meet up once they made it to the "big league."

For his part, Fonda was thoroughly enjoying his new start. Not only was he now making $3000 a week, he was also dating or rumored to be dating seemingly every actress in Hollywood, from Carol Lombard to Greta Garbo. Even better, his old friend Jimmy Stewart had joined him in Tinseltown, and the two were rooming together again. In 1935, Fonda made the film *I Dream Too Much*, and once again critics liked what they saw, with one calling him "the most likable of the new crop of romantic juveniles."

His next role was opposite Fred MacMurray in *Trail of the Lonesome Pine* in 1936, and this film was significant at the time because it was the first movie filmed both in color and outdoors. Later that year, Fonda teamed up with Sullavan in *The Moon's Our Home*, and perhaps not surprisingly, they rekindled their romance for a short time and even discussed getting remarried. Before long, however, they began fighting with each other much as they had back in Massachusetts, and they soon realized it was in everyone's best interest for them to remain just friends.

For all that the Hollywood of the 1930s was known for its scandals and infidelities, the public still liked the idea of a happy ending, especially for their rising stars. As a result, Fonda's public relations team soon began portraying him as a good, respectable young man who was just looking for the right woman to share his life with. An article published in May 1936 claimed, "Henry Fonda says it is all right with him if he gets married by next Christmas. He has just bought a home in Beverly Hills, and although he admits that they are is no immediate prospect of a Mrs. Henry Fonda, the house is all ready for her." As it turned out, Fonda would find his new bride on the other side of the Atlantic. On July 10, Walter Wagner shipped him off to London to star in *Wings of the Morning*, a new film being produced by Alexander Korda. This charming romance was filmed on location in Surrey, England and Kilkenny, Ireland, but even though the film was the first movie filmed in Technicolor in Europe, neither the critics nor the fans found it particularly exciting. However, what was exciting for Fonda was the 28-year-old widow of millionaire George Brokaw, Frances Ford Brokaw, who was petite, blonde, and beautiful. A descendant of the third wife of Henry VIII, she had been born in Canada and raised among the social elite of that country. She had a daughter, four-year-old Frances (called Pan by her family), and a substantial fortune. She actively pursued Fonda in Europe, and then followed him back to America, where the two were married on September 16, 1936. Just over a year later, their first child, named Lady Jane Seymour Fonda after her mother's distant relative, was born. Their second child, Peter, was born three years later.

Henry and Frances

Chapter 3: Wars and Rumors of Wars

"My father can't articulate the way he works. He just can't do it. He's not even conscious of what he does, and it made him nervous for me to try to articulate what I was trying to do. And I sensed that immediately, so we did very little talking about it...he said, 'Shut up, I don't want to hear about it.' He didn't want me to tell him about it, you know. He wanted to make fun of it." - Jane Fonda

After a brief honeymoon, the Fonda's moved to Hollywood, where Henry continued to pursue his acting career. In 1938, he showed up on set to film *Jezebel* and was introduced to his leading lady, the former debutante Bette Davis. While it is unknown what passed between the two in private, their performance together was excellent, with Davis playing a spoiled southern belle living in antebellum New Orleans. Fonda plays her hothead fiancée, who abandons her in the middle of the movie only to return a year later married to another woman. The fiery personalities of both Davis and Fonda translated well to the screen, and *Jezebel* remains a cinematic classic.

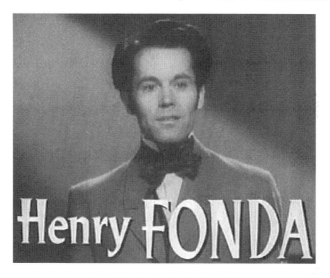

Fonda in the trailer for *Jezebel*

If 1938 was a good year for Fonda's career, 1939 was almost perfect. That year, he was cast in one of his favorite roles, that of *Young Mr. Lincoln*. Famed director John Ford was at his best, insisting that Lincoln be portrayed not as the somber president he would become but as "a jackleg young lawyer from Springfield." Ford also insisted that Fonda was the only actor to play him. *Young Mr. Lincoln* proved to be one of Henry Fonda's most memorable roles and earned him extensive critical acclaim. Congress would later add the movie to the National Film Registry, reserved for films deemed "culturally, historically, or aesthetically significant".

Fonda enjoyed working with Ford on the movie, ensuring they would continue to work together, but he was by no means in awe of the great director. He would later say of Ford, "He was so egomaniacal. He would never rehearse, didn't want to talk about a part. If an actor started to ask questions he'd either take those pages and tear them out of the script or insult him in an awful way. He loved getting his shot on the first take, which for him meant it was fresh. He would print the first take -- even if it wasn`t any good."

John Ford

Having played one of America's favorite men, Fonda next turned his attention to playing one of the nation's most notorious sinners. In 1939, he appeared in *Jesse James* as Jesse's younger brother Frank. This would be Fonda's first major Western, and it would lead to his being cast, again by Ford, in *Drums Along the Mohawk*. In this film, Fonda played opposite Claudette Colbert as an early American couple named Gilbert and Magdalena Morton. Not only was Fonda's acting splendid, the movie itself is beautiful to look at. Ford used Technicolor well, juxtaposing wide mountain vistas with dark cabinet interiors to capture an idealized version of the new American continent.

By this time in his career, Fonda had carved out a niche for himself playing grizzled, determined common men of the soil, which helped convinced audiences that he understood them and where they were coming from. In Depression-era America, he portrayed the everyday man, the neighbor who may have lost his job or the panhandler riding the rails. He came across on-screen as someone who would tell the truth about what he thought of someone else but would never let anyone figure out what he thought of himself. This suffering, taciturn, thoughtful father figure was just what John Ford needed for his latest picture, 1940's *The Grapes of Wrath*, and Ford believed that Fonda was the man for the job. Fonda also believed he was the man for the job; and time would prove that the American public believed he was man for the job. However, the movie's producer, Darryl F. Zanuck, was not so sure. He wanted Tyrone Power to play the protagonist, Tom Joad, so in order to win the role for himself, Fonda had to sign a seven-year contract with Zanuck's studio, 20th Century Fox.

Zanuck

This was a chance move for such a young actor, but it proved to be the right one. *The Grapes of Wrath* earned Fonda his first nomination for an Academy Award. Not only is the movie considered a film classic to this day, many consider it to be the best role that Fonda ever played. Set during the Great Depression, the downtrodden Tom Joad is the kind of hero that everyone suffering during the era could relate to, and he vows to fight for social reforms: "I'll be all around in the dark. I'll be everywhere. Wherever you can look, wherever there's a fight, so hungry people can eat, I'll be there. Wherever there's a cop beatin' up a guy, I'll be there. I'll be in the way guys yell when they're mad. I'll be in the way kids laugh when they're hungry and they know supper's ready, and when the people are eatin' the stuff they raise and livin' in the houses they build, I'll be there, too."

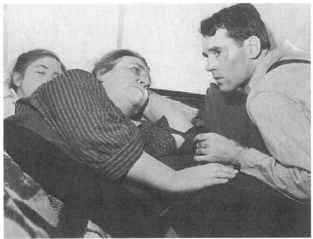

Pictures of Henry Fonda as Tom Joad

Later in the year, Fonda returned to the classic Westerns that he built his career on, playing the title role in *The Return of Frank James*. In this film, Fonda played opposite Gene Tierney, an actress with whom he would team up again in the comedy *Rings on Her Fingers*. In between these two films, he starred with Barbara Stanwyck in *The Lady Eve*, and though this was Fonda's first comedic role on film, the movie was wildly successful and appears on the American Film Institute's list of the 100 funniest movies of all time.

Fonda in *The Lady Eve*

By this time, the United States had joined World War II, and more and more Hollywood actors were joining up. Jimmy Stewart was already flying bombing missions for the Army Air Corps, and Fonda wanted to enlist as well, complaining, "I don't want to be in a fake war in a studio." However, he was still under contract to 20th Century Fox, and John Ford convinced him that he could better use his talents, at least for the time being, making movies to support the war effort. For example, he provided the narration for Ford's documentary about the Battle of Midway, but as the war went on, working in Hollywood was not enough for him. On August 24, 1942, the day after he completed filming of *The Ox-Bow Incident*, Fonda drove to the Navy headquarters in Los Angeles and volunteered for active duty, saying, "I'd like to be with the fellows who handle the guns." While he had hoped to keep his plans quiet, the press heard about what he was doing and dispatched a reporter to follow the story. He reported, "Without the usual Hollywood fanfare, Fonda waited in line with other prospective recruits, took his medical examination and was sworn in. Recruiting officer Lieut. Blanchard said Fonda will be sent to San Diego within a few days and can realize his wish to quote 'handle the guns' by competing for a rating in the gunners mates school. 'It has been my desire to join the service for a long time,' Fonda said, 'And I am glad that I am able to get in and do a little pitching.' While some stars had used their status to go in as officers, Fonda asked for, and received, the designation of apprentice seamen, the lowest rank in the Navy."

Fonda after enlisting in the Navy in 1942

Over the next few years, Fonda would rise through the ranks of the Navy, first as a quartermaster aboard the USS *Satterlee* in Seattle, Washington, and then as a Lieutenant in Washington, D.C. While stationed in Washington, Fonda was offered an unusual opportunity: he was recruited for the new Office of Strategic Services, the predecessor of the C.I.A. Thus, for the rest of the war, he would work in the shadowy world of wartime intelligence. According to records from the era, Fonda had a knack for intelligence and would have made a good undercover agent if not for the fact that his acting career had made his face and voice so well known. Instead, he worked as an analyst, putting to use the excellent memory he had developed through years of learning scripts. For his efforts, he received both a Bronze Star and a Navy

Presidential Unit Citation.

Chapter 4: At Home in Hollywood

"I suppose one human being never really knows much about another. My impressions of Hank are of a man reaching but unreachable, gentle but capable of sudden wild and dangerous violence, sharply critical of others but equally self-critical, caged and fighting the bars but timid of the light, viciously opposed to external restraint, imposing an iron slavery on himself. His face is a picture of opposites in conflict." - John Steinbeck

While the world viewed Fonda's military service as an act of sacrificial patriotism, those nearest to him knew that it was much more. Sadly, by enlisting in the Navy, Fonda was running away from a fight he could not win toward a war that he thought he had some hope of surviving. Unfortunately, the war that Fonda was losing was in his own home, his opponent was his wife Frances, and the collateral damage was being done to their children, Jane and Peter.

The Fonda's had been married nearly a year when Henry began to realize that something was wrong with Frances. At first, he wrote her nervous energy off as the concerns of a young mother-to-be, and after Jane was born, he thought she was just being overprotective. Even when she insisted that he wear a mask while holding his firstborn, or when she constantly worried that the baby might contract some sort of mysterious illness, he went along with her precautions. However, as time wore on, Frances's condition deteriorated. By the time Peter was born in 1940, she had become a neurotic hypochondriac who lived in deathly fear of germs and illness.

Jane Fonda in her 20s

Peter Fonda with Patty McCormack in 1962

Unfortunately, Henry was ill-equipped to handle Frances's worries. Raised in a family where good health was a given and complaining was a sin, Henry expected Frances to pull herself up by her own bootstraps, and when she was unable to do this, he vacillated between over-involvement in his children's lives, often in the form of yelling or excessively harsh discipline, and ignoring his family altogether, spending as much time as possible on the set of whatever movie was working on. As an adult, and an actress in her own right, Jane would later recall, "Dad was so emotionally distant, with a coldness that mother was not equipped to breach." Another family friend, a peer of Jane's, remembered, "We were all afraid of Jane's father in those days. We always felt that he was a time bomb ready to explode."

By the time World War II ended, the family was living full time on their brand-new estate, Tigertail. Located in an up-and-coming Beverly Hills neighborhood, Tigertail was the jewel of the area, and according to a 1948 magazine, it was "probably the most carefully planned home in these United States. Before even the cement was mixed, trees were removed and transplanted on the grounds, flowerbeds were set out, a citrus grove was planted, and gardens were mapped." Sadly, while both Henry and Frances put tremendous effort into physically building the space in which they were raising their children, they put almost no effort into the emotional health of their family. Henry worked more and more, while Frances found her escape in pills. Throughout the war and during the years following, she was hospitalized over and over again for what were referred to during that era as "nervous symptoms." If she wasn't in a hospital bed, she often found her way into the bed of other men, and when Fonda finally returned from the war, it was not to a hero's welcome but to a marital bed and home in which he was no longer welcome. Frances made much of the work she had done (and planned to continue to do) to manage their money, and there were bills and account books all over Fonda's side of the bed. He was forced to sleep in the guest room or elsewhere for the rest of their marriage.

While she had mental health issues, Frances also had plenty of good reasons to separate herself from her husband, both emotionally and physically. During most of the war years, while Fonda was away, Frances had to deal with a paternity suit filed by a woman who claimed that she had a baby as a result of an affair with Fonda. Although the suit was dropped shortly after the war ended, Frances and her daughter Jane both believed that Henry had cheated. In fact, Jane always maintained that her father cheated frequently on her mother, contributing at least in part to Frances's misery and untimely death.

During his first year home from the war, Henry and Frances tried to work their difficulties out. Instead of returning to making movies, Fonda devoted himself to being a gentleman farmer, and he actually became something of a humorous legend for his regular praise of manure for his beautiful lawn and garden. Frances also seemed to be focusing on her family, but in the most unhealthy way possible. She spent most of her days in bed, going over bills and worrying about her children's health. She also expressed increasing concern for her own mortality and fading good looks. She was now in her late 30s, and determined to "not go gently into that good night," she consulted one doctor after another about everything from legitimate ailments to plastic surgery. After a while, Frances's doctors decided that her problems might stem from a hormone imbalance and ordered the gynecological cure-all of the day: a hysterectomy. By this time, the summer of 1946, Henry had returned to making movies and was away filming *My Darling Clementine* in Utah and Arizona, and Frances told him nothing of her plan to have surgery. Instead, she claimed to be flying to New York to visit her oldest daughter, Pan. She checked herself into Johns Hopkins Medical Center, had the surgery, recovered, and returned home before Henry found out that anything had happened.

With so much trouble at home, Fonda continued to make about one picture per year. In 1947, having completed his contract with 20th Century Fox, he went to work for John Ford's new company, Argosy Pictures, and though he would never again be a contract actor, he did enjoy working with Ford on *The Fugitive*. This picture was not the story of a falsely accused Doctor Kimball but about a Mexican priest being pursued, eventually to martyrdom, by a Marxist government. The following year, Fonda returned to Westerns, starring again for Ford in *Fort Apache* as an Army colonel in charge of Western fort, with a beautiful daughter played by the now grown up Shirley Temple.

As things continued to fall apart in his home life, Fonda began to look for another escape. The war was over, but it was being portrayed over and over again on screens and stages across America. It is no surprise then that an old friend from his Broadway days, Joshua Logan, contacted Henry about a part that seemed to be (and in fact was) written for him. Seeing a chance to recapture both some of his youth, at least that portion spent on stage, and some of the glory of his early career, Fonda jumped at the opportunity to bring *Mister Roberts*, a comedy about the Navy, to life on Broadway. Thus, he packed up his gear one more time and left his family behind, this time heading on his way to New York. It was oddly symbolic and fitting that one of the few items he took with him was his own officer's cap, which he wore onstage night after night.

Chapter 5: The Curtain Falls

"People ask me from time to time what it was like growing up with Henry Fonda as my father. I say, Ever see *Fort Apache*? He was like Colonel Thursday." - Peter Fonda

Mister Roberts proved to be the high point of Henry Fonda's stage career, earning him his only Tony Award for Best Actor in 1948. Critics raved about the production, and audiences flocked to see it, but even as Fonda enjoyed both the success and the security he felt away from his family, he nonetheless expressed guilt that he had left his wife and children back at Tigertail. Thus, once it became obvious that he would be staying in New York for some time, he sent for Frances, Jane and Peter. Given the state of their marriage, it may seem surprising that he wanted his wife to join him, and it might be even more amazing that she agreed to come, but in spite of all her problems, Frances was still a dutiful wife and mother. As a result, she sold their beautiful home on its spacious lot and moved across country to New York, where she purchased a home in the fashionable Greenwich neighborhood.

Did Henry Fonda hope that returning to the stage would somehow bring back his youth and optimism? Did he believe that he could leave behind his early 40s and return to his early 20s? Was he looking for the optimism that he felt years earlier about life? It's hard to tell with certainty because Fonda was not the type of man to talk about his emotions, even to his closest friends, but whatever his hopes were, they were soon dashed. Frances fared no better in New York than she had in Tigertail; in fact, while the house that they bought was large and comfortable, it was also dark in a sort of Gothic, Victorian way, not the best home for someone who struggled with depression. She continued to have health problems and had to have surgery in 1949 to repair a problem with her bladder, which left a large scar across her abdomen and only increased her angst about her physical appearance. Frances also continued to worry about not only her health but that of her children. Sadly, while she was correct to worry, she was worrying about the wrong things. Now in her early teens, Jane was developing an eating disorder that would trouble her for years, while Peter remained sickly, catching every cold and virus that went around. A different sort of man would have stepped up and tried to fill in the gaps Frances was leaving in the family's life, but instead of filling in the gaps, Henry worked harder to turn a blind eye to them. Frances would go into the hospital, but Henry would go on stage.

Given the circumstances, it is not terribly surprising that Henry found refuge with someone else during this time. Her name was Susan Blanchard, and she was the 21-year-old stepdaughter of famous lyricist Oscar Hammerstein II. When the two started seeing each other in 1948, Fonda may have assumed that it would be another short-lived fling, but eventually they became more involved and he wanted to marry her. Thus, in the fall of 1949, Henry sat down with Frances, told her about the affair, and asked her for divorce. According to his autobiography, Frances took the news well and put up no resistance; Henry claimed she later wrote to a friend that she wished him better luck with his third marriage than he had with theirs.

Blanchard

Time would soon demonstrate that Frances's supposed acquiescence was either a ruse or something that Henry himself fabricated. In the spring of 1950, Frances once again checked herself in to a luxurious mental health facility that catered to the neuroses of the rich and famous. She seemed to be responding well to treatment, and the doctors were optimistic about her recovery. In fact, they allowed her a short furlough to visit her family. Tragically, this proved to be a tragic decision, because while visiting her oldest daughter, Frances smuggled a razor blade out of the bathroom. She hid it on her body and smuggled it into the hospital, where one week later, in the early hours of April 14, her 42nd birthday, she used the blade to cut her throat and bled to death before she was found.

The doctors at the hospital immediately contacted Henry, who acted quickly to claim the body and plan a small funeral that was only attended by himself and Frances's mother Sophie. He then sent the body to Hartsdale, New York, where it would be cremated and the ashes interred. It was only after he had done all these things that he told his children that their mother was gone. Even then, he did not tell them that she had committed suicide, perhaps believing that, at 10 and 12, the two could not handle the truth. Instead, he told them that she had died of a heart attack while in the hospital.

That evening, Fonda concluded the day in which she claimed his wife's body, held her funeral, sent her remains to be cremated, and told his children that their mother was dead, by going on stage as usual. Obviously, this decision leads to speculation. Was he, as one doctor accused him, "a cold, self-absorbed person, a complete narcissist?" Or was he a grieving, guilt-ridden husband looking to lose himself in a world that he understood better than his own? As is usually the case in such situations, those who despised Fonda believed the former, while those who respected him believed the latter.

A few months after Frances's death, Fonda married Blanchard, and two years later, the two adopted a baby girl named Amy, only to get divorced three years later in 1956.

Mister Roberts ran for another year before closing down in January 1951, and at that point in time, Fonda could have very easily returned to Hollywood and movie making. Instead, he remained on Broadway, starring next in another war thriller called *Point of No Return*, and after that, *The Caine Mutiny Court-Martial*. In fact, it's possible that he might never have returned to Hollywood had it not been for an opportunity to star in the screen version of *Mister Roberts*. Even though he was working again with John Ford, Fonda had certain concerns about the picture, later explaining, "Ford didn't know what to do with *Mister Roberts* that wasn't repeating what was successful in New York. He was trying to do things to the play that would be his in the film."

Fonda had good reason to be concerned about the picture. First, there were the personal issues surrounding his memories of Frances's death. There was also the issue of his age; he was now 45, a bit old to be playing a brash young officer yearning for battle. Finally, he was also becoming less able to cope with the stresses of film making, especially after being away from it for so long. Things finally came to a boil during a violent argument between Fonda and Ford, and in a fit of rage, Ford punched his old friend. Though Fonda vowed never to work with Ford again, he later claimed that he forgave Ford: "I don't know what was in his mind, but I do know Ford was stricken by what he had done, by hitting me."

In spite of his increasing reputation for moodiness, Fonda was still in great demand in Hollywood. He spent the next three years, 1954-56, working opposite of Audrey Hepburn in Leo Tolstoy's *War And Peace*, but this was a different type of war story than he was accustomed to playing. He would complain, "When I first agreed to do it, the screenplay by Irwin Shaw was fine, but what happened? King Vidor used to go home nights with his wife and rewrite it. All the genius of Tolstoy went out the window." Still, his talent shone through, and *War and Peace* was liked by both critics and audiences.

When he completed *War and Peace*, Fonda went on to work with famous director Alfred Hitchcock in *The Wrong Man*. This film was unusual in Hitchcock's repertoire in that it was of an almost documentary nature. Its mysterious, tense mood came from a real-life story based off the book *The True Story of Christopher Emmanuel Balestrero*, and Hitchcock was even able to film part of the movie on location where the incident took place.

After Fonda's marriage to Blanchard ended in 1956, he married Afdera Franchetti, an Italian countess he met while filming in Italy, the following year. But yet again, this marriage did not last very long, and Henry was soon looking for someone new. He found someone else in Shirlee Mae Adams, and after the two began an affair in 1960, he divorced Franchetti in 1961. For Henry Fonda, this marriage would prove to be the one that lasted; he and Adams would remain married until his death.

Fonda and Franchetti

Fonda and Adams

By 1957, Fonda had done enough acting to feel like he was ready to move behind the camera, so he tried his hand at producing *12 Angry Men*. The movie was the big screen version of a successful television movie by the same name, and it was unique because almost all the action takes place within a small jury room. Co-starring with Jack Klugman and E.G. Marshall, Fonda played "juror number eight", the one holdout among a group of men determined to convict a young man of murder. At first, it seemed like it might be a poor choice for his debut as a producer. For one thing, the film was underfunded, because many traditional backers were unwilling to invest in another Broadway to big screen movie, and given the financial constraints, Fonda was forced to shoot it in just 17 days, a difficult place to be in for such a perfectionist. However, in spite of these limitations, critics raved about the film, and Fonda, as the producer, received an Oscar nomination for Best Picture. He also won the 1958 BAFTA award for best actor, as well as an Oscar nomination for the same. "Juror Number 8" was later selected by the American Film Institute as one of the 50 greatest movie heroes of the 20th century. The film was also a financial success, with the public becoming more interested in it after its award nominations. Still, Fonda did not enjoy producing, and he vowed that he would never do it again.

While it is true that Fonda never produced another film, he did serve as a producer for a short-lived Western television series called *The Deputy*. From 1959-1961, he starred as Marshall Simon Fry, the upholder of law and justice in a small town on the western frontier. The part was an easy one for him to play, since he had just completed two other Westerns, *The Tin Star* in 1957 and *Warlock* in 1959. Furthermore, he did not appear regularly on screen, instead working more as a narrator on and off the screen. His deputy, played by Allen Case, did most of the work.

In addition to working on Westerns, Fonda constantly drew upon his experience during World

War II throughout the 1960s, and this was particularly true in *The Longest Day* (1962). In that movie, he had the privilege of playing General Theodore Roosevelt, Jr., son of the late president and one the leaders of the D-Day invasion. Fonda also played the lead in *In Harm's Way* and *The Battle of the Bulge* in 1965.

However, his most famous role of this era was as a long-haired buffalo hunter in *How the West Was Won*. The movie, filmed in five segments, starred almost every famous actor of that day and covered several decades of American history, from 1842 through the 1880s. It is interesting to note that while John Ford directed two of the five segments, Fonda only appeared in the segment directed by Henry Hathaway. Despite the critical acclaim of the film, the 1960s were a strange time for movie Westerns. As Hollywood became increasingly sensitive to its portrayal of Native Americans, it had to retool the typical "cowboy and Indians" tale and make it more palatable for modern audiences. One early example of this was *Once Upon a Time in the West*, directed by Sergio Leone and released in 1968. In it, Fonda played a villain named Frank, and he initially refused the role only to be persuaded to accept it by his friend, actor Eli Wallach. Leone, who also wanted Fonda for the role, also flew to the United States from Italy to persuade the actor. Because the character he was playing was so vicious, Fonda suggested that he don brown contact lenses to make his eyes darker and more sinister, but Leone rejected this idea, stating that he wanted the audience to appreciate the contrast between Frank's evil personality and Fonda's seemingly innocent blue eyes.

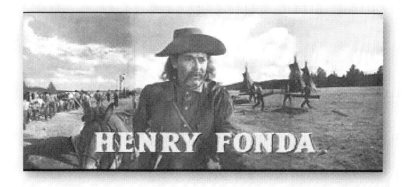

Fonda in *How the West Was Won*

Of course, not every film that Fonda made during the 1960s focused on war or suffering. In 1963, he starred in *Spencer's Mountain*, a charming look at a Depression-era family living in Wyoming. Fonda played the hard-working father of a large clan of rowdy children and elderly parents, but even though the movie was a popular success, Fonda did not care for it because he felt it was too bucolic for such turbulent times. He even speculated that it would set "the movie business back twenty years", but a decade later, the film would inspire the successful television series *The Waltons*. It is interesting to note that these two productions provide a sort of wholesome pair of bookends around the "sex, drugs and rock and roll" decade that began with John Kennedy's assassination and ended with Richard Nixon's resignation.

Five years later, Fonda again played the father of a large clan in *Yours, Mine and Ours*. The movie, based on the true story of a widow and widower who marry and combine their large families, co-starred Lucille Ball. By this time Fonda, though a political liberal, felt that the counter culture movement needed to be addressed. According to Fonda, "They've gone too far now, and we are all so satiated with the extremes, with what they call reality. I refuse to admit this degradation is reality." The highlight of the movie is Fonda's monologue against the sexual revolution. However, one of the leaders of the counter-cultural movement was Fonda's own daughter, Jane. While he was a political liberal, Jane was a far left-winger who became a poster child for the anti-war movement at the height of the Vietnam War. For a time, her political views, piled on top of years of strain, broke their relationship, and the two rarely spoke. To his credit, Fonda also refused to comment publically about his daughter's leanings, maintaining that her political views and private life were her own business and not his to speculate on. Jane would become most notorious for posing with a North Vietnamese anti-aircraft gun during the war, earning her the derisive nickname Hanoi Jane.

One of Fonda's favorite co-stars during this era was his old friend Jimmy Stewart. They starred together in *Fire Creek* in 1968, in which Fonda played the bad guy to Stewart's hero, and they worked together again in 1970 in *The Cheyenne Social Club*, a comedy set in the Old West. One of the funny things about *The Cheyenne Social Club* was that it gave Fonda and Stewart the chance to argue politics on screen. This was something the two men knew something about, since they had had more than one heated discussion over their political beliefs during their friendship. Fonda prided himself on being a liberal Democrat who had even worked with blacklisted actors during the dark days of McCarthyism, but Stewart was a conservative Republican who had already backed his friend Ronald Reagan as governor of California and would later support his election as president. Both men took their beliefs seriously, and they eventually gave up talking about politics with each other in order to save their friendship.

Chapter 6: The Final Curtain Call

"Henry Fonda one time said that every time he had a job, he thought it was gonna' be the last one. And, if you got any sense, you gotta' think that because, you know when somebody's gonna do a dip, some of 'em go pretty far down." - Barry Corbin

While Fonda continued to appear in movies throughout the 1960s, he did not spend all his time working in Hollywood. In fact, he had a reputation for driving himself to exhaustion by working on both the East and West Coasts at the same time. In 1959, he spent the fall in New York playing the lead in a two person play entitled *Silent Night, Lonely Night*. In it, he plays a man who becomes stuck by the weather in a New England inn on Christmas night, and as he talks with his only companion, a woman considering leaving her husband, it is revealed that he is in town to visit his own wife, who is hospitalized in a local insane asylum. One cannot help but see Fonda's attempts to work through his own guilt as it is further revealed that the man feels he drove his wife there by his own philandering. He played the struggle between guilt and justification well, saying at one point, "I imagine if we could hear all the stifled cries for help in the world, it would be deafening."

The following winter, he premiered in *Critic's Choice*, starring as Parker Ballantine, the long-suffering theater critic trying to decide how to handle the terrible play his second wife has written. The play was well-received by real theatre critics and ran for more than 180 performances.

In the early spring of 1962, Fonda took on a new role that was challenging on a social, professional and personal level by playing Charles Christian Wertenbaker in *A Gift of Time*. Wertenbaker was a writer living in France with his family when he was diagnosed with terminal cancer, and after months of suffering increasingly unbearable pain, he took his own life in late 1954. What made his story so compelling was that his wife, Lael, not only assisted with his suicide but wrote and published a book about her husband's death. That book, *The Death of a Man*, brought up the issue of euthanasia for the first time in American culture. Knowing that such a controversial topic would be hard for the public to swallow, Fonda and Olivia de Havilland, who played Lael, spent extensive time in France researching Wertenbaker's death. According to de Havilland, they visited "the radiologist's, [going] into the room where the X-rays were first shown… into all the rooms of the house where the Wertenbakers lived." Fonda added, "We talked to the Wertenbaker's doctor and some his Basque friends. What strong faces they had."

This level of research was as close as Fonda ever got to "Method Acting." He had often avoided the topic in the past, maintaining, "I can't articulate about the Method, because I never studied it. I don't mean to suggest that I have any feelings one way or the other about it...I don't know what the Method is and I don't care what the Method is. Everybody's got a method. Everybody can't articulate about their method, and I can't, if I have a method—and Jane sometimes says that I use the Method, that is, the capital letter Method, without being aware of it. Maybe I do; it doesn't matter."

Ultimately, in spite of Fonda and de Havilland's hard work, the play was too controversial to be popular, and it closed after fewer than 100 performances.

Fonda would act in two more stage productions during the 1960s. In the winter and spring of 1969, he played Jim Bolton in the comedy *Generation*, a humorous look at the "generation gap" in America during that era. Though the movie would bomb, Fonda brought tremendous life and feeling to the stage production, and it ran for months before closing after its 300th performance.

Fonda then concluded the decade with a special engagement run as the Stage Manager in *Our Town*.

In March 1972, Fonda returned to the stage, this time appearing at the Huntington Hartford Theater in Los Angeles. He starred in the lead of *The Time of Your Life*, and joining him in this production were Richard Dreyfuss and Jane Alexander. A few years later, in 1974, he returned to Broadway in one of his most demanding roles, a one man show portraying Clarence Darrow, the lawyer best known for arguing on behalf of a teacher who included the theory of evolution in his curriculum in the Scopes Trial, against William Jennings Bryan. In this simple play, Fonda appeared alone on stage, speaking for the lawyer in his last years of life as he reflected on what he had done and learned in his long law career. Fonda gave a stellar performance and was nominated for another Tony Award for his work, and he might have remained on stage indefinitely, had he not collapsed during a performance in April, 1974. Rushed to the hospital, he was diagnosed with heart arrhythmia and, soon afterwards, prostate cancer. Upon reviewing his options, he chose to have his cancer surgically removed and a pacemaker installed to correct the arrhythmia. After a lengthy recovery, he returned to the play in 1975.

Three years later, he appeared in *First Monday of October*, in which he plays an aging Supreme Court Justice facing yet another trying case. However, stage acting took a larger toll on Fonda then filming did, and after this role, he finally acquiesced to his doctor's instructions and gave up stage work altogether.

Chapter 7: On the Big and Little Screen

"I hope you won't be disappointed. You see I am not a very interesting person. I haven't ever done anything except be other people. I ain't really Henry Fonda! Nobody could be. Nobody could have that much integrity." - Henry Fonda

By the time Fonda was done with the stage, he was over 70 years old, and naturally it was harder to find film roles for an older man, so he turned his attention to television. First, Fonda starred in the ABC Series *The Family* in 1971 and 1972. However, in 1973 he starred in *The Red Pony*, a film based on John Steinbeck's novel in which Fonda played a stern father struggling with his son's love for a horse. The film resonated well with the American public, and it won Fonda an Emmy nomination. A few years later, in 1976, Fonda starred in *Collision Course*, playing General Douglas A. MacArthur opposite E.G. Marshall's Harry Truman. The movie made much of the difficulties in the relationship between the two men and was popular among the politically liberal audiences of the mid-70s.

Fonda also played a significant role in a few popular television miniseries of the late '70s. He starred in *Captains and Kings*, a series based on Taylor Caldwell's famous novel, as Senator Enfield Bassett, along with an all-star cast that included many of the miniseries regulars of the day. In 1979, he also appeared in ABC's *Roots: The Next Generations*, but this series did not reach the popularity that the original Roots had in 1976.

Fonda's most famous role of the mid-70s was in yet another war movie, this time playing Navy Admiral Chester Nimitz in the classic *Midway*. Always enjoying the chance to don a uniform, Fonda gave a stellar performance, playing Nimitz as much more than just a one-dimensional war hero. He also managed to capture the kind of angst that the admiral experienced after ordering his last aircraft carriers into battle. In one of the most famous lines in the movie, Nimitz asks, "Were we better than the Japanese, or just luckier?" Indeed, it's a question that historians of the battle continue to ask today.

Finally, Fonda also did a turn in the popular disaster movies of the late '70s, starring first in a 1977 Italian thriller about a killer octopus, and then going on to appear in *Rollercoaster* opposite Richard Widmark. He joined with Mark Etienne and Fred MacMurray to battle killer bees in *The Swarm*, and he played the President of the United States in *Meteor*. In his last disaster film, he starred in *City on Fire* as Fire Chief Albert Risley, trying to save a city from spreading fires that are going out of control.

Chapter 8: The Sun Sets on a Golden Pond

"I didn't help or discourage them or lead them by the hand. I'm not trying to set myself up as a good father, because I wasn't a good father. But I think I knew instinctively that if they did make it, they would like to know they'd done it on their own. I recognize all the problems my children have had, and I don't claim any credit for what they've become. They've become what they are in spite of me." - Henry Fonda

Fonda's final role, and the one most critics believe was his greatest, would come from an unusual source and for an unusual reason. In 1981, Jane Fonda, by now a successful actress in her own right, bought the rights to a movie called *On Golden Pond*, and her reasons for doing so were more personal than professional. *On Golden Pond* tells the story of the relationship between an adult daughter and her distant father, and Jane would later admit that she purchased the rights to the film in the hopes that her father would agree to star with her in it. In spite of his poor health, and perhaps even because he knew his life was drawing to a close, Fonda agreed to take the role. As a result, he and Jane brought to life an all-too-familiar struggle: an adult child trying to determine what to hang onto and what to let go of in her past, while her parents try to figure out how to repair a broken connection.

Fonda with Katharine Hepburn in *On Golden Pond*

Perhaps because the two were both such good actors, or because the story was so personal, Henry and Jane brought their own personal tension to the screen, and when *On Golden Pond* opened to a limited release in December 1981, it earned rave reviews. The producers, who had been concerned that the story might be too personal to play well, then released it across the nation in January. Not only did the film make almost $120 million in theatres, it also earned 10 Oscar nominations, and Henry Fonda won his first Oscar for Best Actor, over 40 years after his first nomination in the role of Tom Joad. He also won a coveted Golden Globe Award for the same role.

In winning the Oscar for Best Actor, Fonda became the oldest actor to ever win an Academy Award, but sadly, he was too frail and ill by that time to attend the ceremony. Instead, Jane appeared in his place and accepted the award on his behalf. In the acceptance speech, she told the audience, "My father didn't really believe that this was going to happen.... I know that he's watching right now, and I know that he's very, very honored and very happy, and surprised. And I'll bet when he heard it just now I'll bet he said, 'Hey, ain't I lucky,' as though luck had anything to do with it. I know also that he…has always felt a little strange about these things, these competitions, because it's like comparing apples and oranges and he feels very proud to have been among such a wonderful group. My father is so happy, he feels so fortunate to have been able to play the role of Norman Thayer, a character that he loves a lot and understands very well…."

Anyone who has seen *On Golden Pond* knows that the movie ends shortly after Fonda's character, Norman Thayer, nearly dies of a heart attack. In that regard, Henry Fonda would not fare as well as his on-screen counterpart, as he died from heart disease on August 12, 1982. Thankfully, by the time of his death, he had established the kind of outcome with his real life family that was shown in the movie. Jane also mentioned that specifically in the acceptance speech on his behalf, saying, "We all became like a family during the filming and we've sort of stayed together since. People call him up and stay in touch and come to visit him, and so it's like we've stayed a family, and it's made my father very, very happy….. He was very happy, and so was I and are we, to have had our two families together, the Haydens and the Fonda's, on the beautiful shores of that lake so that we could get to know each other more."

The Fonda's had indeed made their peace as a family, and both Jane and Peter, as well as Henry's wife Shirley, were with him when he died. In keeping with his wishes, there was no funeral held for Fonda; instead, his body was quickly cremated and his ashes given back to his family. President Ronald Reagan, who himself had been an actor during the same era, called Fonda "a true professional dedicated to excellence in his craft. He graced the screen with a sincerity and accuracy which made him a legend."

Other accolades would follow, with one magazine calling Fonda "the man we wished we lived next door to." As is often the case with eulogies, the words were kinder than they were realistic. The truth is that Henry Fonda would likely not have been the best neighbor to have, nor was he the best father or best friend someone could have. He was a man full of flaws who managed to overcome them for days and weeks at a time in order to give a good performance on stage and on screen. On the other hand, if all the world's a stage for people to put on performances, Henry Fonda wasn't really that different than anyone else. He was just better at it.

Bibliography

Adrian, Iacob. Film Actors Vol.8 Henry Fonda (2013)

Fonda, Henry and Howard Teichmann. Fonda: My Life (1981)

McKinney, Devin. The Man Who Saw a Ghost: The Life and Work of Henry Fonda (2012)

Mosley, Glenn and Read Morgan. Henry Fonda and The Deputy-The Film and Stage Star and His TV Western (2010)

Clark Gable

Chapter 1: Growing Up in Rural Ohio

"I eat and sleep and go to the bathroom just like anyone else. I'm just a lucky slob from Ohio who happened to be in the right place at the right time." – Clark Gable

William Clark Gable was born on February 1, 1901, the first child of William Henry "Will"

Gable and Adeline Hershelman. He was born in the same small Midwestern town where Adeline had been born and raised, and he grew up an only child for the duration of his upbringing. Although his first name is mostly forgotten today, he was named after his father, and Clark was actually his middle name. Will and Adeline had great difficulty deciding on the name for their son; Adeline preferred "Clark," yet her husband intended to name his son after himself. Ironically, the father of a man Life magazine once called "all man and then some" felt that the name Clark was not masculine enough, an opinion that actually reflected his own insecure masculinity and the way in which that shortcoming affected how he would raise his son. In the end, the compromise was that Clark would be named after his father but identified as Clark for most of his life.

While the name issue was a relatively trivial matter, the argument concerning Clark's name was indicative of the unharmonious marriage between Will and Adeline. From the time of their marriage onward, Will's commitment toward his wife was less than complete, as he spent much of his time out of the house. Even though much of his time was accounted for while working in the oil fields, he paid scant attention to the wishes of his wife, and the saga concerning the naming of their son reflects the manner in which Will was unsympathetic to the best wishes of his wife. The personality clash between Clark's parents is largely attributable to personal backgrounds, and it's easy to see why their marriage would be unsuccessful even from the start. There was a clear religious divide between the two, as William was a devout Methodist but Adeline was Catholic; one of the few times Adeline's preferences was honored occurred when Clark was baptized, despite the fact that William had no desire to have the service performed. In light of the significant religious divide separating them, one could reasonably question why Will and Adeline were married to begin with, and the most likely explanation is simply that it was a marriage of convenience. By the time of their marriage, they were each approaching 30; which was especially confining for Adeline, who had already reached the age in which people of the era considered old for a single woman. Will had his own pressure to raise and support a family, since he had acquired a reputation for gambling and chasing women. During this period, Will had worked as an oil prospector, a trade that was less than reputable (widely seen as a fool's errand), and Adeline's parents could not have been confident that their son-in-law would adequately provide for their daughter. As a result, it was not difficult to predict that the marriage would be rife with acrimony, but there were clear motives for both of Clark's parents.

Will was well aware of the fact that Adeline's parents were not fond of him, and he grew paranoid that her parents would intervene and attempt to break up the marriage (Bret). For this reason, he and his new wife moved to Cadiz, Ohio shortly after the marriage, where he found more steady employment working in an oil field. This career shift was largely borne out of necessity; the oil boom had long come and gone, and there was simply no way of supporting a family without steady employment. However, even after finding a more reputable job, Will continued to treat his wife with a complete lack of respect, spending the vast majority of his time outside of the house and continuing to sleep with other women (Bret).

Complicating the marriage was that Adeline began suffering from severe health ailments even before Clark was born. Given that medical knowledge was relatively rudimentary at the beginning of the 20th century, it is difficult to pinpoint exactly what her afflictions were, but it is believed that she suffered from a heart condition and may also have experienced epileptic seizures (Bret). In any event, her health took an extreme turn for the worse during the spring of 1900, around the time that she became pregnant with Clark. Her health complications nearly prevented Clark from ever having been born; had Adeline opted to have surgery, she would have needed to abort her child. The decision to keep Clark amounted to a form of martyrdom, a belief that her child's fate would prove better than her own. It was clear that she would not live to raise her baby, and she passed away just six months after Clark's birth in February of 1901. The official cause of death was listed as epilepsy, although she may have died due to a brain tumor.

After his wife's death, Will made the unceremonious decision to erase many of his son's ties to his deceased mother. First, the birth certificate was revised to state that Clark had been born in Cadiz. Not only was this factually incorrect, but the fact that Hopedale was the town in which Adeline's family still resided implicitly declared that Will wanted nothing to do with his in-laws. In addition, Will refused to provide his son with a proper Catholic upbringing, sparking outrage from Adeline's family. Clark was nearly cut off entirely from his mother's extended family, yet a truce was established when it was agreed that Clark could spend time with Adeline's brother Charles.

It is unlikely that Adeline's death left Will terribly distraught, and there is a strong probability that they would have eventually opted for a divorce had Adeline lived longer. However, her death left Will in the precarious position of being tasked with raising and providing for his own son. Fully cognizant that he had no relatives who could perform this task, when Clark was two years of age, Will arranged for Clark to live with Adeline's brother Charles and his wife, who lived in rural Pennsylvania. Although he would be too young to remember his experience living with his aunt and uncle, they provided him with stability that had been absent for the previous year-and-a-half of his life.

While Clark was living with his aunt and uncle, Will began dating once again and soon found a new spouse. His second wife, Jennie Dunlap, was the daughter of a coal miner and worked as a seamstress. Given that she lived in the same boarding lodge in Cadiz where Will worked, it was easy for the relationship to progress swiftly, and they married on April 16, 1903, less than two years after Adeline's death. Jennie was Will's age and, like Adeline, had already reached the point at which she was identified as an "old maid." Whether or not her decision to marry Will was a desperate move is unclear, but to her credit, she was entirely willing to assist in raising Clark. In fact, she and Will would not have any children together themselves, so Clark continued to be an only child.

Immediately after marrying Jennie, Will purchased a four-acre property in Hopedale, Ohio, and he took Clark back from Charles. After two years separated from his father, Clark was united once again with Will, but the family situation remained far from perfect. As with his first marriage, there was a sizeable personality difference between Will and his wife; while Will projected an image of hyper-masculinity, Jennie was more artistically inclined, and Clark inherited his own love for art from his stepmother. She taught Clark the piano, and Clark took music lessons. Although Will did not approve of art or literature, he did not forcefully prevent his son from reading or pursuing his own interests. Clark displayed a talent for music, and at the age of 13 he became the only boy in the local men's band.

Naturally, a boy who grew up and became known for his virility was also an athlete. During his youth, Clark had already developed a strong physique, and he played several sports, including swimming, baseball, and track. Not surprisingly, Will approved of the sports. Nevertheless, despite reaching his adult height by the age of 13, Gable was ridiculed throughout his childhood for being gentle and having a high-pitched voice that undermined his rugged physique. He was also meticulously well-groomed, a trait that was instilled in him by his stepmother. Growing up in decidedly non-cosmopolitan rural Ohio, Gable qualified as something of a dandy.

Clark as a young boy

Clark as a teenager

Even as a teenager, Clark bore fundamental similarities and differences to the man he would later become. First, he retained the sturdy frame he possessed as a youth, and it would be years before his body began to go soft. Many of Gable's film performances showcase the athletic virtues he displayed as a teenager, particularly his early 1930s movies. At the same time, one of the fundamental aspects of Gable's star image is that the dandy in him never entirely went away; Christopher Spicer described his attention to detail as an adult:

> "Clark Gable didn't only look clean, he *was* clean. He showered several times a day, never using a tub because he couldn't bear to sit in dirty water. He shaved his chest and under his arms, and his bed linen was changed every day. He was

invariably impeccably dressed in public. His suits and jackets were handmade for him at Dick Caroll's in Beverley Hills and at Brooks Brothers in New York, from where he would order them ten at a time. They were all arranged in his wardrobes by color and size and tagged with the purchase date." (3).

It's immediately clear that Gable was an aesthete of the highest order, but this would not be enough to raise him to the level of the Hollywood elite. Rather, Gable's genius as an actor lay in his ability to combine the rugged masculinity required of a Hollywood leading man with the soft, immaculately-groomed aura of a sophisticated gentleman. While it would be years before Gable would project the assuredness he would display on screen, it is important to recognize that the foundation for his later persona was established even as a teenager. It also explains why Gable once claimed, "I'm no actor and I never have been. What people see on the screen is me."

Unfortunately for Gable, as a teenager he was an aesthete living in a region of the country that expected its men to find employment as manual laborers. Most children in Hopedale ended their schooling altogether after graduating from the 8th grade, after which they worked alongside their fathers. Clark was never an especially committed student, but manual labor wasn't for him either, so he entered Hopedale High School in September 1915. The enrollment for the entire school numbered just 28, with eight in Clark's grade. There were three teaches, one of whom also served as superintendent and another who assumed the responsibilities of the principal (Spicer). Even though Gable didn't care much for studying, high school did serve the productive end of exposing him to acting, and he appeared in school productions. However, during his time at Hopedale High School, several of Clark's best friends left town, devastating him and leaving Clark with little motivation to further his education.

Clark's teenage years were further complicated by a catastrophic business decision made by his father. By the time Clark reached high school, Will had become moderately successful financially, leading him to invest in oil drilling. But when it was discovered that the hole was dry, Will lost a great deal of money, forcing the family to sell their property in the late summer of 1917 (Spicer). Shortly thereafter, they purchased a 74-acre farm near Ravenna, Ohio, a rural town just outside Akron. The town was just 60 miles away from Hopedale, yet Clark struggled with moving to an insular community (not unlike Hopedale) where he had no connections. Upon arriving, he enrolled in Edinburgh Centralized High School, another tiny institution, where he was one of just 24 students (Spicer). His experience there was miserable from the start, and Clark dropped out of school permanently in November of 1917.

Once he was finished with school, Gable had no employment prospects outside of working on his father's farm, and though he worked for his father for a brief while in 1917, he found the work disagreeable. Speaking of the experience years later, he noted that he was simply not cut out to be a farmer: "I fed the hogs and the rest of the stock, plowed in the spring till every muscle ached, forked hay in the hot sun until I was sweating an impressive mop of calluses. I did what I was expected to do on the farm, but it takes a certain knack for farming in the old-fashioned way. I just didn't have what it takes." (Spicer 21).

Not surprisingly, Clark's time on the farm proved short-lived, and Jennie encouraged him to seek employment outside of the farm. He subsequently worked as a water-carrier at one of the local mines, a menial job that paid $5 per day, but by early winter, he had saved enough money to purchase his father's car. After that, Clark and a group of friends left rural Ohio for Akron, which was experiencing rapid industrialization at the time. Clark did not move to Akron with employment prospects lined up; the move was very much a last resort motivated by the fact that he simply could not continue working for his father. Eventually, he was able to find work as a clerk for the Miller Rubber Company, earning $100 per month, less than he had made at the mine. Still, the meager sum was enough for Clark to rent a room, and he quickly absorbed himself in the city life.

Although they were not located far apart, the difference between Clark's previous hometowns and Akron cannot be overstated and. For the first time, Clark was exposed to plays and films, and after viewing a stage production of *Bird of Paradise*, Clark made it his goal to become an actor. In efforts to meet people in the business and ingratiate himself, Gable developed an obeisant attitude toward the local actors, essentially becoming an errand-boy for them. Clark was willing to perform any role so long as it would bring him closer to the performers, and even though he was unable to find acting opportunities himself, Clark's time in Akron was instrumental in nurturing his desire to eventually become a professional actor.

It is impossible to determine whether Clark would have been able to eventually become an actor while living in Akron. Late in 1919, Jennie fell ill and passed away early in 1920, and after he became a widower yet again, Will moved to Tulsa, Oklahoma, where he worked at an oilfield. Unfortunately for the young man, even though Jennie's will stipulated that Clark was to receive $300, he was denied access to the money until he turned 21. Clark was exceptionally close to his stepmother, and it has even been alleged that many of his future relationships were attempts to reconstruct the dynamic he had with her (Bret). He was only 18, but he had already endured the death of his mother and then his stepmother. Finding himself in a vulnerable moment, Clark agreed to join his father in Tulsa.

While many Hollywood stars start off with good fortune, Clark Gable's childhood was filled with family tragedy and feelings of displacement. Given his love for acting and music, it is entirely possible that he would have thrived had he been born in a more urban setting, but he was relegated to outsider status in rural Ohio. It would be several years before he would be able to project the confidence he exuded in his films, but even after reaching Hollywood, he still possessed a melancholic undercurrent stemming from his upbringing. As an adult, Gable was quick to deflect attention from his childhood, and his acting career was very much an escape from an imprisoning landscape. Paradoxically, Clark's youth was quite transitory and saw him shift locations on a number of occasions, yet his early years were at the same time quite static, as he was forced to live in small towns with few outlets for his artistic interests. Ultimately, he would be unable to find any professional satisfaction until he reached his 20s.

Chapter 2: Breaking Away

Clark as a young man

"Every picture I make, every experience of my private life, every lesson I learn are the keys to my future. And I have faith in it." – Clark Gable

After the death of Clark's stepmother, Will encouraged his son to join him in Tulsa, promising Clark that he would find acting opportunities should he relocate. Clark agreed and arrived in Tulsa in 1920, where he joined his father in the oilfields (Bret). It is not entirely clear why Will asked his son to move; he may have grown tired of being estranged from his son, but he had never shown any great commitment to Clark, so it's hard to understand why Will would express interest in seeing his son after Clark had reached adulthood. An even more difficult decision to rationalize is why exactly Clark acquiesced in joining his father in Oklahoma; Will promised acting opportunities, but there is little reason why Clark should have trusted his father, who had never shown any regard for his personal interests. Moreover, Will had always frowned upon

Clark's interest in the arts and would surely have scoffed at the notion of his son actually becoming an actor. It was ultimately an act of trickery that brought Clark to Oklahoma, where there were no acting jobs to be found, and Clark was trapped into working as a manual laborer.

Life in the oilfields was only marginally better for Clark than working on his father's farm. The pack-like mentality of the oil workers forced Gable to subdue the gentler aspects of his personality, and he adopted the rowdy lifestyle that was par for the course for the oil men. He began drinking heavily and picking up prostitutes, and it should be noted that a love for women and alcohol were aspects of Gable's personality that never went away, even after the public spotlight was cast upon him in Hollywood. He later admitted to liking brothels, saying of them, "When it's over it's over. No questions, no tears, no farewell kisses." He also talked at length about his love of women, noting, "Types really don't matter. I have been accused of preferring blondes. But I have known some mighty attractive redheads, brunettes, and yes, women with grey hair. Age, height, weight haven't anything to do with glamour… I am intrigued by glamorous women…A vain woman is continually taking out a compact to repair her makeup. A glamorous woman knows she doesn't need to."

Of course, the reckless attitude Gable assumed while living in Oklahoma is not only attributable to the standards set by his peers but can also easily be read as an expression of alienation. He was trapped in a job he had no enthusiasm for, and he was unable to access the inheritance money bequeathed to him by his stepmother until he turned 21. There was, therefore, very little that Gable could do to remedy his situation from 1920 through early 1922, and he toiled away alongside his father.

Naturally, Clark leapt at the chance to relocate after receiving his inheritance. In February 1922, immediately after his 21st birthday, Gable quit his job in Tulsa and left for Meadville, Pennsylvania, where he collected his money. He also started going by the name Billy, and he took up jobs that made him travel around the country. First, he left Meadville for Kansas City, where he worked for a traveling tent show assisting with the set design (Bret). This job was not dissimilar to his earlier stints as a helper to the acting troupe in Akron, and it once again brought him in close proximity to actors. The major difference was that his position with the Kansas City troupe enabled him to travel with the company, and he traveled outside of the region. When the group experienced hardship and their act was terminated in Montana, Clark and the group's pianist left for Bend, Oregon, where his friend's family resided. The exact job that Clark found in Oregon is unclear; it is believed that he either worked as a necktie salesman or as someone tasked with unloading shipments from the loading deck (Bret). Whichever job he held, Clark's first job in Oregon was a clear step up from his experience in Tulsa, but not as personally preferable to his time with the acting troupe.

Eventually, Clark found an acting opportunity with the Astoria Players, a local stock company, where he worked in the familiar position of helping with the set design. At this point, he had shown great difficulty in advancing beyond this necessary but decidedly unglamorous position, and it was only after one of the actors left the company that Gable actually received an opportunity to act. The company was not terribly successful, but Gable benefitted from the practice, since he was entirely untrained and still possessed an unusually high-pitched voice. Gable lasted less than one year with the company, which collapsed at the start of 1923. Immediately thereafter, he returned to Oregon, where he worked for *The Oregonian* as a deliveryman and assistant in the newspaper office (Bret).

During his spare time, Gable continued to hone his skills, and in June 1923, he caught his biggest break yet when he met Josephine Dillon, an actress of moderate fame who was in town scouting actors for her own drama troupe. After auditioning, he was accepted and was finally in a position where he could receive acting instruction from someone with a substantial degree of success within the industry. For this reason, 1923 stands as one of the most significant years of Gable's entire career, and the year in which he truly solidified acting as his career.

Josephine Dillon

Thanks to Dillon's tutelage, Gable improved his many deficiencies as an actor. First, he improved his posture and learned how to comport himself with greater poise. In 1923, Gable was also underweight (possibly as a result of hepatitis, although this is not entirely substantiated), and Dillon assisted him in building his body up to the point that he could find roles as a leading man. Finally, she improved his elocution and helped train him to lower his voice. The tutelage he received from Dillon was not especially dissimilar to the formal training that most actors go through. The American public may be largely unaware of the tremendous work that goes into constructing an actor's appearance, but before Gable could attempt to make a name for himself in Hollywood, he had to first succeed in making himself fit for the gaze of the camera.

After guiding him through the technical aspects of being an actor, Dillon used her connections to secure acting opportunities. First, she secured a position for Clark in the Forest Taylor Stock Company, which was based in Portland and enabled Clark to gain consistent acting experience. In June 1923, Gable and Dillon arrived in Hollywood, and they were married the following year. Of the five wives Gable would marry over the course of his life, his marriage to Dillon is surely the most difficult to explain. She had long been rumored to be a lesbian, and she was 17 years older than Clark. (Bret). The most probable rationale is that Gable married her out of the belief that doing so would make Dillon more likely to continue helping him further his career.

However, immediately after arriving in Hollywood, Gable had no success finding acting opportunities. He even worked in an auto garage for awhile, as he had always been a skilled mechanic, but later in 1923, he was able to find a small role in a film, thanks to a connection of Dillon's. That same year, he also made the decision to go by the name Clark again, and he also added two years to his age, holding himself out as a 24 year old. These steps completed his makeover, fully preparing him for his illustrious Hollywood career.

Chapter 3: Life in Hollywood

"It's a chain of accidents. When you step into Hollywood, you wind yourself into thousands of chains of accidents. If all of the thousands happen to come out exactly right - and the chance of that figures out to be one in eight million - then you'll be a star." – Clark Gable

As with most actors, Clark Gable was unable to find significant acting parts in his first films and instead appeared as an extra. The lone exception was actually his first film, *White Man*, in which he had a very small role. He was able to find consistent acting opportunities, including two films released in 1924 and 10 the following year. Even though his acting performances were quite minor, he was also able to earn a decent living; in his first film, *White Man*, he earned $150 per week. The films in which he was cast as an extra paid considerably less (roughly $15 per day), but he was hardly a starving actor, especially with Dillon supporting him.

Many of his earliest films were actually quite significant on their own, even though he did not have major roles. For example, Gable's second film, *Forbidden Paradise* (1924), was directed by the legendary Ernst Lubitsch. In fact, Clark's first major acting opportunity was to have been in Erich von Stroheim's *The Merry Widow* (1925), but he clashed with the famous director and was relegated to once again appearing as an extra. For the first two years of his career, Gable stayed very busy but could not find his first big break. Throughout the decade, he was unable to progress through the Hollywood ranks, but his situation was far less dire than it might appear. He had the luxury of being able to depend on Dillon, who spoiled him and subsidized him quite generously.

Furthermore, when it became clear that Clark would have difficulty finding any major opportunities from the outset, he simply turned his attention to the theater. As the 1920s progressed, he began receiving increasingly more prominent acting opportunities, bringing him outside of California. In 1927 and 1928, he accepted a position with the Laskin Brothers Stock Company in Houston. After this stint was completed, he moved to New York City with Dillon and acted on Broadway.

Gable was successful in the theater and had every reason to believe that he would have a successful career as a Broadway actor, but by the end of the decade the theater began to suffer for several reasons. First, the arrival of synchronized sound in the movies made the cinema considerably more popular than the stage, as audiences were captivated by the prospect of watching singing and dialogue onscreen. But even more importantly, the Great Depression compromised the success of the theater, and actors were unable to continue finding acting opportunities. Thus, after several years acting in plays, Gable once again turned his attention back to Hollywood, moving back to California in 1930. That same year, he and Dillon divorced, putting an end to a strange marriage.

The timing makes it seem as though once he had a contract with MGM, Gable no longer relied on Dillon to advance his career and therefore found it possible to cut all ties with her, but Gable also had another pressing reason to divorce his first wife. At the time, he was involved in an affair with another woman, a Texas socialite named Marian Franklin Prentiss Lucas Langham, who went by "Ria." Clark and Ria were married in the immediate aftermath of his divorce, and they settled into Hollywood together. Unlike Dillon, Langham was firmly entrenched in the upper class, and her financial assistance had actually helped Clark with his theater career during the 1920s. As a theater patron, she and Gable met through the stage. As with his first marriage, Clark would continue to sleep with myriad women, but what his marriage lacked in fidelity it made up for in duration. He and Ria remained married for most of the decade before divorcing in 1939. Although Langham and Dillon were vastly different in their backgrounds, one similarity was that they were each far older than Clark. Langham was 47 at the time of their marriage, a substantial age discrepancy that lends credence to the belief that many of Gable's wives were surrogates for his deceased mother or stepmother.

Ria

Fortunately for Clark, his success on Broadway enabled him to find more appealing acting roles than he had found during his first stint in Hollywood. In 1930, he signed a contract with MGM that allowed him to no longer have to act as an extra. His first film upon returning was *The Painted Desert* (1931), which cast him as a brazen former criminal. As the role would suggest, Gable's niche early in his career was as a criminal, a far cry from the genteel performances he would later give. During the 1930s, gangster and crime films were exceedingly popular, and Gable proved to be successful playing men of ill repute. Clark's first headlining role was in the 1931 film *Sporting Blood*, in which he starred as a gambler who succeeds at the horse races and successfully evades the police, but he was able to reveal a broader acting talent with *Possessed* (1932), which paired him with Joan Crawford. In the film, Gable stars as a lawyer who has an affair with Crawford and in the process helps her progress through the societal ranks. The film focuses most heavily on Crawford's character, yet Gable benefitted from being able to portray a romantic dimension that had not been part of his earlier, more physical performances. Crawford later said Gable " was a king wherever he went. He walked like one, he behaved like one, and he was the most masculine man that I have ever met in my life."

Gable and Crawford in *Dance, Fools, Dance*

Two other significant films for Clark during 1932 were *Red Dust* (1932) and *No Man of Her Own* (1932). *No Man of Her Own* is notable for being the first (and only) film in which Gable appeared alongside Carole Lombard, who would later become his wife. Meanwhile, in *Red Dust*, Gable was paired with Jean Harlow, the first of six films he would appear in with her. Directed by Victor Fleming, *Red Dust* features an action-packed plot set in French Indochina, and the action plot and romantic plot converge as Jean Harlow's character becomes Gable's love interest and nurse. The film showed that Gable was capable of combining his skills as a physical actor with romantic comedy, an achievement that cannot be underestimated. Indeed, the ability to succeed in both realms at the same time meant the difference between being a B-actor and being a major star.

Gable and Jean Harlow in _Red Dust_

Chapter 4: Gable Tackles 1930s Hollywood

"They see me as an ordinary guy, like a construction worker or the guy who delivers your piano." – Clark Gable

In 1932 and 1933, Gable continued to find appealing acting opportunities, and altogether, he appeared in four films both years. In 1932, he noted, "I have been in show business for 12 years. They have known me in Hollywood but two. Yet as picture-making goes, two years is a long time. Nevertheless, my advice has never been asked about a part in a picture. I found out I was going into 'Susan Lenox' in Del Monte. Read it in a paper. When I walked on the set one day, they told me I was going to play 'Red Dust' in place of John Gilbert. I have never been consulted as to what part I would like to play. I am paid not to think." But he also admitted that he tried to avoiding bad parts, stating about his acting, "I worked like a son of a bitch to learn a few tricks and I fight like a steer to avoid getting stuck with parts I can't play."

Off the movie set, Gable attracted attention for having an affair with Joan Crawford, and he quickly developed a reputation for being a womanizer. A famous story holds that Gable once looked at a publicity photograph of leading MGM actresses and remarked without hyperbole that he had slept with each of them. The inability to remain faithful stands as the greatest similarity and one of the only similarities linking him with his father. Even though Clark's endless stream of affairs positioned him in a less-than-noble light, he is a prime example of the adage that any publicity is good publicity, as his pursuits off the movie set furthered his image as one of the sexiest men in Hollywood. For his own part, Gable once said, "Hell, if I'd jumped on all the dames I'm supposed to have jumped on, I'd have had no time to go fishing."

By 1933, Clark was commanding a robust salary of $2,000 per week from MGM. For the most part, they were able to keep him busy and thereby maximize their investment in the process, but there were also periods in which they had no films available for him. As a result, MGM was eager to lend Gable to Columbia, which offered to pay him $2,500 per week to appear in *It Happened One Night* (1934). Gable had not been their first choice for the role (nor was Claudette Colbert, his costar), but Gable had shown that he could handle romantic comedy and was thus considered a serviceable replacement for Robert Montgomery, who had turned down the role. As Linda Mizejewski wrote, "In key moments of *It Happened One Night*, Gable brings to the character of Peter some of the tough-guy grittiness from his MGM image but he also shows that he is able to mock it or play against it" (103). It was, therefore, an unlikely set of circumstances that saw Gable appear in his most significant film to that point in his career.

Gable with Claudette Colbert in *It Happened One Night*

It Happened One Night was one of a number of prominent Depression-era films directed by Frank Capra, who specialized in wholesome, sentimental films that restored the promise of the American Dream. This motif resurfaces in *Mr. Deeds Goes to Town* (1936), *You Can't Take it With You* (1938), *Mr. Smith Goes to Washington* (1939), and (later) *It's a Wonderful Life* (1946).

Capra's style held great appeal to the American public not only because his films suggested that everything would get better for the impoverished American viewer but because he seamlessly combined pathos with comedy in a way that was profoundly heartening for the downtrodden viewer. In *It Happened One Night* (1934), Gable stars as a newspaper reporter who has lost his job and witnesses Ellie, a wealthy socialite (played by Colbert) eloping with a man against her father's wishes. Realizing that Ellie's father has offered a reward to whoever can return his daughter to him, Gable's character threatens to cash in on his knowledge, but over the course of the film he and Colbert's character fall in love and the film concludes with their marriage.

It is not difficult to understand why *It Happened One Night* had such great appeal for the Depression-era audience. The weaving together of the reconciliation of class difference with the romantic plot allowed viewers to dream on the possibility that they might be able to meet someone who could help them overcome their unfortunate economic condition. The witty dialogue - in the proper screwball comedy tradition - also made the Gable-Colbert pairing particularly sexy, albeit in a covert way that circumvented the censorship standards of the Hays Code. For these reasons, the film stands as one of the most successful films of all time, becoming the first movie to win all five of the most decorated Academy Awards: Best Picture, Best Director, Best Screenplay, Best Actor, and Best Actress. The film could not have gone better for Gable, who not only garnered critical acclaim but also returned to MGM having proven that he could deliver an Oscar-winning performance.

After going back to MGM, Clark was once again paired with Jean Harlow, starring with her in *China Seas* (1935) and *Saratoga* (1937). *China Seas* reprised the formula of casting Gable as an uber-masculine adventure hero, this time as a sea captain who reveals his romantic side as the film unfolds, eventually culminating in his union with Harlow's character. *Saratoga* was the more significant film, not only because of its more alluring plot but because of the fact that Harlow died during the production. In a freak occurrence, Harlow died of kidney failure, and the film was completed by using body doubles. Because audiences were eager to watch Harlow's final performance, *Saratoga* performed well at the box office, and it received strong reviews as well. In the film, Gable plays Duke, a racetrack bookie who eventually wins over Harlow's character, who drops her engagement with a wealthy suitor in order to be with Duke.

Gable and Harlow

The death of Jean Harlow complicated Gable's position within MGM, as the studio had suddenly lost one of its premier romantic pairings. Fortunately, Gable had acted alongside Myrna Loy on a couple of occasions, and each of his 1938 films cast him with her. The first of these, *Test Pilot* (1938), was especially successful and was nominated for an Academy Award for Best Picture. The film relied on Gable's ability to portray the action hero, and he was well-suited for the role of a fighter pilot. Like the films he appeared in with Jean Harlow, the plot involves Gable curbing his reckless instincts in the interest of the romantic plot. Gable's acting was particularly successful for the way that he combined the brashness of the action hero with the sophistication of the romantic comedy hero. As a result, in roles such as *Test Pilot*, he revealed an exceptional ability to appeal to both men and women. *Test Pilot* is an example of Gable's ability to be romantic and masculine in a 'natural' way that was simultaneously sophisticated and genuine. According to Linda Mizejewski, this naturalness formed the cornerstone of Gable's appeal: "Clark Gable's stardom in the 1930s was tied to cultural ideals and contentions about masculinity, and he went on to become one of the great masculine icons of American cinema. He became known as an actor who always 'played himself,' who expressed his rugged manliness without 'acting' on-screen, a reputation that he shared with icons John Wayne and Gary Cooper." (97).

Mizejewski recognizes how Gable (as well as John Wayne and Gary Cooper) succeeded due to his ability to provide a model for masculinity that was accessible and not tied to wealth or pretension. He was a heartthrob for women and an idol for men, and there was no actor more powerful than him by the end of the decade. He once humorously claimed, "This power that I'm supposed to have over women was never noticed when I was a stage actor on Broadway. I don't know when I got it. And by God, I can't explain it." He also talked about his popularity, asserting, "I don't believe I'm king of anything, but I know why they like to think I am. I'm not much of an actor, but I'm not bad unless it's one of those things outside my comprehension. I work hard. I'm no Adonis, and I'm as American as the telephone poles I used to climb to make a living. So men don't get sore if their women folks like me on the screen. I'm one of them, they know it, so it's a compliment to them. They see me broke, in trouble, scared of things that go bump in the night, but I come out fighting. They see me making love to Jean Harlow or Claudette Colbert and they say, 'If he can do it, I can do it,' and figure it'll be fun to go home and to make love to their wives."

As the 1930s drew to a close, Gable's marriage with Ria Langham had grown stale, and they had actually not lived together in years. Obtaining a divorce was a mere formality, and the divorce was made official in 1939, motivated in no small part by the fact that Gable had fallen in love with actress Carole Lombard. Just three months after the divorce was finalized, he and Lombard married. It is important to note that Lombard differed significantly from each of his earlier wives; where they were substantially older than him, Lombard was four years younger; unlike Dillon and Langham, one could not argue that Lombard was a substitute for his deceased stepmother. In this regard, Gable's third marriage was more adult than his earlier ones and he and Lombard were not only married but lived together as well. Gable was already 38 years of age, yet he had at last found a woman to whom he was committed.

Gable and Carole Lombard

Chapter 5: Gone with the Wind

Gable in 1938

"The public interest in my playing Rhett puzzled me. I was the only one, apparently, who didn't take it for granted that I would." – Clark Gable

By 1939, Clark Gable had already won an Academy Award and proven that he could successfully command high box office receipts. However, his most famous film was yet to come. That year, he starred in *Gone With the Wind*, arguably the most beloved film ever made in Hollywood and certainly one of its most famous. The film has been mythologized into American culture to the point that Rhett Butler's final parting line to Scarlett - "Frankly, my dear, I don't give a damn." - has become part of the American lexicon. At the same time, there is a wide gulf between the love expressed toward the film by the American public and the relative contempt toward it exuded by critics. Alan David Vertrees discussed this dynamic, writing, "What are we to do with *Gone With the Wind*? The most popular and commercially successful film of all time, embraced by popular historians and journalistic critics while generally reviled by 'serious' scholars and cinephiles, *Gone With the Wind* stands as both a monument to classical Hollywood and a monumental anomaly" (ix).

Gable and Vivien Leigh in *Gone With the Wind*

No matter how much highbrow audiences might disparage *Gone With the Wind*, it is not difficult to understand the appeal that it continues to have on its audience. The sweeping, dramatic plot centers on the vain Scarlett O'Hara (played by Vivien Leigh) and her attempt to find a spouse. Set in the American South during the Civil War and the Reconstruction era, Leigh's southern belle encapsulates the decadence of the South in its declining state. Her character is simultaneously egotistical and unlikeable, but Scarlett also exudes just enough pathos to appeal to a wide audience. The film also benefits from having one of the most celebrated romantic pairings of all time, as Gable's Rhett Butler, a wild and wealthy Southern gentleman, is the ideal match for Scarlett O'Hara. Despite spanning nearly four hours in length, the baroque plot has an almost unmatched ability to captivate viewers.

Given the ideal match between Clark Gable and Vivien Leigh, it may come as a surprise to learn that Gable had no intention of appearing in the film. Gary Cooper had already turned down the role of Rhett Butler and allegedly claimed, "Gone With the Wind is going to be the biggest flop in Hollywood history. I'm glad it'll be Clark Gable who's falling flat on his nose, not me." It was only through Lombard's urging that Gable agreed to take on the role (Harris). Gable was also the actor that producer David O. Selznick wanted. Always careful of cultivating his image, Gable explained his reservations about taking the role: "I found myself trapped by a series of circumstances over which I had no control. It was a funny feeling. I think I know now how a fly must react after being caught in a spider's web. Scarlett doesn't always love Rhett. It's the first time that the girl isn't sure that she wants me from the minute she sets eyes on me."

As it turned out, Gable was as suave as ever playing Rhett Butler, but he admitted it was a difficult role: "I discovered that Rhett was even harder to play than I had anticipated. With so much of Scarlett preceding his entrance, Rhett's scenes were all climaxes. There was a chance to build up to Scarlett, but Rhett represented drama and action every time he appeared. He didn't figure in any of the battle scenes, being a guy who hated war, and he wasn't in the toughest of the siege of Atlanta shots. What I was fighting for was to hold my own in the first half of the picture - which is all Vivien's - because I felt that after the scene with the baby, Bonnie, Rhett could control the end of the film. That scene where Bonnie dies, and the scene where I strike Scarlett and she accidentally tumbles down stairs, thus losing her unborn child, were the two that worried me most." Olivia de Havilland explained how she had to try to get Gable to cry during one of the scenes, "Oh, he would not do it. He would not! Victor (Fleming) tried everything with him. He tried to attack him on a professional level. We had done it without him weeping several times and then we had one last try. I said, 'You can do it, I know you can do it and you will be wonderful.' Well, by heaven, just before the cameras rolled, you could see the tears come up at his eyes and he played the scene unforgettably well. He put his whole heart into it."

The saga over casting the leading man was just one step in the long and complicated history of the film's production. From the start, the legendary Selznick had great ambitions for the film, going so far as to purchase the film rights to it before the novel it was based off was released in 1936. The book became an instant classic, selling a million copies within 6 months, after which it was awarded the Pulitzer Prize in 1937 (Taylor). That Selznick had the savvy to purchase the film rights to the novel before it was even distributed to the public reflected his love for adapting literary classics, an aspect of his personality that frequently leads critics to dismiss him as a slave to the novel. Despite this, however, Molly Haskell explains that Selznick assumed a great deal of risk with the production, and the book's grand narrative represented its saving grace:

> "It's easy to poke fun at the literary, and sometimes pseudoliterary, ambitions of Selznick, yet he could have lost his reputation as well as his shirt, could have been a laughingstock…There were many good reasons (mostly financial) that so few studios were eager to bid on the book, but there was one overwhelming argument in its favor: the generalized nature of the story, the very lack of historical detail with which critics reproached it, allowed it to speak of timeless love and loss, of family and romance, of a titanic struggle against national catastrophe that reverberated with all the struggles, past and to come, in a young nation's history." (35).

Haskell's explanation alludes to the way in which, despite much of the film being set in the Civil War era, the film still had great relevance in 1930s America, a landscape that was itself struggling with many of the same themes explored in the novel, such as economic loss and racism. In addition, broad themes such as family loss and broken romances were captivating to any audience. Selznick's interest in producing the film may have stemmed from his love for the novel, but it is clear in any case that the plot was well-suited for the screen.

For all of Selznick's literary leanings, it is also true that he was committed to transforming the text into a visual spectacle that made the film far from a mere retelling of the book. Alan David Vertrees discusses how during the production of *Gone With the Wind*, Selznick balanced his need to remain faithful to the novel with his desire to produce a great work of visual art:

> "Selznick developed the script with one eye on [Margaret] Mitchell's novel (and on the public's response to it) and the other on his visualization of the finished film. Indeed, the preliminary design of the film—not only as story but also as spectacle and cinematic achievement—was in many ways as important as the script itself. Selznick saw *Gone With the Wind* not only as an adaptation of an enormously popular novel, but also as a display of the full potential of cinematic art." (xii).

The technical accomplishments of *Gone with the Wind* are on display throughout the film, as it was one of the earliest and most successful examples of Technicolor. In addition, Selznick hired Victor Fleming (who directed *The Wizard of Oz* that same year) to direct the film and the famed Max Steiner to arrange the score. As a result, Selznick was rewarded with a film whose technical virtuosity went almost unmatched.

It is easy to become enraptured by the sweeping plot and bravura formal stylings of the film, yet viewers should not cast a blind eye to the ideology of *Gone With the Wind*. In particular, the film displays a casual racism that was not uncommon in 1930s Hollywood yet cannot be brushed aside by 21st century viewers. The most flagrant example of racial inequality concerns Scarlett's relationship with her black servant, Mammy, who displays no interest in breaking free from her submissive condition. The film also contains discriminatory language, and while one could argue that it merely followed the material in the book, the failure to remove the racist underpinnings of the plot amounted to an implicit acceptance of the offensive subject matter.

Gone With the Wind was awarded with 10 Oscars at the 1940 Academy Awards, an achievement made all the more impressive when considering the competition it faced. It is no accident that 1939 is often considered the greatest year in Hollywood film history, as *The Wizard of Oz*, *Mr. Smith Goes to Washington*, *Ninotchka*, and *Young Mr. Lincoln* were also among the famous films released that year. However, the showering of awards, particularly the Academy Award given to Hattie McDaniel, sparked an outcry from the National Association for the Advancement of Colored People (NAACP). In response, McDaniel refused to criticize either her role or the film as a whole. Ultimately, the Academy Awards saga itself was indicative of how *Gone With the Wind* is a cherished American classic on the one hand, but also a film that has caused great outrage from a significant portion of American society.

Nevertheless, Gable was now at the peak of his career, and he noticed the change that *Gone with the Wind* had on how people viewed him. He once noted, "Damn it. I never conceived of this. When I rode through Atlanta's streets today it wasn't like an opening at Grauman's Chinese at Hollywood. It wasn't like anything I ever experienced in my life. It was almost too big for me to take. And I hope to heaven when I leave here tomorrow night, after everybody has seen the picture, that I leave as Rhett Butler and not Clark Gable."

Chapter 6: Late Career

"I don't want a lot of strangers looking down at my wrinkles and my big fat belly when I'm dead." – Clark Gable

In the aftermath of *Gone With the Wind*, Gable continued to act at a prolific rate, though none of the films achieved any great success. His life remained quiet and comfortable until January 1942, when he was suddenly widowed after Carole Lombard died in a plane crash. She and her mother had gone on a tour selling war bonds, and the plane crashed near Las Vegas. Lombard was the first female casualty to die as a result of World War II, and despite flying to the scene of the accident, there was nothing Gable could do to amend the tragedy. The death plunged him into a deep depression, and despite finishing the film in which he was acting at the time, *Somewhere I'll Find You* (1942), Gable was ultimately unable to mask his heartbreak and even lost 20 pounds. Actress Esther Williams pointed out that after Lombard's death, Gable "was never the same. His heart sank a bit."

During World War II, Hollywood studios made every effort to prevent their stars from enlisting, since actors were valuable commodities. Even if they emerged from combat without suffering any wounds, their time away from the studio still constituted a substantial financial loss. However, with his wife having just passed away, there was little resistance that MGM could justifiably make, and Gable enlisted in the Air Force, where he was first given a special assignment. Eventually, he progressed through the ranks and was appointed First Lieutenant. In 1943, he accompanied the 351st Bomb Group to England and was promoted to Captain, spending 1943 in England at the RAF Polebrook with the 351st Bomb Group. While there, he was involved in combat and eventually earned an Air Medal and Distinguished Flying Cross. The following year, he was appointed to the rank of Major, but he was relieved from active duty in June 1944. Even so, it was not until 1947 that he resigned his commission.

Gable in Britain in 1943

Gable and Jimmy Stewart during World War II

Despite reticence from the studios, it was not terribly unusual for actors to enlist in the service in some capacity. What distinguished Gable's experience in the Armed Forces from those of many of his peers in Hollywood is that he displayed a fierce commitment to progressing through the ranks and serving the country to his fullest capacity, even after (and perhaps because) his wife had lost her own life due to World War II. In many ways, serving his country constituted an entirely separate career for Gable, one that monopolized his time and attention for two years. When he returned, both his professional and personal lives were vastly different.

When Gable joined the war, he was still near the top of the Hollywood elite. Upon returning, he still qualified as a major name in Hollywood, but his box office appeal was somewhat ambiguous; he had been away from the camera for three full years, and he was also in his mid-40s. Gable's first film after returning was *Adventure* (1945), a relatively minor romantic comedy that paired him with Greer Garson and featured the memorable publicity slogan "Gable's back and Garson's got him." The film is not well-remembered, and it was Gable's activity off the movie set garnered more headlines. In 1944, he joined the Motion Picture Alliance for the Preservation of American ideals, an organization housing many of Hollywood's more conservative figures. In joining the organization, Gable distanced himself early on from any allegations that may have otherwise been directed toward him during the Red Scare that subsumed Hollywood in the years to come.

During the late 1940s, Gable's romantic pursuits continued to generate publicity. He and Joan Crawford, who had been involved in an affair early in Clark's career, were once again romantically involved. The relationship did not last, and Gable then began seeing Sylvia Ashley, an actress and model from Britain. Ashley was well-known for having been the widow of screen legend Douglas Fairbanks, at least until she and Gable married in 1949. Three years younger than Clark, the age dynamics of the relationship more closely resembled Gable's third marriage than his first two. Despite being more age-compatible than either of Gable's first two wives, however, the marriage with Ashley was doomed to fail. After three years together, they obtained a divorce, and by 1952, Gable was once again single.

The late 1940s and early 1950s were bittersweet for Gable's career. On the one hand, he continued to secure major acting roles, but he found his opportunities less than fulfilling. One of his most significant post-war films was *The Hucksters* (1947), which paired him with Ava Gardner for the first time, although Deborah Kerr served as his chief co-star for the film. In the film, Gable plays a wealthy man who returns from World War II with the ambition of earning a fortune. He discards all of his money and works his way up the socioeconomic ladder from square one. The film has a parallel between that main plot and the romantic plot, in which he must similarly prove his worthiness to Kay (Deborah Kerr), the socialite with whom he falls in love. The film received lukewarm reviews but did lead to two additional films starring both

Gable and Ava Gardner: *Lone Star* (1952) and *Mogambo* (1953). The latter film is particularly noteworthy, as it remade *Red Dust*, one of Gable's earliest films. The film, which not only co-starred Ava Gardner but also Grace Kelly, was directed by John Ford. With such a famous cast and an acclaimed director, the public was understandably optimistic, but it is now almost entirely forgotten. The adventurous plot, set in Africa, was full of novelty, but the relatively thin narrative kept it from becoming a classic.

Gable and Ava Gardner in *The Hucksters*

Gable began to grow frustrated with the roles that were made available to him, and in 1953 he decided against renewing his contract. This decision wasn't unusual, because by 1953 it was a common practice for major stars to operate as independent contractors. What made Clark's case different from that of other stars, like Cary Grant, is that the lack of appealing opportunities was more a reflection of his age and status within the industry. Simply put, he was in the process of slipping from the list of most marketable stars in Hollywood.

His next major career move came in 1955, when he and Jane Russell founded a production company together. The first and only film produced by Gable was *The King and Four Queens* (1956), which was directed by the famous Raoul Walsh and co-starred Jane Powell. Despite being nearly 55 years old at the time of filming, Gable starred in the action film, playing the role of a cowboy who romances a group of widows (and their mother-in-law) in the hopes of inheriting their fortune. By this point in his career, Gable was hardly up to the task of playing an action hero, but the comedic elements of the plot supplied his performance with an irony that makes the film somewhat tongue-in-cheek in its treatment of Clark's masculinity. At the same time, producing the film was so taxing that Gable would not produce another film.

As the 1950s progressed, Gable's health began to deteriorate, and his career slowed down as well. Between 1956 and 1961, he averaged just one film per year. In 1958, Gable fully admitted, "My days of playing the dashing lover are over. I'm no longer believable in those parts. There has been considerable talk about older guys wooing and winning leading ladies half their age. I don't think the public likes it, and I don't care for it myself. It's not realistic. Actresses that I started out with like Joan Crawford and Barbara Stanwyck have long since quit playing glamour girls and sweet young things. Now it's time I acted my age. Let's be honest. It's a character role, and I'll be playing more of them. There's a risk involved, of course. I have no idea if I can attain the success as a character actor as I did playing the dashing young lover, but it's a chance I have to take. Not everybody is able to do it."

His life off the movie set began to settle down as well when he married Kay Spreckels, a former fashion model and actress who he had known for years. In fact, their first date had taken place over a decade before they were married, and it ended up with Gable botching an attempt to cook dinner for her at his ranch. When an accident left them both covered in gravy, Gable said to her, "Well, the first date you have with me and you end up in the gravy; at least you won't forget it. I imagine I've made quite the impression on you."

Like Gable, Spreckels had already been married a number of times, but she and Clark had a strong rapport, and their marriage was successful. She later said of him, "Looking back I wonder if there are many people who even in 25 or 30 years of marriage find the happiness that Clark and I had in those five years and four months." She also added, "Sometimes I would try to tease Clark into telling me some tasty morsels about his former leading ladies, but I might as well have banged my head against a stone wall. He simply refused to gossip. He'd break into that schoolboy grin that I found so irresistible and say, 'She's a fine girl. A fine girl.' That's the only thing I didn't like about my remarkable husband, for I'm a gal who likes a bit of gossip, now and then."

Kay Spreckels

By the end of the decade, Gable began showing his age. On the movie set, he struggled to hold his posture, particularly during long takes, and his weight also ballooned. In an effort to hide his escalating weight, his 1958 film *Teacher's Pet* was filmed in black-and-white, but even with the cosmetic tactics, it was impossible not to notice that Gable was losing his athleticism and virility. In response to this, he began to shift away from roles that demanded great physicality and shifted toward more comedic parts. One such film, *It Started in Naples* (1960), received strong reviews and was even nominated for an Academy Award for Best Art Direction. The romantic comedic plot paired Gable with Sophia Loren, with Clark playing the role of an American lawyer and Loren an Italian nightclub singer. The lighthearted film cast Gable in a charming light without demanding the physical prowess of his earlier performances.

Clark Gable's final film, *The Misfits*, was the most notable of his final years, especially because it included Marilyn Monroe and her husband, Arthur Miller. Monroe had long fantasized about Clark Gable, even going so far as to tell people that he was her father, and Miller wrote the script for the film specifically with Monroe in mind (Taraborelli). The movie was made when their marriage was in a state of disarray, and Monroe's life as a whole had already begun the downward spiral that culminated with her death in 1962. As the title suggests, the film casts each of the characters in a less than favorable light. Monroe stars as Roslyn Tabor, a divorcee who becomes romantically involved with Gable's character, an aging cowboy named Gay Langland. The plot mainly consists of the rowdy exploits of the main characters, whose reckless behavior masks a deep underlying ennui.

The Misfits is not only remembered for its famous cast but also for the subtext surrounding the cast. The film serve as a meta-commentary on Monroe's lifelong infatuation with Clark Gable, and Montgomery Clift's performance as a jaded rodeo performer makes reference to Clift's own personal insecurities. Far from a traditional Western with a macho hero, the film instead adopts a mood of alienation and discontent, leading Georgiana Banita to characterize it as the rare Western with an absent image of patriarchy.

Furthermore, the somber plot was mirrored with a difficult production that taxed everyone involved. Naturally, Monroe had caught Gable's eye, and he said of her, "Everything Marilyn does is different from any other woman, strange and exciting, from the way she talks to the way she uses that magnificent torso." But by 1961, Monroe was heavily addicted to sleeping pills, and her sporadic attendance kept everyone irritable. Gable himself complained, "The title sums up this mess. Miller, Monroe and Clift - they don't know what the hell they're doing. We don't belong in the same room together."

Even worse, the production took a great toll on Gable, whose health quickly deteriorated as he began suffering from a heart condition. It is possible that his heart condition was exacerbated by an extreme diet he took in order to lose weight and attempt to transform his body into proper physical condition for the role, and it didn't help that Gable actually insisted on performing his own stunts, one of which involved being dragged hundreds of feet. Whatever the cause, Gable's health took a sharp turn for the worse during the making of the film, and when he died on November 16, 1960 from the effects of a severe heart attack, the film had not yet been completed.

Although his death was undeniably untimely, Lesley Brill notes that the off-screen drama of *The Misfits* was appropriately suited to the tragedy of the actors involved: "Made in the midst of 'real life dramas,' *The Misfits* undertakes an imaginative exploration of pain and change and death. If the circumstances surrounding its production do not finally affect the images and words of the movie itself, they nonetheless attach to it an aura of tragic richness as an avatar of its ill-fated cast. The biographies of its makers resonate forlornly with the sadness of much of its story." (76).

Given the star-crossed fate of the cast members, *The Misfits* film remains a film of great sadness, one that put an abrupt end to Clark Gable's life and imbued the narrative with an overarching melancholy. The tragedy of Gable's death was made all the more pronounced by the fact that Gable's wife, Kay, gave birth to their son just months after his death.

Clark Gable will forever be best known for starring in *Gone With the Wind*, a film that is firmly entrenched within the canon of American film classics and arguably the most beloved film ever made. The fact Gable starred in such a well-loved film reflects his status as a screen legend of the first order, but it is also important to remember that he displayed great ability in other films as well. In fact, his lone Academy Award victory came not for *Gone With the Wind* but in recognition of his performance in *It Happened One Night*. In an age in which Hollywood was dominated by gangster heroes on the one hand and screwball comedy and musical actors on the other, Gable was able to combine rugged masculinity with refined sophistication in a way that was truly unprecedented. If he was, for a brief period, more popular than either Cary Grant (the romantic comedy actor par excellence) or Gary Cooper (premier action hero), it is not because he beat them at their own game but because he was able to combine the two. As Doris Day put it, "He was as masculine as any man I've ever known, and as much a little boy as a grown man could be – it was this combination that had such a devastating effect on women."

At the same time, the sophisticated veneer of Clark Gable's career masked a life filled with persistent tragedy. His mother and stepmother both died when he was young, and the death of Carole Lombard magnifies how even after reaching stardom, Gable's life continued to involve deep sorrow. Having died just before his 60th birthday, Gable was denied a chance at old age, and he seemed poised to transition to a life of quiet domesticity, with his acting career nearing its end and a new existence as a father on the horizon. Had he lived longer, it is unlikely that his career would have taken new directions. The tragedy of his death lies not so much in lost career opportunities but rather in the fact that Gable was denied the chance to raise a family.

Even though he died before he retired, it is impossible to deny that Clark Gable had a pronounced effect on Hollywood film history. In the throes of the Great Depression, he offered a hero that male and female viewers alike could identify with, displaying an acting style that was highly athletic yet at the same time very genteel. It is no accident that women like Marilyn Monroe fantasized over him; he was the ideal model for an upstanding American gentleman and comported himself seemingly without flaw. Even after returning from World War II and entering his late career, Gable offered a level of charm that few could match, and despite dying prematurely, his ability to continue starring in films even as he approached old age attested to his popularity. Still, it will always be the 1930s films, particularly *It Happened One Night* and *Gone with the Wind*, that dominate discussions of Clark Gable, who will forever be recognized as one of the titans of Hollywood's Golden Age.

Bibliography

Banita, Georgiana. "Re-Visioning the Western: Landscape and Gender in *The Misfits*." *John Huston: Essays on a Restless Director*. Eds. Tony Tracy and Roddy Flynn. Jefferson: McFarland & Company, 2010. 94-110. Print.

Bret, David. *Clark Gable: Tormented Star*. Cambridge: Da Capo Press, 2008. Print.

Brill, Lesley. *John Huston's Filmmaking*. Cambridge: Cambridge University Press, 1997. Print.

Harris, Warren G. *Clark Gable: A Biography*. New York: Three Rivers Press, 2005. Print.

Haskell, Molly. *Frankly, My Dear: Gone With the Wind Revisited*. New Haven: Yale University Press, 2010. Print.

Mizejewski, Linda. *It Happened One Night*. United Kingdom: John Wiley & Sons Ltd, 2010. Print.

Spicer, Christopher J. *Clark Gable: Biography, Filmography, Bibliography*. Jefferson: McFarland & Company, 2002. Print.

Taraborelli, J. Randy. *The Secret Life of Marilyn Monroe*. New York: Grand Central Publishing, 2009. Print.

Taylor, Helen. *Scarlett's Women: Gone With the Wind and Its Female Fans*. United Kingdom: Virago Press Limited, 1989. Print.

Vertrees, Alan David. *Selznick's Vision: Gone With the Wind and Hollywood Filmmaking*. Austin: University of Texas, 1997. Print.

James Cagney

Chapter 1: From Street to Stage

"It was just everyday living. With me, it was fighting, more fighting, and more fighting. Life then was simply the way it was: ordinary, not bad, not good, just regular. No stress, no strain. Of course, no one had much of anything but we didn't know that we were poor." – James Cagney

On July 17, 1899, James Cagney was born on the tough streets of the Lower East Side of Manhattan, and at the time his family was so poor that they didn't bother keeping careful records of family births and addresses, so the actual location of his birthplace remains a mystery. His father, James Francis Cagney, worked any job he could find and was, at one time or another, a bartender, a boxer and (at the time of his second son's birth) a telegraphist. Cagney's mother, Carolyn, was a first generation American with roots in Ireland and Norway, and it was from her that Cagney inherited his red hair, blue eyes and hot temper.

Cagney was the second of seven children, but two of Cagney's siblings died within months of their birth, which the family attributed to their poverty. As Cagney put it in his own autobiography, there was almost a third: "I was a very sick infant. My mother, only 20 – a mere child herself – was terribly worried, of course. What bothered her most, next to my possible demise, was the fact that I hadn't been baptized. As a good Catholic, she felt that if I were to die before I was given a proper name, I'd never be allowed into heaven. She bemoaned this again and again to her brother: 'He hasn't got the name – he has to have a name!' Now, my uncle was a pretty rough Irishman. He humored her for a while, but Mom continued to cry the house down about my lack of identity. Finally he turned on her and said, 'Carrie, for God's sake, shut up! Stop your crying and call the kid Ikey!" At that time, the Lower East side was characterized more than anything else by its diversity, ensuring Cagney grew up surrounded by people who had come to America from all over the world. He would later be grateful for this type of upbringing, noting, "The polyglot nature of my neighborhood is the basic reason why all my life I've had such an appreciation and understanding for dialects. I ought to – I was surrounded by them. Indeed, I was 22 before I ever heard an elderly man who spoke without an accent…"

Like most living in the heart of New York City at that time, the young boy always had a job. At one time, it was as an office boy for the *New York Sun* making $5 a week, all of which he gave to his mother. Later, he worked at the New York Public Library for $12.50 a month. He also played semi-pro baseball and he was so good at amateur boxing that he once finished runner-up for the lightweight boxing title in New York State. He wanted to turn professional, but his mother warned him he would have to beat her first, so he soon gave up the idea. Cagney later recounted his time working as a young kid positively, explaining, "It was good for me. I feel sorry for the kid who has too cushy a time of it. Suddenly he has to come face-to-face with the realities of life without any mama or papa to do his thinking for him."

After it was clear he wasn't going to be a boxer, Jimmy next turned to a less suitable but more lucrative line of work: serving as a maître d' at an upscale tea room. His job at the tea room may seem strange, considering Cagney's tough guy image, but he was certainly more rounded than the average street tough. In addition to boxing and playing baseball, he also took tap dancing lessons, and friends that knew him as a young man recall him as "Cellar Door Cagney" thanks to the knack he had for dancing up the side of slanted cellar doors.

Nor was young Jimmy Cagney all brawn and no brain. After graduating from Stuyvesant High School in 1918, Cagney enrolled in Columbia University as an art major, but by this time, the United States had entered World War I. Assuming that the war would go on for a number of years, and already having an ear for German gained as a child, Cagney also decided to major in the language. This immediately benefited him when it came to joining the Student Army Training Corps, a predecessor of the Army ROTC, and Cagney might have gone on to a career in the military had fate not intervened. The war ended in November 1918, and an influenza pandemic swept through the world, taking the life of his father and leaving his mother a young widow pregnant with her seventh child. This sudden turn of events forced Cagney to drop out of school and move home to help make ends meet.

Thankfully, Jimmy Cagney had some sort of photographic memory, which not only helped him excel in school but also opened the door for his acting career. Like so many other would-be actors, his interest in performing began with the movies. Cagney's aunt lived in Brooklyn near the Vitagraph Studios, and while visiting her, Cagney would hang over the edge of the fence surrounding the studios and watch movies being filmed, especially those involving his favorite actor, John Bunny.

John Bunny

Eventually, Jimmy would follow his older brother Henry into the amateur dramatic club at the Lenox Hill Neighborhood House, where he worked primarily behind the scenes as a stagehand. At the time, the younger Cagney had no interest in acting, but that all changed one night when Harry became too ill to carry on with his part. The director, Florence James, called on Jimmy to take his brother's place, and because of his excellent memory, Jimmy had no problems learning the script. He went on stage that night with the lines memorized and mimicked his brother's acting movements, which he had remembered from watching rehearsals. Naturally, the applause from the audience proved to be a thrill for him and left him wanting more.

Chapter 2: The Boxer Who Danced

"You know, the period of World War I and the Roaring Twenties were really just about the same as today. You worked, and you made a living if you could, and you tried to make the best of things. For an actor or a dancer, it was no different then than today. It was a struggle." – James Cagney

Jimmy might have been bitten by the acting bug, but playing bit parts in dramatic companies was not going to pay the bills, so he also got a full-time job at Wanamaker's Department Store in 1919. Undeterred, he was still working there when he auditioned for a small part in *Every Sailor*, a war time musical with a chorus made up of service men dressed as women. He later explained the unusual nature of this first part: "And that is how I began to learn dancing, as a chorus girl. I faked it to begin with. I would stand in the entrance, catch the real dancers, and steal their steps. Thereafter, in all the dancing shows and acts I did, I learned by watching." While it would certainly surprise many to hear that the classic Hollywood tough guy played his first part in drag, it didn't faze Cagney at all because when he was acting, "I am not myself. I am not that fellow, Jim Cagney, at all. I certainly lost all consciousness of him when I put on skirts, wigs, make-up, powder, feathers and bangles." It certainly didn't hurt that they were paying Cagney $35 a week, which he considered "a mountain of money for me in those worrisome days."

Though Carrie was proud of her second son's success, she still wanted him to return to college and get a degree. He refused to go back, but he did leave the department store and take a position as a runner for a local Broad Street brokerage house, and in his off time, he continued to audition, eventually getting a part in the chorus of *Pitter Patter*. He was paid over $50 a week, but he sent $40 of it to his mother. More accustomed to hard work than the life of an actor, Cagney also made additional money by working as a dresser and carrying luggage for the other actors. The show proved to be Cagney's first part in vaudeville.

While working on the ticker counter, Cagney met Frances Willard "Billie" Vernon, a 16-year-old member of the female chorus line, and they soon fell in love and married in 1922. They then moved into a sort of early style of commune called Free Acres that was established in Berkeley Heights, New Jersey. Cagney and his wife would tour together with an act called "Vernon & Ide", and later, he would replace Archie Leach, of the Parker, Brandon and Leach act. The name Archie Leach doesn't mean much to anyone anymore because Leach later changed his name to Cary Grant.

Cary Grant

Cagney and his wife with actors Jack Oakie and Joan Marsh

In 1924, Vernon and Cagney moved across the country to Hawthorne, California to try to break into the movies, even though they were so poor at that time that they had to borrow the train fare from a friend who was also an aspiring actor. At first, Cagney tried to support himself and his wife by teaching dancing, but perhaps not surprisingly, there were already plenty of dance schools near them and thus not enough clients. Cagney was unable to make ends meet, forcing the couple to give up on their dream of making it out West. They borrowed more money to move back to New York. These were obviously hard times, and Jimmy never forgot them, or what it took for them to make it through. More than 50 years later, he would give his wife the credit, saying "the rock solid honesty and the sterling character of this little gal made it possible our going comparatively unscathed through the years when we were in dire straits. And when I say dire straits, I mean 'dire' and I mean 'straits.' It was rough. At times no food in the larder, big holes in the shoes. When I didn't have a penny, she was out working. Life seemed just a never ending sequence of damned dingy, badly furnished rooms with a one burner plate. There were many times when I was sorely tried and decided to get out of the acting business, to go out and get any kind of job that would bring in the weekly paycheck. But every time I mentioned it, my Bill told me with pleasant firmness, no."

Fortunately, Cagney fared better on the stage than he did in the movies. In 1925, he was cast as a tough guy in the play *Outside Looking In*, and his work in that production earned him a far more comfortable living at $200 a week. Since he had no experience doing dramatic acting, Cagney later admitted he thought he got the part because his hair was redder than that of the other performer he was competing against, but regardless, the play was popular and garnered Cagney a number of positive reviews. One critic in *Life* magazine noted, "Mr. Cagney, in a less spectacular role makes a few minutes silence during his mock-trial scene something that many a more established actor might watch with profit". Burns Mantle, a stage critic who founded and wrote for *Best Plays*, claimed *Outside Looking In* "contained the most honest acting now to be seen in New York."

However, Cagney faced another major setback in 1926, when he was promised but then lost a part in George Abbott's Broadway. Believing that they would be sailing to England to perform the show in London's West End, Jimmy and Billie had their luggage loaded on to a ship and had given up the lease on their apartment, but the day before they were to leave, Cagney was told that he no longer had the part. Cagney's wife later recalled that after this turn of events, "Jimmy said that it was all over. He made up his mind that he would get a job doing something else."

That something else turned out to be something familiar. To make ends meet, Cagney tried his hand again at teaching dance, and this time, his students were fellow professionals, so he was able to make more money. More importantly, he was also able to hear about new plays opening, which is how he secured a role in *Women Go on Forever*. For four months, Cagney taught dance all day, and danced across the stage all night. By the time the play ended, he was both physically and mentally exhausted.

The following year, Cagney was cast in *Grand Street Follies of 1928*, and this time, he was also made the choreographer. The Follies were a hit, which led to the reprisal of the show the following year as the aptly named *Grand Street Follies of 1929*. In vaudeville, as in life, Cagney soon learned that nothing succeeds like success; his successful roles in the Follies led to a part in *Maggie the Magnificent*. Though the critics didn't much care for the play, they praised Cagney's performance, and Cagney praised director George Kelly for his professionalism: "On *Maggie the Magnificent*'s first day of rehearsal, he said to us, 'Now, boys and girls, we have hired you because we know you were experienced. I will benefit of all that experience. We think you know your business. Anything that occurs to you, please let me know – because I can't think of everything. So – if you would do me the favor of speaking up? All right now, let's get to work.' Naturally, with such a complete professional in control, there was no need for us to give him anything." Cagney also said he learned "what a director was for and what a director could do. They were directors who could play all the parts in the play better than the actors cast for them."

Chapter 3: The Public Enemy Becomes a Public Hero

"Though I soon became typecast in Hollywood as a gangster and hoodlum, I was originally a dancer, an Irish hoofer, trained in vaudeville tap dance. I always leapt at the opportunity to dance films later on." – James Cagney

Following *Maggie the Magnificent*, Cagney and his co-star Joan Blondell were cast in a new play called *Penny Arcade*. As with the previous play, the critics did not like *Penny Arcade*, but they loved Cagney and Blondell, and when Al Jolson saw the couple's talent, he bought the rights to the play for $20,000 and then turned around and sold the play to Warner Bros., with the caveat that they would hire Cagney and Blondell to re-create their parts on screen. Warner Bros. cast the two, giving Cagney a three week contract for $1500 to play tough guy Harry Delano, and this type of part would prove to be his bread and butter for the rest of his career. Despite the fact it was his first film, Cagney refused to be cowed into doing stuff he didn't like, including a scene he wouldn't shoot: "There was a line in the show where I was supposed to be crying on my mother's breast...'I'm your baby, ain't I?' I refused to say it. Adolfi said 'I'm going to tell Zanuck.' I said 'I don't give a s*** what you tell him, I'm not going to say that line.'" By holding firm, Cagney had the line removed from the script.

Joan Blondell

The film adaptation of *Penny Arcade*, titled *Sinners' Holiday*, was released in 1930, but Cagney's on screen career began not so much with a bang but with a whimper. The studio liked him, but they weren't sure how much they liked him. Thus, when the shooting ended, Warner offered him a seven-year contract for salary of $400 a week, but the studio added an unusual stipulation that specified it could drop him at the end of any 40 week period. In other words, Cagney could find himself out of work after any 40 week period, but since he had no better offers and still needed to support his family, he took the contract. When looking at Cagney's decision sign with Warner Bros., it's essential to keep in mind his background. $400 a week was a substantial amount of money for a family that had grown up broke, and by this time, the stock market had crashed and many Americans had no work at all. At the time, getting paid $400 a week to stand in front of the camera was easy money in his mind, though he would soon change his mind.

Cagney's next picture was *Doorway to Hell*, and it was followed by several other gangster films, including *Little Caesar*, in which he played opposite Edward G Robinson for the first time. Over the next few years, these two men would come to define what it meant to be a gangster in a Hollywood film. But ultimately, Cagney's big break became in 1931 when he was cast in *The Public Enemy*. The very nature of the casting for that film is the stuff of Hollywood legend, as Cagney would later recall: "Then came *The Public Enemy*. The story is about two street pals – one soft-spoken, the other a really tough little article. For some incredible reason, I was cast as the quiet one; and Eddie Woods, a fine actor but a boy of genial background, well-spoken and well-educated, became the tough guy. Fortunately, Bill Wellman, the director, had seen *Doorway to Hell*, and he quickly became aware of the obvious casting error. He knew at once that I can project that direct gutter quality, so Eddie and I switched roles after Wellman made an issue of it with Darryl Zanuck."

Robinson in *Little Caesar*

Wellman clearly made the right decision, because *The Public Enemy* soon became one of the first films to ever gross more than $1 million. Not only did the public love the movie, the critics loved it. A reviewer in the *New York Herald* said that Cagney's performance was "the most ruthless, unsentimental appraisal of the meanness of a petty killer the cinema has yet devised." Some critics have cited the film as changing the way that the public would perceive good guys versus bad guys, asserting that Cagney's portrayal of Tom Powers as a murderer with a heart of gold introduced the genre to Hollywood. However, Cagney always disagreed, pointing instead to Clark Gable in *Night Nurse* as being the first "good bad guy".

The movie attempted to be so realistic that Cagney was actually punched in the face in one scene, and another called for him to duck from live gunfire, but the most famous scene in the movie comes when Cagney's character angrily picks up half of a grapefruit and shoves it into his girlfriend's (played by Mae Clarke) face. The shocking nature of the scene, and the surprise on Clarke's face, led many to assume that it was an impromptu move on either Cagney's part of the director's part, and that Clarke wasn't told what was coming her way. For her part, Clarke claimed that she knew the grapefruit was coming, but that she had been told it wouldn't actually be included in the movie itself: "I'm sorry I ever agreed to do the grapefruit bit. I never dreamed it would be shown in the movie. Director Bill Wellman thought of the idea suddenly. It wasn't even written into the script." Even today, movie experts refer to it as one of the most significant moments in film history, and naturally, Cagney had his own take on the issue: "When Mae Clarke and I played the grapefruit scene, we had no idea that it would create such a stir...I was not to hear the end of that little episode for years. Invariably whenever I went into a restaurant, there was always some wag having the waiter bring me a tray of grapefruit. It got to be awfully tiresome, although it never stopped me from eating it in the proper amount at the proper time."

Cagney was glad to have work, and he appreciated the money he was making, but he was still the scrappy tough guy from the Lower East Side who refused to be pushed around by anyone. For instance, when Douglas Fairbanks, Jr. organized a charity drive, the studio insisted that every actor participate, but Cagney refused, saying that while he was glad to donate to charity, he would not be forced to do it. This incident and subsequent others would eventually earn him the title "The Professional Againster" in Hollywood.

While shooting *The Public Enemy*, Cagney was also working with Edward Robinson on *Smart Money*. Warner liked the way the two men interacted on screen, so the studio wanted them to get back together in another film as soon as possible. In spite of the fact that he had never hit a woman in real life, Cagney was once again called upon to assault his leading lady in *Smart Money*. This time, he had to slap his co-star, Evelyn Knapp. However, things were changing in Hollywood at the beginning of the 1930s, as motion pictures, once considered a novelty, were becoming more mainstream in American society. With that came an outcry from conservative Americans and religious groups to limit the amount of sex and violence in pictures. Needless to say, they did not appreciate films in which men assaulted women, and they also didn't like criminals being portrayed as having redeeming qualities. Warner decided to take Cagney's career in another direction by casting him with Joan Blondell in a comedy, *Blonde Crazy*, but this new direction wouldn't last long.

Chapter 4: Working For and Against Warner Bros.

"There were many tough guys to play in the scripts that Warner kept assigning me. Each of my subsequent roles in the hoodlum genre offered the opportunity to inject something new, which I always tried to do. One could be funny, and the next one flat. Some roles were mean, and others were meaner." – James Cagney

The Public Enemy was so popular that movie theaters were running the movie 24 hours a day just to keep up with demand; in fact, one legendary anecdote about the movie related by Cagney is that Joan Blondell's ex-husband figured out the times the grapefruit scene would be on and would duck into the theater to catch it as often as possible. Given the movie's popularity, Cagney realized that he was bringing in a lot of money for Warner Bros. but was not being paid as much as many of the other actors whose films were not doing as well. He approached the executives at the company and demanded a raise, and when they refused and also insisted that he spend his extra time promoting other films, Cagney quit, turned his apartment in Hollywood over to his brother Bill, and moved back to New York. He would describe his rationale for this move: "The trouble surfaced when I realized that there were roughly two classes of stars at Warner's: those getting $125,000 a picture – and yours sincerely, who was getting all of $400 a week. That $400 soon stopped because I walked."

While it was obviously a risky decision, it was also a wise one, because the popularity of *The Public Enemy* and *Blonde Crazy* had the public clamoring to see more of him. While Jimmy was gone, his brother was able to persuade Warner to renew his contract and pay him $1000 a week, after which Cagney returned to Hollywood and began working on *Taxi*. This film marked both a first and a last in his career. The first was his dancing, as he performed an excellent number on screen for the first time. The last was getting shot at with live ammunition. At the time, studios regularly shot at their actors with live rounds because blanks were considered too expensive, and Cagney had taken it for granted that it was part of the job. However, during the filming of *Taxi*, something happened that changed his mind: "…one of the machine-gun bullets hit the head of one of the spikes holding the backing planks together. It ricocheted and went tearing through the set, smacked through a sound booth, ripped across the stage, hit a clothes tree, and dropped into the pocket of someone's coat." From that point forward, Cagney refused to put himself in the line of fire, and that decision may have saved his life on the set of *Angels with Dirty Faces* because an errant bullet passed through the place where he would have otherwise been standing.

The film *Taxi* also contains one of the most misquoted lines in movie history. At one point in time, Cagney yells at his enemy, "Come out and take it, you dirty, yellow-bellied rat, or I'll give it to you through the door!" For some reason, this line began to be quoted all over the nation as, "MMMmmm, you dirty rat!" To this day, impressionists still use it when impersonating Cagney.

Warner may have thought that they had won the battle with Cagney over his salary, but they were wrong. Cagney returned to Hollywood for $1000 a week, but he believed that his work was worth $4000 a week, which is what Edward G. Robinson and other actors of the era were making. Cagney again demanded a raise and again threatened to quit if he did not get it, but this time, the studio called his bluff and suspended him. Cagney responded that if that was their attitude, he would quit acting altogether and return to Columbia University to become a doctor. Finally, after six months of wrestling, Frank Capra was able to persuade Cagney to accept $3000 per week, along with top billing and the assurance that he would have to film no more than four movies a year. This success would lead to Cagney becoming one of the leading members of the Screen Actors Guild when it was founded in 1933.

1933 and 1934 had Cagney making multiple movies for Warner Bros., and as is usually the case, some were better received than others. *Footlight Parade* was particularly popular, and Cagney enjoyed making it because it allowed him to sing and dance on stage again. The dance sequences, choreographed by the famous Busby Berkeley, are considered some of the best of the era. Cagney's other favorite movie of that time was *Here Comes the Navy*, not so much because of the quality of the film but because he got to work with Pat O'Brien, who would become one of his best friends. Ironically, the movie was filmed aboard the USS *Arizona*, several years before it would be sunk by the Japanese at Pearl Harbor.

Cagney and Blondell in *Footlight Parade*

Cagney and Gloria Stuart in *Here Comes the Navy*

By 1935, Cagney was considered one of the 10 biggest moneymakers in Hollywood, but when asked if this was the big moment when he realized he was a star, he replied with his usual honesty: "Nothing of the sort! I never gave it a thought, never thought of it at all. Whatever was going on in my Hollywood life I regarded as completely transitory. I looked on it only as doing a job, and that job happened to work out. And the answer to all this is, where did I go nights? I sure wasn't going around picking up the kudos – or the kiddos. I just stayed home."

Cagney finally got to be on the other side of the cops and robbers game in *G-Men*, this time playing an FBI agent tracking down a wanted criminal. After that, he made his first and only foray into Shakespeare by portraying Nick Bottom in *A Midsummer's Night's Dream*. Needless to say, he would not try such a role again.

Instead, Cagney next made a third film with Pat O'Brien, this one called *Ceiling Zero*, but in this film, Warner again challenged Cagney's contract. First, they listed O'Brien above him in the credits, a clear violation of his top billing clause, and the company had already pushed Cagney by having him make five movies in 1934, another violation. He had let this pass, but the billing issue proved to be the final straw. He sued the studio for breach of contract, and after again leaving Bill to handle his professional and business matters, he returned to New York. When looking at his contract battle with Warner, particularly his preference to renegotiate over and over again, it may seem that Cagney was stubbornly insistent on having his way at all costs, but he cast his actions in a different light: "Top billing is an entitlement that means money in the bank, and I was protecting my entitlement. I walked out because I depended on the studio heads to keep their word on this, that, or other promise, and when the promise was not kept, my only recourse was to deprive them of my services. I'd go back east and stay on my farm until I had some kind of understanding. I'm glad to say I never walked out in the middle of a picture, the usual procedure when an actor wanted a raise."

Back in New York, Cagney began shopping around for property outside the city and claiming that he would just settle down to farm. Though he grew up in the city, Cagney had been interested in farming ever since his mother took him to hear a talk on soil conservation when he was a young man. Thus, while he was off from work, he purchased his first farm. Located on Martha's Vineyard, it consisted of 100 acres of bucolic quiet, but his wife didn't care for the place at first; Billie was concerned about the money and work it would take to make the deteriorated old house and out buildings habitable. Jimmy persisted, however, and she soon came to love it too. For his part, Carney maintained that the Vineyard "represented for me the place where I could always go to find freedom and peace…"

Of course, the Cagney's would have to work hard to maintain their peace, especially after Jimmy's fans learned where they lived. In order to avoid multiple strangers showing up at his door, Cagney spread the rumor around the area that he had hired an armed guard to patrol the place. This led to a comical situation when his pal Spencer Tracy came to visit. Tracy's cabbie would not pull up on to the property, explaining to him "I hear they shoot!" Thus, Tracy had to walk up the dirt road on foot to get to the house.

Jimmy Cagney the actor might have disappeared altogether and been permanently replaced by Jimmy Cagney the gentleman farmer had it not been for Edward L. Alperson, who represented Grand National Films, a new studio that offered Cagney $100,000 per film plus 10% of whatever the movies made. Cagney accepted this deal and returned to Hollywood to make *Great Guy* and *Something to Think About* for Grand National. These movies are unique among his performances of that era in that he plays a more sympathetic "good guy" rather than a criminal, but while his performances were critically acclaimed, the movies themselves were low-budget and looked it. Grand National ran out of money before it could make any more films, and Cagney once more found himself looking for a new project.

Cagney did not have to look for long; he won his case against Warner Bros., setting a new precedent for actors who had formally been bound by the studio system. More than that, the studio actually invited him to return to work for them, this time offering him a contract for $150,000 per film, with a clause guaranteeing that he would have to make no more than two movies each year. He could also choose which pictures he made. Always a family man, Jimmy insisted that his brother Bill be made the assistant producer of any movies he was cast in.

Cagney's victory against Warner Bros. proved to be a triumph in the politics of Hollywood, and it also led him to become involved in other political matters, a decision that would later cause him some problems. In 1936, the specter of war was consuming Europe, with Hitler and the Nazis in Germany and Mussolini rattling his saber in Italy. The world was watching, and though most Americans were still isolationists, Cagney believed that the Nazis needed to be stopped. As a result, he joined the Hollywood anti-Nazi League, unaware that the League was actually a Communist front. This would come back to haunt him later.

In the meantime, Cagney was back working for Warner Bros. After working with Pat O'Brien in *Boy Meets Girl* in 1938, Cagney teamed up with him again in the classic *Angels with Dirty Faces*. Cagney had had his eye on this role for some time and had hoped to make it for Grand National. In it, he stars as recently released gangster Rocky Sullivan, and while trying to track down an old pal who owes him money (played by Humphrey Bogart), Sullivan runs into another old friend, Jerry Connolly. Played by O'Brien, Connolly is now a priest working with at-risk kids, many of whom idolize Rocky. He tries to persuade Sullivan to go straight but fails, and Sullivan ends up being sentenced to the electric chair.

Cagney and O'Brien in *Angels with Dirty Faces*

In the moments leading up to his execution, Connolly visits Sullivan and pleads with him to "turn yellow", so that the kids who have so admired him will lose their respect for him and his criminal ways. Sullivan refuses to humiliate himself and insists that he will walk to the chair like a man. However, at the last moment, he falls to his knees before his executioners and pleads for his life. For years, critics would speculate over whether Sullivan's seeming cowardice at the last minute was a real last ditch attempt to save his life or feigned to appease Connolly, but Cagney would never say: "Through the years I have actually had little kids come up to me on the street and ask, 'Didya' do it for the father?' I think in looking at the film it is virtually impossible to say which course Rocky took – which is just the way I wanted it. I played it with deliberate ambiguity so that the spectator can take his choice. It seems to me it works out fine in either case. You have to decide."

Critics hailed Cagney's performance in *Angels with Dirty Faces* as one of his best, and he received his first Oscar nomination for Best Actor, but he ultimately lost out to Spencer Tracy, who ironically won it for playing a priest in *Boys Town*. However, Cagney did snag the coveted New York Film Critics Circle award for best actor, and it would hardly be his last Academy Award nomination.

By 1939, hard work and a hard-nosed approach to business had made Cagney the studio's highest paid actor. In fact, his annual salary of $350,000 was second only to Cary Grant's in the entire industry. While Warner probably didn't appreciate the route Cagney took to get to that position, the studio also knew it was money well spent. Cagney finished up the year with *The Roaring Twenties*, his last film with Bogart and the last gangster movie he would make for a decade. As usual, he received good reviews, with Graham Greene remarking, "Mr. Cagney, of the bull-calf brow, is as always a superb and witty actor".

Cagney with Bogart and Jeffrey Lynn in *The Roaring Twenties*

The Roaring Twenties marked the end of another era for Cagney, although this time the change was more subtle. As noted earlier, Hollywood was under increasing scrutiny for the moral message of its films, and during the 1930s, most of Cagney's gangster characters were portrayed as having turned to a life of crime because of being raised in abusive and/or poor environments. As the 1940s dawned, public perspective was shifting, and from this time on, large-scale violence was seen as part of a mental illness or, at the very least, a lack of self-control.

Chapter 5: Yankee Doodle Dandy

Cagney in *Yankee Doodle Dandy*

By 1941, Jimmy and Billie Cagney had been married almost 20 years, but they still had no children, so they decided to adopt an infant boy whom they named James Cagney, Jr. A few years later, they would adopt a girl and name her Cathleen. Tragically, while Jimmy and Billie remained close throughout their marriage, they had a difficult relationship with their children. James Jr. died two years before his father following a long period in which the two were estranged, and Cathleen would remain estranged from her father until his death.

Jimmy Cagney is best known for playing gangsters with one notable exception: his portrayal of George M. Cohan in *Yankee Doodle Dandy*. Both critics and Cagney himself believed it was his best role ever, and there are a number of reasons (in addition to Cagney's talent) *Yankee Doodle Dandy* was such a hit. One is that the crew began filming the picture on December 8, 1941, the day after the bombing of Pearl Harbor, so it goes without saying that everyone working on the project was in a state of what one person called "patriotic frenzy." Cagney's co-star, Rosemary DeCamp, noted the cast and crew had a feeling that "they might be sending the last message from the free world" out to the country. At the premiere, the company sold seats for up to

$25,000 each, donating the money to the U.S. Treasury in the form of war bonds, and in that one evening they raised almost $6 million for the war effort.

Another factor that made the film a hit involved the parallels between Cohan's and Cagney's lives. Both men got their start in vaudeville, they both struggled hard before finding success, they both were devoted to their families, and they had both been married to the same women for many years, which was no small feat in Hollywood then (or now).

Cohan

Both the public and the critics loved the movie. *Time* wrote, "*Yankee Doodle Dandy* (Warner) is possibly the most genial screen biography ever made. Few films have bestowed such loving care on any hero as this one does on beaming, buoyant, wry-mouthed George M. (for Michael) Cohan. The result is a nostalgic, accurate re-creation of a historic era of U.S. show business." As far as Cagney's performance was concerned, they were equally enthusiastic, noting, "Smart, alert, hard-headed, Cagney is as typically American as Cohan himself... It was a remarkable performance, probably Cagney's best, and it makes Yankee Doodle a dandy." Perhaps the biggest praise came from Cohan himself; when he saw Cagney's performance in the film he exclaimed, "My God, what an act to follow!"

Of course, one of the reasons Cagney succeeded in the role was the very reason he was cast for it: "Psychologically I needed no preparation for Yankee Doodle Dandy, or professionally either. I didn't have to pretend to be a song-and-dance man. I was one…In just about every interview, in most conversations, one question emerges unfailingly: what is my favorite picture?…A discerning critic like Peter Bogdonovich can't understand why I choose *Yankee Doodle Dandy*…The answer is simple…Once a song-and-dance man, always a song-and-dance man. In that brief statement, you have my life story: those few words tells as much about me professionally as there is to tell….Its story abounds in all the elements necessary for a good piece of entertainment. It has solid laughs [and] great music. And how much more meaningful are those patriotic songs today in view of all our current national troubles! *Yankee Doodle Dandy* has lots of reasons to be my favorite picture." When Cagney wrote those words in 1974, the troubles he referred to were very different than those faced at the time of the film's release, but *Yankee Doodle Dandy* stood the test of time. Even today, it remains an American favorite.

Not surprisingly, considering the both the nature of the film and the year in which it was released, *Yankee Doodle Dandy* was nominated for eight Academy Awards. It won three, including Cagney's win for Best Actor. When accepting his award, he remained humble, saying, "I've always maintained that in this business, you're only as good as the other fellow thinks you are. It's nice to know that you people thought I did a good job. And don't forget that it was a good part, too."

Following his success with *Yankee Doodle Dandy*, Cagney teamed up with his brother Bill to create Cagney Productions, and their plan was to make movies themselves and then release them through United Artists. However, Cagney was in no hurry to get back to work; instead, he returned to his farm on Martha's Vineyard to rest up. After that, with the war still ongoing, he joined the United Service Organizations (USO) and began touring military bases and visiting soldiers. At each base, he would recreate scenes from *Yankee Doodle Dandy*, as well as some of his early song and dance work.

In September 1942, Cagney returned to Hollywood and was elected as president of the Screen Actors Guild. The following year, Cagney Productions released its first film, *Johnny Come Lately*, starring Cagney as a newspaperman in the late 19th century. According to Cagney, "…our biggest accomplishment in *Johnny Come Lately* was to establish as one of the hallmarks of Cagney Productions the liberal use of good supporting actors. As Time magazine said about this, 'Bit players who have tried creditably for years to walk in shoes that pinched them show themselves in this picture as the very competent actors they always were. There has seldom been as good a cinematic gallery of U.S. small-town types.'"

Jimmy and his brother took a real chance with *Johnny Come Lately* because most of the larger studios were focusing on making war films, and that's what the American public seemed to want. While the film did receive some positive reviews and made a reasonable amount of money, it was not the type of hit Cagney was used to making. Thus, instead of beginning to work on another film right away, he went on another USO tour, this time to England.

Cagney enjoyed his time in England and worked hard to entertain the troops stationed on military bases there. He often gave multiple performances in a single day of his main act, "The American Cavalcade of Dance", a history of dance in 20th century America, and finishing with numbers from Yankee Doodle Dandy. The only thing that Cagney wouldn't do was give interviews to reporters covering the tour; when some British reporters approached him one time, he responded, "I'm here to dance a few jigs, sing a few songs, say hello to the boys, and that's all."

When Cagney came home, he quickly got to work on Cagney Productions' next film, *Blood in the Sun*. Always willing to try something new, Jimmy trained with martial arts expert Ken Kuniyuki and a former policeman named Jack Halloran to do his own stunts in the film. After the failure of *Johnny Come Lately*, the brothers hoped that the spy thriller set in Japan would be more appealing to American audiences. However, while *Blood in the Sun* was popular with critics and even won an Academy Award for Best Art Direction, it was a box office failure. Compounding that failure, Cagney had spotted a photo of a young war hero named Audie Murphy and believed that Murphy had the looks and poise to make it in pictures, so he invited him to Hollywood for a screen test. Unfortunately, Cagney didn't recognize the acting talent of the future actor and thus sold his contract to another company shortly after.

While trying to line up the rights for Cagney Productions' third movie, Cagney starred in *13 Rue Madeleine*, a spy picture that paid him $300,000. The film was a success, and Cagney used the money he made to produce *The Time of Your Life*, an adaptation of the Broadway play by the same name that appealed to critics but not to audiences. The problem was not Cagney's acting ability but the unwillingness of the public to accept him in the role of Joseph T., a quiet, philosophical people watcher.

During the years following World War II, Cagney became increasingly active in local and national political circles, an interest that had been sparked in the 1930s when he opposed the "Merriam Tax," a form of "under the table" bribes given by studios to the campaign of Frank Merriam, California's candidate for governor. Each actor was expected to donate a day's pay to Merriam's campaign, but out of principle, Cagney not only refused to make the required contribution, he also threatened to donate a week's salary to Merriam's opponent.

At first, Cagney considered himself to be a political liberal, and he supported Franklin Roosevelt's election and policies. He was also involved in what he later described as a "liberal group...with a leftist slant". However, when another member, future president Ronald Reagan, warned him about the direction the group was taking, he and Reagan resigned. Furthermore, his one-time involvement in the Anti-Nazi League caused him problems as the Red Scare and Cold War became everyday facts of life in post-war America, but thankfully he was ultimately cleared by the notorious House Un-American Activities Committee.

Furthermore, while serving as the president of the Screen Actors Guild in 1942 and 1943,

Cagney led the Guild's opposition to the Mafia. There had been rumors for years about a group affectionately dubbed the "Irish Mafia" that Cagney himself was allegedly a member of, consisting of a group of Irish-American actors that like to get together for dinner and drinks, but by the early 1940s, Cagney found himself up against the real thing, an organized crime family that wanted to get their cut of the Hollywood action. Unlike many of his fellow actors, Cagney has seen guys like these before, and even after his wife got a call telling her that she was now a widow, he was unperturbed. When they stepped up their threats by hiring a hit man, Cagney contacted his friend George Raft, who apparently had his own underworld ties. He "made a call", and the hit was called off.

While Cagney had liked Roosevelt, he was not as fond of Harry Truman, so in 1948 he voted for a Republican candidate (Thomas E. Dewey) for the first time in his life. The next two decades saw him become firmly entrenched as a conservative, and Cagney explained this transition in his autobiography: "I believe in my bones that my going from the liberal stance to the conservative was a totally natural reaction once I began to see undisciplined elements in our country stimulating a breakdown of our system. From what I've seen of the liberal attitudes toward the young and the permissive attitude in the schools and everybody pulling every which way from center, I consider these all inimical to the health of our nation. Those functionless creatures, the hippies, for example, just didn't appear out of a vacuum."

Chapter 6: Mr. Cagney Meets Mr. Roberts

"Made it ma! Top of the world!" – Cagney's character in *White Heat*

The string of failed pictures left Cagney's own production company in deep debt, so Cagney made a deal to return to Warner Bros. with his company coming in as part of the deal, and the first picture made under the new agreement was *White Heat* in 1949. Unlike his previous characters, many of whom seemed to have a good reason for killing, Cagney's character (Cody Jarrett) was the mentally ill son of a man who had died in an insane asylum. He also had serious mother issues, even sitting in his elderly mother's lap at times. Not surprisingly, he dies a dramatic death at the end, killed in a massive explosion after gunning down some of his own men and shouting one of the most famous final quotes in a movie, "Made it ma! Top of the world!".

Cagney in *White Heat*

The studio called the movie the story of a "homicidal paranoiac with a mother fixation", and Cagney didn't disappoint. His performance in *White Heat* is considered one of his best, and in one of the most famous scenes, he did an impromptu take in the scene where Jarrett learns of the death of his mother that fellow actors didn't know was coming. His portrayal was so realistic and terrifying that it frightened some of his fellow cast members. The critics and the public both loved *White Heat*, but Cagney wasn't as happy with it. In spite of being America's "Yankee Doodle Dandy," he was still struggling against his gangster archetype, and by this time he was also the father of young children. As such, he told one reporter, "It's what the people want me to do. Someday, though, I'd like to make another movie that kids could go and see."

Cagney and Virginia Mayo in *White Heat*

In light of these feelings, it's no surprise that he jumped at the chance to star in another musical, this time opposite one of his favorite leading ladies, Doris Day. The musical was called *The West Point Story*, and Cagney said of it in his autobiography, "There was some critical thinking and hollering about the key plot line: the assignment of a Broadway musical director to actually live the life of a West Point cadet for some weeks. Such a thing just couldn't happen, some critics said. Only it did. Both Westbrook Pedlar and George M. Cohan did just that at various times."

However, Cagney's next film, *Kiss Tomorrow Goodbye*, brought him back to portraying a gangster, mostly because Cagney Productions, which had been purchased by Warner Bros., was deeply in debt. Having been raised to always pay his own bills, Cagney would not declare bankruptcy, and he insisted on making and marketing *Kiss Tomorrow Goodbye* to make money. Though the critics did not care for it, the public did, and they bought enough tickets to pay off Cagney's creditors. The company made just one more film, *A Lion is in the Streets*, and then shut down.

Cagney particularly enjoyed his next role as Martin "Moe the Gimp" Snyder in the 1955 movie *Love Me or Leave Me*, which he called "that extremely rare thing, the perfect script." Doris Day played his wife, Ruth Etting, in this biographical piece, and since Snyder was Jewish, it allowed Cagney to use the accent he had mastered when he was growing up on the Lower East Side. He also mastered Martin's limp to such an extent that Snyder himself asked Cagney how he did it. Cagney simply replied, "What I did was very simple. I just slapped my foot down as I turned it out while walking. That's all." Critics loved the film, and Cagney was nominated for another

Academy Award. He certainly would've won is the award was chosen by co-star Doris Day, who called Cagney "the most professional actor I've ever known. He was always 'real'. I simply forgot we were making a picture. His eyes would actually fill up when we were working on a tender scene. And you never needed drops to make your eyes shine when Jimmy was on the set."

Doris Day

Cagney in *Love Me Or Leave Me*

Next, Cagney worked with legendary director John Ford on *What Price Glory?*, but Cagney was not crazy about working with the famous director because Ford insisted the film be shot as a regular picture rather than the musical Cagney had signed on to make. Cagney would later refer to Ford having a "slightly sadistic sense of humor," which included allowing him and another actor to be injured in a motorcycle collision on set. The two nearly came to blows, as Cagney later recounted, "I would have kicked his brains out. He was so goddamned mean to everybody. He was truly a nasty old man." On another occasion, as Ford yelled at him, Cagney got back in his face, "When I started this picture, you said that we would tangle asses before this was over. I'm ready now – are you?" After that, Ford finally backed down.

John Ford

Given his dislike of Ford, it is somewhat surprising that Cagney agreed to make his next picture, *Mister Roberts*, with him, but Cagney wanted to work with his friend Spencer Tracy, who was supposed to play opposite him in the film. It was only after he had agreed to make the movie that Tracy was replaced by Henry Fonda, but he enjoyed working with Jack Lemmon, whom he described as "a nice young fella". In his autobiography, Cagney recalled the following story:

> "I realized that upcoming was a scene with Jack, as Ensign Pulver, that I'd found so funny in the reading that I realized it would be marvelously so in the playing. The difficulty was that it was so funny I had serious doubts about my ability to play it with a straight face. I talked it over with Jack. I said, 'We've got some work ahead of us. You and I'll have to get together and rehearse that scene again and again and again until I don't think it's funny anymore.' He agreed because he had the same feeling about the scene. So we got together and did it and did it and did it. But every time I came to the payoff line in the scene, 'Fourteen months, sir,' I just couldn't keep a straight face. Finally, with enough rehearsal we thought we had it licked. We came to filming time.

"….This is one hell of a funny little scene: the commanding officer of a naval vessel finally meeting an ensign who had been ducking him during their voyage for well over a year. I used to collapse every time Jack said 'Fourteen months, sir,' but when we filmed it, I was able to hang on just barely. What you see in the film is the top of Mount Everest for us after our rigorous rehearsals. It still kills me every time I think about it."

Cagney wasn't the only one who thought the scene (and the entire film) was hilarious. The movie received three Oscar nominations, including one for Best Supporting Actor for that "nice young fella," Lemmon.

Chapter 7: The Gangster Goes Straight

"The last curtain call is usually the best. When it's time to go, you should go." – James Cagney

Following the completion of *Mister Roberts*, Cagney bought a new 120 acre farm in Dutchess County, New York. He named it Verney farm and poured tremendous effort into making it a working business, and over time, he bought more of the surrounding property, growing the farm to 750 acres. His agricultural efforts earned him an honorary degree from Rollins College in Florida, but rather than just accept the award, he insisted on submitting a paper on soil conservation to justify receiving his degree.

One feature that all Cagney's farms had in common were their horses. When Cagney was born in 1899, horses were still the primary mode of transportation in America, and as a city boy, his family obviously owned no horses, but he always jumped at the chance to get to sit on the back of the nag that pulled the milk truck. As an adult, he enjoyed buying, breeding, raising, training, and talking about horses, and Giant Morgans, of the big feet, were his favorite breed.

By this time, Cagney was 56 years old but still going strong both physically and mentally. He made his next movie, *Tribute to a Bad Man*, for MGM. This film, one of his few Westerns, had actually been written for Spencer Tracy, but Tracy was unable to complete filming due to health issues, so Cagney took over. *Tribute to a Bad Man* did well at the box office, leading MGM to cast Cagney opposite Barbara Stanwyck in *These Wilder Years*. Cagney liked Stanwyck from their time together in vaudeville years earlier, and in an off-screen scene reminiscent of something out of the movies, the two old stars entertained their younger cast members with song-and-dance numbers from their youth.

Stanwyck

Unlike many of his counterparts, Cagney had no interest in appearing on television, but in 1956, he agreed to appear in *Soldiers From the War Returning* as a favor to his old friend, Robert Montgomery. Montgomery had his own series and needed a powerful performance to open the new season with, but when reporters cornered him with questions about future television appearances, Cagney made his position clear: "I do enough work in movies. This is a high-tension business. I have tremendous admiration for the people who go through this sort of thing every week, but it's not for me."

Having had success with several other biographical films, Cagney portrayed famous actor Lon Cheney in *Man of 1000 Faces*, and the critics ate his performance up, with one reporter calling it one of the best performances of his career. It also did well at the box office, earning a good return for its production company, Universal Studios.

During this era, it was common for well-seasoned actors to try their hand at directing, so in

1957, Cagney made his first and only venture behind the camera to shoot *Shortcut to Hell*. A remake of 1941's *This Gun For Hire*, the movie was based on the novel *A Gun For Sale* by Graham Greene. At first, Cagney believed that he would be a very effective director; when he made the movie for his friend, producer A.C. Lyles, he did it as a favor, and for his own enjoyment, refusing to be paid. This appealed to Lyles, since he had very little money invested in the picture, which Cagney was able to shoot in just 20 days. He would later say that 20 days as a director was plenty for him, remarking, "We shot it in twenty days, and that was long enough for me. I find directing a bore, I have no desire to tell other people their business".

Over the next few years, Cagney made a few other movies, and by this time, he had enough money and prestige to be picky about what he wanted to do, so these roles were some of his best. He was happy to play the role of the labor leader in *Never Steal Anything Small*. In this musical, one of the last he would ever make, he enjoyed a hilarious song and dance number with Cara Williams, who portrayed his girlfriend in the film.

After *Never Steal Anything Small*, Cagney took off and flew to Ireland, where he filmed *Shake Hands with the Devil* with the well-known English director Michael Anderson. Cagney's reasoning for playing an Irish Republican army officer was more personal than professional; for one thing, Cagney felt he could use some of his off time in Ireland to trace his family's roots. Also, he was increasingly concerned about the level of violence spreading in the country, and he was attracted to *Shake Hands with the Devil*'s anti-violence message. The critics loved the film, and many considered it one of the best performances of his final years of acting.

In 1960, Cagney brought his production company out of mothballs to produce *The Gallant Hours*, and critics loved his portrayal of Adm. William F "Bull" Halsey, who led the Guadalcanal campaign in the Pacific. Though the film was set during World War II, it was not a classic war movie but more of a psychological thriller, with the focus being on the impact of command on Halsey himself. Critics loved the movie, with one reporter saying, "It is Mr. Cagney's performance, controlled to the last detail, that gives life and strong, heroic stature to the principal figure in the film. There is no braggadocio in it, no straining for bold or sharp effects. It is one of the quietest, most reflective, subtlest jobs that Mr. Cagney has ever done."

Cagney's final career film prior to retirement was the comedy *One, Two, Three*. Director Billie Wilder insisted that he was the only one to play an ambitious, overworked Coca-Cola executive trying to establish a presence in West Berlin. While the film itself was funny, Cagney's experience in making it was nothing to laugh about. He was the consummate professional and accustomed to working with tight scripts and well-rehearsed actors, so when one scene took 50 takes to get right, he was at his wit's end. He also complained about one of his co-stars, "I never had the slightest difficulty with a fellow actor. Not until *One, Two, Three*. In that picture, Horst Buchholz tried all sorts of scene-stealing didoes. I came close to knocking him on his ass." For the first time in his long career, he actually considered walking out on the movie, but he stuck it out and completed the film. During his time on set, he also made a visit to the Dachau concentration camp on one of his days off, which made a lasting impact on his life.

Cagney retired after returning to America, and unlike many men who have enjoyed fame and success, Cagney relished retirement. He spent most of his time on his farms, with occasional trips to both coasts to go sailing. Though he often struggled with seasickness, Cagney was an avid sailor, and he kept seaworthy craft on both the West and East Coast so he could sail whenever he got the chance.

Cagney also took up painting during his retirement, and to improve, he took instructions from the famous Sergei Bongart, who later asserted Cagney was so talented he could have been a professional artist had he started younger. He even proudly displayed two of Cagney's works in his own home, but Cagney always admitted he was nothing more than an amateur and refused to sell any of his work. The only exception was one painting, which he sold to Johnny Carson for charity.

When not painting, sailing or farming, Jimmy and Billie Cagney spent time in New York, where they enjoyed hosting parties at a little place called the Silver Horn restaurant. Over time, they became close friends with the owner, Marge Zimmerman, and later, when Cagney's health began to fail because of diabetes, Zimmerman became a valued friend and caretaker for the couple. She took it upon herself to refine recipes and cook dishes that helped Cagney manage both his diabetes and his cholesterol, which was also out of control. Under her careful care, Cagney lost weight and became healthier than he had been in years.

In 1974, Cagney made a rare public appearance to accept an American Film Institute Lifetime Achievement Award. Charlton Heston hosted the event, Frank Sinatra introduced Cagney, and so many stars showed up for the ceremony that one reporter quipped that if a bomb should go off in the building, the movie industry in America would be over. For his part, Cagney had fun at the ceremony, teasing impressionist Frank Gorshin by saying, "Oh, Frankie, just in passing, I never said 'MMMMmmmm, you dirty rat!' What I actually did say was 'Judy, Judy, Judy!'". Cagney's joke was a reference to another popular misquote of him, that one being attributed to Cary Grant.

A few years later, in 1977, Cagney had a small stroke, and though he recovered, he was no longer able to enjoy many of the physical sports that he had in the past, including dancing, which he had done to keep fit, and horseback riding, which he enjoyed for the thrill. He also became depressed and gave up painting. Zimmerman and Billie both devoted all their efforts to caring for and encouraging him, with the former becoming their full-time companion, and together, the two women persuaded Cagney to come out of retirement for one role, the small but critical part of New York Police Commissioner Rhinelander Waldo in the film version of the novel *Ragtime*.

Ironically, this American classic was shot in London, and since he never liked flying, Cagney traveled to England on a cruise, the *QEII*. When he arrived at Southampton, the cruise line officials were shocked to find their honored guest and most important passenger mauled by hundreds of fans. While Cagney's performance in *Ragtime* was strong, his co-stars had some problems; seasoned but younger actors missed their cues and forgot their lines in the face of the legend. One of them, Howard E. Rollins, Jr., recalled, "I was frightened to meet Mr. Cagney. I asked him how to die in front of the camera. He said 'Just die!' It worked. Who would know more about dying than him?" Rollins' reference to Cagney's many death scenes as a gangster aside, Cagney enjoyed playing the part, and in spite of increasing back pain, he remained on set after he was done filming to help the younger actors learn their lines.

In spite of his failing health, Cagney remained a star right up until the end of his life. When he and Pat O'Brien showed up at the Queen Mother's birthday performance at the London Palladium, the monarch rose to her feet at their entrance, the only time she stood up during the entire performance. A few years later, Cagney, now wheelchair-bound, appeared on television in *Terrible Joe Moran*, the story of an aging retired boxer. In flashback scenes, the director was able to make use of some of Cagney's early boxing footage in 1932's *Winner Take All*.

Terrible Joe Moran would be his final appearance, because Cagney died two years later on Easter Sunday morning of 1986 at his Dutchess County farm. His funeral mass was held at St. Frances de Sales Roman Catholic Church, with sitting president and old friend Ronald Reagan delivering the eulogy. Afterward, his body was buried at Hawthorne, New York's Cemetery of the Gate of Heaven.

Fittingly, Cagney wrote his own eulogy via the end of his autobiography, and as was his habit, he was more interested in talking about others than himself; in this case, he told his fans, "Thanks, too, for buying the ticket that gave me this lovely and deeply loved farm whence these words come. And, above all, the very numbers of those tickets prompt me to say: grateful thanks for giving a song and dance man across the years all those heartwarming encores."

Bibliography

Bergman, Andrew. James Cagney : The Pictorial Treasury of Film Stars (1974)

Cagney, James. Cagney by Cagney (2010)

Clinch, Minty. James Cagney (1982)

Federal Bureau of Investigations. James Cagney - The FBI Files (2012)

McCabe, John. Cagney (2013)

Schickel, Richard. James Cagney, A Life In Film (Movie Greats) (2012)

James Cagney: Paperback Book (Applause Legends) (2000)

Warren, Doug. James Cagney: The Authorized Biography (1983)

Spencer Tracy

Chapter 1: Hellion

"I never would have gone back to school if there had been any other way of learning to read the subtitles in the movies." – Spencer Tracy

When Spencer Tracy was born, his father John had turned himself into a wealthy self-made man who came from a devoutly Catholic family and whose ancestors had come to America from Ireland during the Great Potato Famine. His father and grandfather had made their money working for the expanding American railroad system in Wisconsin, doing well enough to send John all his siblings to St. Mary's High School. John went on to the University of Notre Dame, and two of his three sisters became nuns.

Meanwhile, Caroline Tracy's background could not have been more different from her future husband's. Her family had been in America since colonial times, they had made their money in milling grain, and they were pillars of the First Presbyterian Church. Caroline was a great (and pampered) beauty, and her father was not about to let her marry any Irish Catholic upstart. At the same time, John Tracy's father was not any happier about his son marrying outside his faith. Together, the two fathers agreed that the young couple must not see each other anymore, and to this end, Tracy, Sr. placed both John and his brother Will under a strict 10 o'clock curfew.

To get around this predicament, John's sister Jenny intervened on behalf of the young lovers. She would later recall, "I would sit up on the stairs or at the upstairs window and wait for those two to come home. I would sneak down and open the door so that they would be able to come in the house, and God knows sometimes it was two or three o'clock in the morning and I would have sat there all night. My nerves were ruined when I was a very young girl." Thankfully, Jenny's nerves were not wasted; on August 29, 1894, John and Carrie were wed in her father's home by a Catholic priest. A few days later, the newlyweds packed their belongings and move to LaSalle, where John had taken a job with a new bank.

Unfortunately, John's problems with alcohol, which Carrie must have thought would eventually go away as he got older, cost him his job and drove the young couple back to Freeport within a year. The young couple subsequently moved in with John's family, and it was there that their first son, Carroll Tracy, was born on June 15, 1896. Not long after Carroll's birth, Carrie and John left the crowded Tracy house and moved in with her parents, since their larger home had a staff on hand to see to the needs of both mother and baby. All the while, the couple still wanted a home of their own and finally found one in early 1899 in Merrill Park, a pleasant neighborhood in Milwaukee.

It was in this house that their next child, also a boy, would be born on April 5, 1900. Before Spencer was born, Carrie had wanted a girl and had not even thought of a name for a boy. When Jenny Tracy asked Carrie what the boy would be named, Carrie replied, "I'm so disappointed that he's a boy. He was supposed to be Daisy after my good friend Daisy Spencer." That gave

Jenny the idea of having the boy named Spencer. Once that was settled, Jenny also helped the parents come up with Spencer's middle name while carrying her 17 day old nephew to the St. Rose Catholic Church for the baptism. They decided to honor their sister Bonnie by giving little Spencer the middle name of Bonaventure, thus naming him after a saint.

The two may have had some reason to rethink their decision when the priest, learning that the child he was baptizing would be named Spencer Bonaventure, asked sincerely if the baby was a boy of girl. But they ran into even more trouble when Carrie learned that her newborn son had been saddled with the name of a saint so obscure that she had never heard of him. Instead, she insisted that the baby's birth certificate read "Spencer Bernard Tracy" and thus, at the age of less than three weeks, little Spencer Tracy had experienced his first brush with the incompatibility between who he was and who others thought he should be.

This discrepancy would only become more pronounced as the boy grew older. For instance, Carroll was a quiet and studious boy, and since he was four years older than Spencer, Carrie and John assumed this was how well-bred little boys behaved. However, Spencer was the polar opposite of his brother, preferring to run and tussle and throw things rather than playing quietly. This led his Aunt Emma to once moan, "He's a throwback." Even mothers of other rambunctious little boys noticed Spencer's hyperactivity, and one woman from the neighborhood later remembered, "He was in dresses when I first saw him. He was bubbling with life. I don't believe he ever sat still. I can't remember him sitting down in a chair or reading a book. His brother Carroll … liked to stay inside and listen to the talk of his elders …but Spence was always outside with the boys."

By that time, the family had moved again, this time to a roomy home in the neighborhood of Bay View, just outside of Milwaukee. John Tracy left this home faithfully every Sunday morning and walked with his two young sons to Catholic mass at Immaculate Conception, but church was one of the few places where little Spencer did not get into trouble. The activity of singing, standing, sitting, kneeling, then standing or kneeling again kept him busy, and the beauty and pageantry of the service kept his mind fixed on the altar. Their mutual faith would prove to be a bond between father and son that would last a lifetime, but it was a different case with Spencer's mother. Rejecting her husband's "papist" beliefs, Carrie Tracy was more interested in her son's education, so she enrolled him in the still-new class called "kindergarten" when he was 5 years old. Perhaps not surprisingly, little Spencer did not find his classes on Trowbridge Street as interesting as the mass at church, and he would later recall:

> "I began to show signs of wanderlust at seven. I wandered completely out of the neighborhood and struck up an acquaintance with two delightful companions, Mousie and Rattie. Their father owned a saloon in a very hard-boiled neighborhood. It was a lot more fun playing with them than in was at school. Being sentimentally Irish, that common-enough episode in a kid's life was to have a

lasting effect on my future. For the first time I saw my mother cry over me. I resolved in an immature way never to make her cry again. I don't mean to initiate that I became a model boy. I didn't."

During Spencer's early childhood, his family would move two more times, each time living even closer to school just so Carrie could keep a better eye on Spencer and try to make sure he got there and back each day without getting into trouble. Even then, however, Spencer got along better with rougher boys than those in his comfortable neighborhood. He would often bring these young ruffians home with him, where his mother would fill them up with cheese sandwiches. Carrie would later remember these times somewhat fondly, explaining to one reporter:

> "I can honestly say that back of every one of Spencer's exploits was something fine like sympathy, generosity, affection, pride, or ambition. There was not a mean bone through in him. True, he broke windows with the same alarming and expensive regularity boys do today. And he would get embroiled in fights to help a friend, fights, incidentally, from which Carroll invariably would have to rescue him because he was so thin and sickly a child until he was 14 that he could never finish on his own what he was quick to start or join in…even though it meant added work for me and bigger bills for John to pay at the stores, neither of us could find it in our hearts to punish or discourage him from such a fine philosophy."

Unfortunately, the rest of Carrie's side of the family was not so tolerant. Spencer and Carroll spent summers back in Freemont with both sets of their grandparents, and while Spencer's parents were more tolerant of the boy's shenanigans, his grandparents tended to try to find activities for Spencer that got him out of the house and out from under their feet. This often meant giving the boy a nickel and sending him to see a silent picture show. It was here, in the darkened theaters, that Spencer first discovered the joy of being lost in a story.

Chapter 2: Young Man About Town

"It helped me develop memory for lines that has been a godsend since I started stage work; it gave me something of a stage presence; and it helped get rid of my awkwardness. Also, I gradually developed the ability to speak extemporaneously". – Spencer Tracy, explaining the debate club's influence on his acting career.

When Spencer was about 9 years old, his parents became sufficiently concerned about his behavior to make a major change in his education. They removed him from the local public school and enrolled him in St. John's Cathedral School, trusting the Dominican Sisters who ran the school to mold and shape their wayward son into a more disciplined young man. Surprisingly, Spencer actually thrived at the rigorous Catholic school. For one thing, serving as an altar boy gave him his first outlet for public performance; while he was sincerely devout, he also enjoyed the experience of putting on the "costume" of robe and surplice, carrying the props of incense and candles, and reciting the lines of the mass in response to the intoning priest. During this period, life at home also improved, in no small part due to the fact that John finally came to terms with his alcoholism and completely gave up drinking. Unable to socialize at the local bar anymore, he stayed home in the evenings and the family had friends over instead. In the days before radio or television, talented children were often called upon to perform for adults before going upstairs to bed, and Spencer thrived during this time by learning magic tricks and small vaudeville style acts to perform for company. He also put on shows in the family's basement, charging his friends one or two pins to attend a performance.

Spencer continued to perform when given a chance, but he also turned his mind to earning money. He got his first job as a lamplighter in 1912, and he continued to work at random odd jobs even when his family moved to a wealthy neighborhood in Milwaukee in 1916. Now that he seemed more settled and responsible, his parents felt secure enough about his future to remove him from the sisters' charge and enroll him in Wauwatosa High, a local public school. However, this proved to be a disaster, and Spencer soon flunked out. He later explained his failure, "I might have enjoyed school if I had been doing the thing I wanted to do. My trouble was not having a definite ambition or goal on which to concentrate. I wanted to be doing something that would hold my interest, but I had no idea what it would be."

Needless to say, Spencer was soon sent back to Catholic school, first St. John's, and when the family moved to Kansas City, Spencer was sent to Rockhurst Academy, a Jesuit school that soon straightened him out. He explained, "I remember Rockhurst as a big building and I remember pursuing to the best of my abilities the study of Latin and geometry. I also remember that there were some boys at Rockhurst and in Kansas City who were mighty good fighters." Unfortunately, John Tracy's job played out in 1917, so the family returned to Milwaukee and Spencer was enrolled in the exclusive Jesuit school Marquette Academy. Now mature enough to balance his studies and other pursuits, Spencer did well in school, and he also established an amateur drama company with fellow future actor Bill O'Brien. Meanwhile, he also remembered feeling like he may have found his first true brush with a potential vocation, later saying, "The influence is strong, very strong, intoxicating. The priest are all such superior men---heroes. You want to be like them---we all did. Every guy in the school probably thought some more or less about trying for the cloth. You lie in dark and see yourself as Monsignor Tracy, Cardinal Tracy, Bishop Tracy, Archbishop---I'm getting goose flesh!

Once the United States entered World War I, however, Spencer began looking forward to new and more distant horizons. He explained, "Well, it was wartime. 1917. And the uniform seemed more appropriate than the habit. Or more glamorous. Everybody was joining up. So we did, too. Caroll and Pat and I went into the Navy. And I guess that's where Cardinal Tracy started turning into Admiral Tracy." The Pat he was referring to was his good friend and fellow actor Pat O'Brien, who was at Marquette Academy with Tracy.

Pat O'Brien with Anne Jeffreys in *Riffraff* (1947)

Eventually, Spencer, who was admittedly "itching for a chance to go and see some excitement", decided to lie about his age and enlist. Tracy recalled that he "knew very well where there was a U.S. Marines recruiting station, for I'd seen it lots of times before", so one day he walked into the office and told the man at the desk, "I want to join the Marines." However, he found himself unable to lie about his age when the time came, so he ultimately waited for the four months it would take him to turn 18. By the time this happened, recruitment of soldiers was at a fevered pitch, and Pat O'Brien later remembered, "The bands played, the drill parades started, the Liberty Bond drives were on, and Spence and myself and some of the others left school one afternoon and went downtown to the enlistment headquarters of the Navy." While O'Brien ended up rethinking his enlistment, Spencer signed up, and though the war ended before he saw any fighting, Tracy would always praise the effect basic training had on his life: "The training, the discipline, and the healthy life not only did me good physically but mentally as well. I realized for the first time that a man must make his own way in life, that he must assume certain responsibilities, and that a man can't receive too much education, because the Navy demand alert minds."

Tracy in 1919

Tracy was discharged from the Navy on February 19, 1919, with a rank of seaman first class, after which he joined the rest of the released veterans in looking for work. Thanks to his father's connections, he soon secured a job as a truck driver, but his father had bigger dreams for him and wanted him to attend college. This required Tracy to give up the freedom of the open road and return to high school. He enrolled in Northwestern Military and Naval College and stayed there just long enough to gather the credits needed to graduate and get into college. Thanks to his father's hard work to track down every possible academic credit Spencer might have, and to ferret out "war credits" granted to high school students who had left school to enter the military, Spencer Tracy finally graduated from high school and entered Ripon College in February 1921. He was about to turn 21, and he later recounted how he had reached this point in life, "Back there in Milwaukee, I don't remember ever seeing an actor and I certainly never thought about it when I was in the Navy. In fact, when I was in the Navy I thought I wanted to be a sailor. And maybe if the family hadn't been so dead set on me finishing high school, I would've stayed in the Navy, but when I got out, I did go back to high school and then---I don't know---automatically, I suppose, college."

At first, Tracy planned to focus his attention on the sciences with an eye to entering medical school, but his public speaking classes changed all that. He excelled in this area, leading one of his professors to later say, "I remember very vividly the occasions when we were working on problems of impression and his speeches would actually leave the class in tears. His dramatic instinct was shown in his surpassing ability in telling a story. There was always the proper sequence of events, the gradual rise to a climax, the carefully-chosen ending." Public speaking led naturally to acting, and Tracy landed the lead in the college's production of *The Truth*. Clark Graham, who directed the piece, remembered Tracy having "a clipped firmness of expression indicating poise, self-control, and confidence." The play was a huge success thanks to Tracy, whose stage presence in one tense scene was so powerful that it frightened even his leading lady. According to a review in the college newspaper, "Mr. Tracy proved himself a consistent and unusually strong actor in his most difficult straight part. His steadiness, his reserve strength and suppressed emotion were a pleasant surprise to all who heard him as [Tom] Warder." As the curtain rang down that opening night, John Tracy's hopes for his son graduating college died and Spencer Tracy's plan to act was born.

When he was passed over for the lead in the school's next play, Spencer teamed up with a friend to form their own theatrical troupe. They staged *The Valiant*, with Tracy playing a convicted murderer determined to protect his kid sister from knowing who he really was. He shocked the audience by reciting the details of a battle in which the brother supposedly died heroically, only to then turn on a dime and recall the poetry the two had shared as children. The reviews were gushing, with one journalist commenting that Tracy played his role "in such a masterful way that the audience felt with him the emotions he portrayed."

After that, the crew, now informally calling themselves "The Campus Players", took their show on the road and performed *The Valiant* for local campus audiences. Tracy later told a reporter what happened next:

> "I must have been a real pain in the ass arguing all the time with everybody because one of the professors there finally stopped me and sucked me into being on the debating team. From there I suppose it was only a short hop to the drama club. Then, well, you know how it is. Every guy starts to tell you how good you are and you start to believe it. Even so, nothing would've happened probably if our debating

team hadn't been invited to debate up at Bowdoin College in Maine, and on the way we had to stop off in New York for a day. And I went over to the American Academy of Dramatic Art---I'd seen about it somewhere---and auditioned for Franklin Sargent. They must've been pretty short of men because he offered me a scholarship. When I got out of college, I went to New York and took him up on it. Pat was there, too. Pat O'Brien. We'd known each other as kids. We had a room together somewhere in the West Fifties. We were in the same class. Neither one of us very impressive. I don't know why. We sure tried."

Tracy began classes with the American Academy of Dramatic Art in April 1922, and much to his own surprise and pleasure, he was allowed to join the senior class there and thus participate in the local stock company. His first play, *The Wedding Guest*, was well-received when it opened in October 1922, and just three months later, Tracy found himself on Broadway for the first time, playing a silent robot in the show *R.U.R.* A few months later, in March 1923, he graduated from AADA and launched his career as a "real actor." He would later praise the academy for shaping his career, saying, "I shall always be grateful to the American Academy of Dramatic Arts for what I was taught there---the value of sincerity and simplicity, unembellished and un-intellectualized."

Chapter 3: The Stage

"There were times when my pants were so thin, I could sit on a dime and know if it was heads or tails."

Unfortunately for Tracy, the real world of acting was not as easy to break into as college shows had been. After graduating, he moved to White Plains, New York and joined a local acting company there called the Wood Players, but much to his surprise and consternation, he was not immediately given leads in every play. Instead, he was given small roles that the director felt were more suitable to his experience (or lack thereof). Quickly becoming disappointed with the direction his career was taking, Tracy sought comfort in the arms of Louise Treadwell, a fellow actress and member of the Wood Players. The two would continue dating off and on until they were married on September 10, 1923.

Louise and Spencer Tracy

During this time, Tracy moved to Cincinnati, but he quickly found he had the same problem there that had plagued him in New York: there were plenty of aspiring actors and few good parts. Right after he and Louise married, he landed a small role on Broadway in *A Royal Fandango*, appearing with Ethel Barrymore, the first star he had ever worked with, but the play closed after only 25 performances. Although this was probably due more to the stars' failures than Tracy's, he later admitted that his ego "took an awful beating", and he almost quit acting altogether.

It was perhaps during this trying time that Tracy cheated on his wife for the first time, but regardless of when it first occurred, infidelity would continue to plague their marriage for as long as he lived. Now a married man with a baby on the way, Tracy moved his young family to Winnipeg in January 1924, where he landed his first professional leading role. When that gig ended almost as soon as it began, Tracy returned to America and went to work for William H Wright, a well-known stock manager who was putting together a new production starring a well-known actress named Selena Royle. Tracy and Royle had good chemistry, and after the play proved a success, Tracy's performance also caught the attention of another Broadway producer who offered him the lead in *The Sheepman*. Ultimately, the play opened poorly in Connecticut and closed without ever reaching Broadway.

Selena Royle

When Spencer's son John, was born in June 1924, he considered settling down and trying to be a good father, but Louise knew the pressure her husband was under and therefore was reluctant to share with him the news that John was deaf. She first hid her suspicions, and then the doctor's confirmation, until after the baby's first birthday, but when Tracy noticed that his son was not learning to talk like other children his age, Louise had to share her secret with her husband. Spencer was inconsolable, believing that his son's deafness was somehow a punishment for his own adultery, but instead of trying to make up for his perceived wrong by showering the boy with extra attention, Tracy withdrew from his family and spent more time away from home. Things did not improve even when their second child, a girl they named after Louise's mother, was born in July 1932. It is indicative of his mixed feelings about the children that Tracy, a devoted if not devout Catholic, allowed them to be raised Episcopalians by their mother instead of in his own faith.

Returning to what he knew, Tracy made a few more plays with local stock companies until 1926, when George M. Cohan offered Tracy a role in a play called *Yellow*. By this time, Tracy had made up his mind that if he failed one more time as an actor, he would leave the stage altogether and get a "real job." Fortunately for both Tracy and the world, *Yellow* was a rousing success; upon opening on September 21, it was well-received and ran for over 130 performances. This was the beginning of a long and profitable friendship between Tracy and Cohan, and Tracy would later claim, "I'd have quit the stage completely if it hadn't been for George M. Cohan." For his own part, Cohan called Tracy "the best goddamned actor I've ever seen!"

Cohan

Cohan was so pleased with Tracy's performance in *Yellow* that he had another part written especially for Tracy in his next play, *The Baby Cyclone*. When that play opened on Broadway in September 1927, it became Tracy's first big hit. Next came *Whispering Friends*, and in 1928, Tracy took on a role in *Conflict* after the other star, Clark Gable, had to drop out.

Tracy continued to give solid performances on stage, which led to him landing the lead in *Dread*, written by Owen Davis, the famous Pulitzer Prize winning dramatist. *Dread* might very well have been Tracy's big break had it not opened on October 28, 1929, the day before Wall Street collapsed and the Great Depression began.

Concerned about his ability to find work in such a bad economy, Tracy considered returning home to Milwaukee and his family, but before he could he was contacted in early 1930 about a lead in a play called *The Last Mile*. This time, he would play a serial killer waiting on death row for execution. The producer who hired him, Herman Shimla, later said that he chose Tracy because "beneath the surface, there was a man of passion, violence, sensitivity and desperation: no ordinary man, and just the man for the part." His choice was a good one, and when *The Last Mile* opened in February, Tracy was given a standing ovation that lasted for 14 curtain calls. The play went on to run for more than 280 performances.

Around this time, directors were coming from Hollywood to scout actors for motion pictures. It was the beginning of a new era, with sound pictures replacing silent films. Tracy got small parts in two shorts called *Taxi Talks* and *The Hard Guy*, but he initially had little interest in making movies. Though he "had no ambition in that direction and...was perfectly happy on the stage", when famous director John Ford approached Tracy and offered him a lead role in his next film, Tracy agreed to do a screen test. Ford's company, Fox Film Corporation, was not entirely pleased with Tracy's looks and stage presence, but fortunately, Ford had enough clout in Hollywood to get his way. Ford cast Tracy in *Up the River*, which premiered in 1930 and also starred Humphrey Bogart, and as soon as they saw Tracy's work, the Fox executives changed their minds about Tracy and offered him a contract. Needing the money to help care for his wife and deaf son, who had also contracted polio by now, Tracy signed the contract and thus moved his family to the West Coast.

John Ford

Chapter 4: Con Man, Policeman, Captain, Priest

"I've never known what acting is. Who can honestly say what it is? ... I wonder what actors are supposed to be, if not themselves ... I've finally narrowed it down to where, when I begin a part, I say to myself, this is Spencer Tracy as a judge, or this is Spencer Tracy as a priest or as a lawyer, and let it go at that. Look, the only thing an actor has to offer a director and finally an audience is his instinct. That's all." – Spencer Tracy

As Spencer Tracy and his family headed to California, the Fox Company was in its infancy and committed to growing as many stars as it could from its new finds. With that in mind, they supported Tracy all the way, giving him a significant role in the film *Quick Millions* in 1931 and arranging as many opportunities as possible for him to meet with the press. Even after *Quick Millions* did not do well, Fox still believed in Tracy and his talent and continued to give him roles in one movie after another. Nevertheless, none of these films did well, due more to the poor quality of the scripts and the filming than Tracy's acting ability, but it still looked like the actor might have to leave Hollywood and go back east to stage work.

With his career seemingly on the ropes, Tracy's seventh movie, *Disorderly Conduct*, became his most profitable movie since *Up the River*, but despite the popularity of his first and seventh full-length films, most of the public had not yet heard of Spencer Tracy. Dissatisfied with the quality of the roles he was being offered, Tracy threatened to leave Fox when his contract ran out in 1932, but the company still believed in him and wanted to recoup some of their investment. They offered to raise his salary to $1500 per week, but in spite of the money they were paying him, Fox continued to cast Tracy in what could most kindly be described as "B movies". He appeared in *Me and My Gal* in 1932 and later, while on loan to Warner Bros., in *20,000 Years in Sing Sing* with Bette Davis.

Spencer Tracy in *Disorderly Conduct*

Tracy finally received the professional attention he was craving when he starred as Tom Garner in *The Power and the Glory* in 1932. Written by Preston Sturges, *The Power and the Glory* tells the story of Garner's rise to power and wealth during the golden days of the railroad industry. Critics loved the film, with one effusing that "this sterling performer has finally been given an opportunity to show an ability that has been boxed in by gangster roles ... [the film] has introduced Mr. Tracy as one of the screen's best performers". Another critic added, "No more convincing performance has been given on the screen than Spencer Tracy's impersonation of Tom Garner." Tracy never considered himself a good-looking man, once commenting that his face was "as plain as a barn door" and wondering why people would "pay thirty-five cents to look at it", but he became more appealing in the movie *Shanghai Madness* in 1933.

Tracy seemed to be on the verge of joining the ranks of premiere Hollywood leading men, but when his next two movies failed to gain any serious attention, Tracy increasingly turned to the bottle for comfort. After a two week binge held up the filming of *Marie Galante* in 1934, Fox pulled him from acting and had him hospitalized for detox and treated for alcoholism. When Tracy was well enough to go to trial, they also sued him for the $125,000 they lost due to delays in filming. Needless to say, Tracy was not pleased at having to pay up, and he would only remain with Fox for two more pictures.

Tracy and Loretta Young in *Man's Castle* (1933)

Chapter 5: Becoming a Star

"It is up to us to give ourselves recognition. If we wait for it to come from others, we feel resentful when it doesn't, and when it does, we may well reject it." – Spencer Tracy

Upon leaving Fox in April 1935, Tracy went to work at Metro-Goldwyn-Mayer, which was at that time looking for a new leading man. Given his reputation as a drunk who was hard to work with, it might seem surprising that MGM even hired Tracy, but critics loved him and MGM producer Irving G. Thalberg saw something in him that he believed he could make great. He insisted that MGM handle Tracy with kid gloves and went out of his way to cast him opposite of the best actresses of the day. Thus, during the mid-1930s, Tracy played in *Whipsaw* opposite of Myrna Loy and in *Riffraff* opposite of Jean Harlow. Neither of these films were very successful, and they actually had the backward effect of portraying Tracy as a hanger-on being carried by beautiful women.

This perception permanently changed in 1936 when Tracy starred in *Fury*, playing a man who is nearly hung by a lynch mob and then goes on to punish those who mistreated him so badly. This time, Tracy hit the jackpot. Not only was Fury popular with critics, the viewing public also loved it, so much so that Fury went on to make $1.3 million, a princely sum at the time. Tracy's biographer James Curtis explained the effect the movie had on Tracy's career, noting that "audiences who, just a year earlier, had no clear handle on him, were suddenly turning out to see him. It was a transition that was nothing short of miraculous...a willingness on the part of the public to embrace a leading man who was not textbook handsome nor bigger than life."

Just a month after *Fury* was released, Tracy's next movie, *San Francisco*, came out. In that movie, he starred with Clark Gable as a priest trying to help singer Mary Blake (played by Jeanette MacDonald), and even though he only had 17 minutes of screen time in the whole movie, his role was pivotal and powerful. In fact, the role was so powerful that it garnered Tracy his first Oscar nomination for Best Actor. *San Francisco* went on to be the biggest Hollywood moneymaker of 1936, leading biographer Donald Deschner to conclude *Fury* and *San Francisco* were the "two films that changed his career and gave him the status of a major star." Tracy's next picture, the screwball comedy *Libeled Lady*, was also a hit, making it his third in less than a year. Part of Tracy's success may have stemmed from the fact that he was "on the wagon" at the time, and without the complications of alcohol clouding his judgment, Tracy was able to focus more clearly on his roles and give them everything he had. This paid off, especially as he gained a new reputation as a professional actor who could be counted on.

During what is now known as the golden era of Hollywood, it was not uncommon for actors and actresses to film several movies every year, and this was as true for Spencer Tracy as it was anyone else. Even after the successes of 1936 (and no doubt due in part to them), in 1937 he appeared in four feature-length films. The first, entitled *They Gave Him a Gun*, was a box office failure, but his second film, *Captains Courageous*, is still considered a classic today. In the film, Tracy plays the captain of a poor Portuguese fishing boat that picks up the spoiled son of a wealthy tycoon. Ironically, the man who struggled being a father in real life did a remarkable job on screen becoming a father figure to the boy and introducing him to the rough-and-tumble life of 19th century manhood. Though Tracy resented having both his character's foreign accent and curly hair, he was great in the role and won the Oscar for Best Actor in 1937, even though he not there to receive it. As he humorously explained in an interview:

"I knew I was going to lose. Three of the five were Metro: Bob and Bowyer and me. So the studio couldn't very well campaign for one of us or pass the word without getting a million-dollar beef from somebody. They were boxed in. Warners was pushing you the hard; and, of course, Selznick was all out for Freddie. And remember that not only was Selznick the greatest operator in the history of Hollywood, but in this case he had what most people including me thought was the best performance to plunk for. God damn, that Freddie was good. Anyway I don't have to tell you… I may be a long about some things but not about acting. I know I'm pretty good, and in *Captains* I was a little better, maybe Barry. I mean, I'm a good actor, but I'm a son of a bitch if I thought I had an expression in my box to put on my face when they announced the winner, Frederick Mark and sitting there in soup and fish, to top it off. And I sure didn't want to reach for the kind of liquid help I was going to need to get through anything like that not in that particular group. So…It was a situation. The studio was insisting I show there was going to be hell to pay if I didn't. Finally I got an idea. Dr. Dennis you know Howard was not only my doctor, he was my friend. And I went to him and laid it on the line. I told him I couldn't go through with it. So he said, quote 'well, what you want me to do? Pick it up for you and make a speech?' And I said, 'No, Denny, but you know my hernia….' Well what can I tell you? Denny was a friend, and he shot me into the hospital and I didn't have to go to the Academy's god damn banquet. Of course, I did have to have the operation. And you can imagine what I felt like lying there, and all those itchy bandages around my middle, and plenty of pain when the word came through, I'd won it?"

Tracy in Captains Courageous

Fortunately, Tracy wouldn't have to wait long to get another chance to accept an Oscar. Based on his rapport with young Freddie Bartholomew in *Captains Courageous*, Tracy was cast as the famous founder of Boys Town, Father Edward J. Flanagan, in the movie *Boys Town*. The role made him so nervous that he admitted, "I'm so anxious to do a good job as Father Flanagan that it worries me, keeps me awake at night." Ultimately, Tracy did an excellent job and the movie was another box office smash, resulting in yet another Oscar nomination in 1938. When he won it that year, he became one of the only actors to ever receive two Academy Awards for Best Actor in a row. This time, he explained how he got ready for winning the award:

"When I got the one for Boys Town, I got up and made my speech and I don't remember the words exactly but something to the effect that I didn't deserve it, that it belonged to Father Flanagan and that all I'd done was let his light shine through me and so I wanted to thank him for the privilege of impersonating him and accepting the award for him. Something like that. And I sat down. In those days used to go back to your seat after getting it. I guess I must've overdone it a little, because Frank Morgan was sitting right behind me, and he leaned forward and whispered, 'I didn't see you in the picture, Spence, but you sure deserve that statue for the performance you just gave up there!'"

The next day, Tracy sent the statuette itself to Flanagan.

In many ways, Tracy always had a problem reconciling his love for the church and his love for acting, sex and liquor. He once confessed to a friend that he thought he might have missed his true calling, saying, "Every time I play a priest, and I've done my share, Father Flanagan in those two *Boys Town* ones and Father Mullin in *San Francisco* and Father Doing in *The Devil at 4 o'clock* every time I put on the clothes and the collar I feel right, right away. Like they were mine, like I belonged in them, and that feeling of being, what's the word, an intermediary is always very appealing those were always my most comfortable parts...."

Chapter 6: Tracy and Hepburn

"I can get a divorce whenever I want to. But my wife and Kate like things just as they are." – Spencer Tracy

After his experience of filming four films in one year, Tracy understandably decided to take a year off, and he did not return to the big screen again until 1939, when he starred as Henry M. Stanley in *Stanley and Livingstone*. Apparently, his absence only made the hearts of his fan grow fonder, because the survey in October of that year found Tracy to be the most popular movie actor in America.

Though Tracy was very popular with his audience, he was not so well loved within the confines of his own home. After years of conflict going back to the birth of their first son, Spencer and Louise Tracy separated in 1933. Unlike many stars at that time, Tracy was open about his marital problems, and he and Louise both told the press that they had no intention to divorce but would remain separated. For the next year, Tracy had an affair with Loretta Young, whom he had met while filming *Man's Castle*, but in 1935, he broke off his relationship with Young and returned home to Louise and his children. While they would never separate again, they wouldn't live together as man and wife in the traditional sense either. By the early 1940s, Tracy was no longer living at home, instead preferring to stay in various hotels and the beds of various actresses that he met while filming. He is alleged to have had affairs with Joan Crawford in 1937 and Ingrid Bergman in 1941.

Following his year-long break in 1940, Tracy returned to moviemaking with a vengeance, making another four movies in 1940. The first, *I Take this Woman*, did not do well, but *The Northwest Passage*, his first color movie, was very popular. Continuing with this historical theme, Tracy played Thomas Edison in the movie *Edison, The Man*, and though the movie itself was not considered very good, critics continue to be impressed by Tracy's acting. Tracy's fourth movie of 1940, *Boomtown*, starred Clark Gable and Claudette Colbert, as well as Heddy Lamar. The media frenzy leading up to the movie was tremendous, and its opening crowd rivaled that of *Gone With the Wind*.

In the spring of 1941, MGM gave Tracy a new contract that paid him $5000 a week and expressly stated he would not be required to make more than three pictures a year. From this point forward, he would not only be listed as the star of every movie that he appeared in but also almost always have top billing. A few months later, MGM, always happy to make use of a good idea by releasing a sequel to *Boys Town* called *A Man at Boys Town*, but it was something of a box office failure. Next, Tracy tried his hand at playing the title role in *Dr. Jekyll and Mr. Hyde*, and even though he was never crazy about his face, he preferred showing it to the screen naturally rather than being made up in the heavy theatrical makeup that he was forced to wear as Mr. Hyde. Lawrence Olivier once teased him for not liking stage makeup, saying "I admire so much about you, Spence, but nothing more than the fact that you can do it all they are faced." When Olivier asked Tracy if he felt naked without makeup, Tracy replied, "Only when I have to say a lousy line."

In 1941, Tracy began filming *Woman of the Year*, a film that would mark the beginning of one of the most famous off-screen and on-screen love affairs in Hollywood history. As one of Hollywood's most popular actresses at the time, and fresh off the success of *The Philadelphia Story*, Katharine Hepburn was allowed to select the director and co-star of her choice for *Woman of the Year*, and she chose George Stevens as director and Tracy as the leading man. The film featured Hepburn and Tracy as newspaper journalists engaged in a battle of the sexes that evolves into romance. Although the film's title and plot are progressive insofar as Hepburn appears as a career woman, it was less progressive than *The Philadelphia Story*. While that has led some critics to criticize *Woman of the Year* for the gender politics at work, the film's treatment of gender is no different from that of the subsequent films Hepburn appeared in with Tracy. Much of this dynamic is simply due to the image of the short and stout Tracy, whose figure embodied patriarchy.

Regardless of the actual roles the two stars played, Hepburn was determined not to be intimidated by her leading man. Since she was rather tall and knew that Tracy was only a little over 5'10, Hepburn showed up at their meeting wearing some of her highest heeled shoes. The film opened to rave reviews, and one critic summed the situation up: "To begin with, it has Katharine Hepburn and Spencer Tracy in the leading roles. This in itself would be enough to make any film memorable. But when you get Tracy and Hepburn turning in brilliant performances to boot, you've got something to cheer about." Other critics agreed, with one writing, "Her performance is a constant pleasure to watch. Mr. Tracy is an excellent foil for her in this particular instance. His quiet, masculine stubbornness and prosaic outlook on life is in striking contrast to her startling brilliance. They make a fine team, and each complements the other." Another reviewer, James Agee, writing for *Time*, noted, "Actors Hepburn and Tracy have a fine time in Woman of the Year. They take turns playing straight for each other, act one superbly directed love scene, and succeed in turning several batches of cinematic corn into passable moonshine. As a lady columnist, she's just right. As a working reporter, he is practically perfect. For once, striding Katharine Hepburn is properly subdued."

Hepburn in *Woman of the Year*

These comments, and many more, would come to apply to the two in real life as well as in their films. The unmarried Hepburn soon fell in love with Tracy, and he with her. The relationship was surprising on many levels. Tracy was already married, and due to religious beliefs, he was unwilling to receive a divorce. And while he was only 7 years older than Hepburn, his soft features and wrinkled face made him appear much older than her as well. It's somewhat surprising that Hepburn would embark on another relationship with an older man after previous relationships with older men didn't turn out well, but even though they never married, Tracy and Hepburn would remain committed to each other with unwavering mutual devotion, not only off the set but in films as well. In fact, it's possible that the lack of an actual marriage appealed to Hepburn, who by this time had not only turned down Leland Hayward but also the eccentric Howard Hughes, whom she had also dated. At the same time, Tracy wasn't any more faithful to Hepburn than he had been to his wife. He continued to engage in romantic affairs, including one with Gene Tierney, whom he met while filming *Plymouth Adventure.*

Perhaps one of the strengths of Spencer Tracy's relationship with Katharine Hepburn was that he treated her like a lady and also considered her his equal in every way. This applied even in cases where it didn't seem to matter very much. For instance, one writer took him to task for being billed above Hepburn on movie posters, saying "Well, after all, she's the lady. You're the man. Ladies first?" To which Tracy replied, "This is a movie, chowder head, not a lifeboat." Meanwhile, unlike Tracy, who prided himself on the ease with which he appeared on stage, Hepburn took her acting career very seriously. This led to some interesting discussions between the two, including one time when Hepburn asked Tracy in front of friends what he felt the secret to acting to be. Looking at them wryly, he said, "Well, it's taken me 40 years of doing it to learn the secret. I don't know that I want to give it away." They insisted, and he finally replied, "Okay, I'll tell you. The art of acting is: LEARN YOUR LINES!" With that, he left the room.

It is at least conceivable that Tracy and Hepburn would not have gotten away with such torrid adultery given the era, but their screen presence was so powerful that MGM was more than willing to help protect their mutual reputations. While their relationship was an open secret in Hollywood, few outside the city knew about it until near the end of Tracy's life. Over the next three decades, the two would make nine movies together, all of them box office hits.

As soon as he finished *Woman of the Year*, Tracy began work on *Turkey Flat*, but even his star power could not save that movie. However, as that film was falling flat, *Woman of the Year* was a smash hit, so MGM cast Tracy and Hepburn together again in *Keeper of the Flame*. Unlike the comedic *Woman of the Year*, *Keeper of the Flame* was a dramatic mystery, and even though the critics did not care for it, the public loved it enough that the film made even more money than *Woman of the Year* had.

By this time, the United States was firmly ensconced in World War II and Hollywood was doing its part, so it was only natural that Tracy's next three movies were about war. The first, entitled *A Guy Named Joe*, became his most popular movie to date, while the next, *The Seventh Cross* (1944), told a harrowing story of an escape from a concentration camp. Tracy's third war picture, *30 Seconds over Tokyo*, was about American bombers running campaigns over Tokyo. The combined receipts of these three movies made Spencer Tracy MGM's most profitable star of

1944.

Exhausted from three movies in 12 months, Tracy again took a year off, returning in 1945 to again star with Hepburn, this time in *Without Love*. Though the usual chemistry between the two actors was there, and the viewing public responded well, the critics panned the movie, declaring it not up to Tracy's usual standards. At this point, Tracy took a short time off from making movies to return to Broadway in a play called *The Rugged Path*, written by Robert E Sherwood. Unfortunately, producing the show proved to be more challenging than anyone had anticipated, as the director later recalled, "In the ten days prior to the New York opening all the important relationships had deteriorated. Spencer was tense and unbending, could not, or would not, take direction". The production only ran for 81 performances before Tracy quit, saying, "I couldn't say those goddamn lines over and over and over again every night ... At least every day is a new day for me in films ... But this thing—every day, every day, over and over again." As that quote would suggest, *The Rugged Path* was the last play for the actor who had once loved the stage so much that he was reluctant to act in films.

After that last stint on Broadway, Tracy returned to Hollywood and Hepburn in *The Sea of Grass*, a classic Western released in 1947. Yet again, the critics were not crazy about their work together but the public loved them. Tracy followed *The Sea of Grass* with *Cass Timberlane*, which also starred Lana Turner.

Tracy in *The Sea of Grass*

In 1948, Frank Capra asked Tracy and Hepburn to star in *The State of the Union*, which has Tracy playing a presidential candidate who is pressured to adopt a platform supporting big business. Hepburn plays his estranged wife, who reemerges and steers him toward a more socially-committed platform. The film marked just how far Hepburn had transformed from the early roles that had marked her as pretentious. Hepburn had always been liberal, but with films such as *State of the Union*, she exuded a concern for the working class, and the fact that she appeared in a Frank Capra film demonstrated her turn toward a more socially compassionate identity.

Hepburn and Tracy in *Adam's Rib*

The following year, in 1949, Tracy appeared as the villain in *Edward My Son*. The director, George Cooper, was surprised that Tracy did not like the part and was even more disappointed when critics criticized him for miscasting Tracy in the role. Always the professional, Tracy admitted, "It's rather disconcerting to me to find how easily I play a heel." However, *Edward My Son* would be one of Tracy's worst films and one of the few he ever made for MGM that actually lost money.

After Tracy starred with Jimmy Stewart in a World War II themed movie, *Malaya*, he returned to his bread-and-butter: the screwball comedy *Adam's Rib*. Once again, he starred with Katherine Hepburn as married lawyers who oppose each other in court. Hepburn displays a concern for social welfare while she defends a woman who murdered her husband in self-defense, but after defeating Tracy in court she resumes her marriage as though nothing had happened. The film is another example of how Hepburn portrayed career women but did so within the confines of traditional gender relations and marriage.

As the description of the roles suggests, the roles were written specifically for Tracy and

Hepburn, whose energy together was infectious and magical. *Adam's Rib* remains a popular comedy today, and one reviewer aptly described their chemistry together: "As we say, Mr. Tracy and Miss Hepburn are the stellar performers in this show and their perfect compatibility in comic capers is delightful to see. A line thrown away, a lifted eyebrow, a smile or a sharp, resounding slap on a tender part of the anatomy is as natural as breathing to them. Plainly, they took great pleasure in playing this rambunctious spoof."

Chapter 7: Old Man Tracy

"The kids keep telling me I should try this new 'Method Acting' but I'm too old, I'm too tired and I'm too talented to care." – Spencer Tracy

"I'm disappointed in acting as a craft. I want everything to go back to Orson Welles and fake noses and changing your voice. It's become so much about personality." – Spencer Tracy

By 1950, Spencer Tracy was 50 years old, and based on the standards of that time in Hollywood, a middle-aged man was more suited to play father figure roles than that of virile leading men. One of his first roles of this kind was also one of his most famous. Tracy played Stanley Banks in *Father of the Bride*, a comedy in which he plays the father of bride Elizabeth Taylor and captures on-screen the role of every man who has ever tried to survive planning and paying for a wedding. While the movie was more of a vehicle for Taylor, audiences and critics alike praised Tracy's performance. *Father of the Bride* is still regularly seen on classic movie channels, his performance garnered him yet another Oscar nomination for Best Actor, and the movie earned more money than any other of his films to date. Along with the sequel, *Father's Little Dividend* (released the following year), *Father of the Bride* again propelled Tracy to the top of Hollywood's list of male actors.

Tracy and Taylor in *Father of the Bride*

After starring as a lawyer in *The People against O'Hara* in 1951, Tracy joined Hepburn to make *Pat and Mike* in 1952. Written for them by the same writers who developed *Adam's Rib*, Pat and Mike became the pair's most popular movie ever, with critics and viewers alike praising its charm and comedic timing. By then, Tracy was in his early 50s and Hepburn was 45, and they arguably looked even older than that, so the film might have been more appropriate if filmed earlier in their careers.

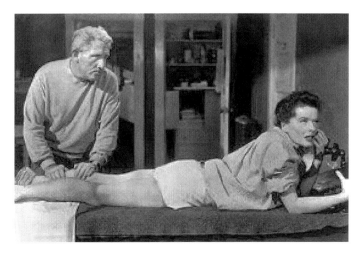

Hepburn and Tracy in *Pat and Mike*

Later that year, Tracy starred with Gene Tierney in *Plymouth Adventure*, another historical drama in the spirit of *Captains Courageous*, but *Plymouth Adventure* lacked the charm and quality writing of *Courageous* and fell flat at the box office. Tracy won his first Golden Globe award and earned a nomination for the British Academy Film and Theatre Award (BAFTA) for his next role, this time as a father in *The Actress*, but the critically acclaimed movie was a complete dud at the box office, with the producer lamenting "that film ... got more [acclaim] from the critics than any film I ever made in all the years, and we didn't make enough to pay for the ushers in the theatre."

Tracy returned to Westerns in 1954, starring in the film *Broken Lance* for 20th Century Fox and then appearing in a 1955 Western, *Bad Day at Black Rock*, as the one-armed misfit in a small western town. This role earned him the best actor prize at the Cannes Film Festival, but a few months later he was forced to quit in the middle of *Tribute to a Bad Man* because the altitude in Colorado, where they were shooting, made him sick. Tracy faced altitude sickness again in 1956 while filming *The Mountain* in the French Alps, but this time he was able to soldier through and completed the project. By that point, Tracy had left MGM for good, and he would remain an independent actor for the rest of his life.

Upon returning to America, Tracy also returned to Hepburn and a new comedy they filmed together called *Desk Set*. Even though he always loved working with Hepburn, Tracy was becoming increasingly undependable and almost did not complete the film. His lack of enthusiasm showed on-screen as well, and *Desk Set* became the least popular of the movies that he made with Hepburn.

Tracy and Hepburn in a publicity image for the 1957 film *Desk Set*.

In 1957, Tracy began work on *The Old Man and the Sea*, and unlike his recent roles, Tracy was enthusiastic about this film. However, his weight was considered a drawback in his portrayal of a rugged fisherman, and when he was urged to go on a diet in preparation for shooting, he refused to do so. He later described the movie as the most difficult he ever filmed, primarily because he had built his career around reacting to others on stage but appeared in most of the scenes alone in this film, but his acting was still superb enough to receive an Oscar nomination and a nomination for the British Academy Film Award. Reviewer Jack Moffitt wrote of Tracy's performance that it was "so intimate and revealing of universal human experience that, to me, it almost transcended acting and became reality."

28 years after filming their last movie together, Tracy reunited with director John Ford to make *The Last Hurrah* in 1958, in which Tracy played an Irish-American hoping to be reelected mayor. While the National Board of Review chose Tracy as 1958's best actor, *The Last Hurrah* was something of a box office failure. Now 60 years old and looking even older than that, Tracy began to wonder if it was time for him to retire, but then came the opportunity to play Clarence

Darrow in the famous movie *Inherit the Wind*. Based on the famous 1925 Scopes monkey trial, *Inherit the Wind* pitted Tracy's Clarence Darrow against William Jennings Bryan (played by Frederick Mark), and the film is now considered a classic and some of Tracy's best work. He received nominations for an Oscar and a Golden Globe award, but the public did not care as much for the movie, possibly due to the cultural sensitivity over the subject matter at the time.

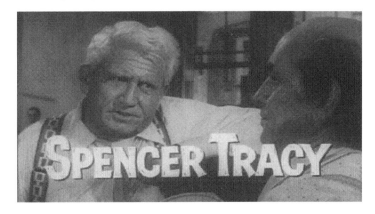

Tracy in *Inherit the Wind*

Tracy donned a Roman collar one last time in 1961 to play a priest in *The Devil at 4 O'Clock*. At first it looked like he might have to drop out of this picture because of some conflicts in his other filming schedule for *Judgment at Nuremburg*, but his costar Frank Sinatra and *Judgment*'s director, Stanly Kramer, were able to work things out so that Tracy could finish the film. While the critics did not love *The Devil at 4 O'Clock*, the public did, and it proved to be the most profitable film of the last decade of his career.

On the other hand, 1961's *Judgment at Nuremburg* is considered one of the best movies of the decade. The movie tells the story of the trials held for Nazi war criminals at the end of World War II, and the author, Anna Mann, wrote the character of Judge Haywood specifically for Tracy. For his part, Tracy said that it was the best script he ever read, and the film culminates in a 13 minute speech delivered by Tracy from the bench. Much to everyone's surprise, the 61-year-old actor nailed the entire speech in one take, earning an ovation from everyone on set after the scene was finished. Mann later wrote in a letter, "Every writer ought to have the experience of having Spencer Tracy do his lines. There is nothing in the world quite like it."

Due to his work on *Judgment at Nuremberg*, Tracy was not able to complete his role in *How the West Was Won*, but that movie's director, John Ford, was satisfied when Tracy agreed to do the narration for the film. By now in poor health, Tracy summoned his energy for one more film with Stanley Kramer, *A Mad, Mad, Mad, Mad World*, which became a '60s classic. Tracy only had a small role, but it required all his personal and professional energy to complete his role in just nine days, and the film went on to be the most profitable film of that year.

By the time *Its A Mad, Mad, Mad, Mad World* was finished, it seemed likely that Tracy would never act again, and indeed, he turned down one film after another, preferring to live quietly in a small house he shared with Katherine Hepburn. Despite being just 62 years old, Tracy had developed a severe heart disease, exacerbated by his bouts of alcoholism, and Hepburn moved in with him in his Beverley Hills apartment to provide constant nursing care. From the end of 1962 until 1967, Hepburn also appeared in no films, devoting herself exclusively to caring for Tracy.

However, in 1967, Tracy agreed to star as the father in Stanly Kramer's *Guess Who's Coming To Dinner*. The film, which paired Tracy and Hepburn for the last time, was directed by Stanley Kramer and co-starred Sidney Poitier and Katharine Houghton, Hepburn's niece. The film is notable not only for being the final collaboration between Tracy and Hepburn but also because of its sensitive treatment of the still-controversial topic of interracial marriage. Tracy had once joked that "the physical labor actors have to do wouldn't tax an embryo", but by this point, Tracy's poor health meant he was only able to work only two or three hours each day, and he filmed his last scene on May 24, 1967.

Tracy in *Guess Who's Coming to Dinner*

When *Guess Who's Coming To Dinner* was released later that December, it garnered Tracy the rare posthumous Oscar nomination for Best Actor. Just 17 days after filming his final scene, Tracy got out of bed early on June 10 and made his way to the kitchen for a cup of tea. Hearing him get up, Hepburn followed him into the kitchen, and as she later explained, "Just as I was about to give [the door] a push, there was a sound of a cup smashing to the floor—then clump—a loud clump." Spencer Tracy had suffered a sudden heart attack and was dead before his body hit the ground. As she rushed to his side, Hepburn recalled, "He looked so happy to be done with living, which for all his accomplishments had been a frightful burden for him."

The Tracy family planned an elaborate Requiem Mass for Spencer for June 12 that was held at Immaculate Heart of Mary Catholic Church in East Hollywood. Directors, actors, and other famous contemporaries showed up, and the only person dear to Tracy who was not there was Katherine Hepburn. Always the lady, she stayed away out of respect for Louise Tracy and her children. After the mass, Spencer Tracy was buried at the Forest Lawn Memorial Park in Glendale, California.

Many actors through the years have succumbed to being typecast and/or letting their personal lives so influence the parts that they played that they always seemed to be playing themselves. This was even truer during Hollywood's Golden Era, when every audience knew John Wayne's character would be a tough cowboy and Mae West would play a "bad woman" with a good heart. However, no one could ever accuse Spencer Tracy of having a type. After all, he might be a priest in one picture and a drunken bum in the next. He played famous lawyers and death row inmates with equal passion.

His roles did not seemingly reflect his personal life, but anyone who took a closer look would find that Tracy himself lived a life that was just as diverse as the parts he played. He could be a raging alcoholic but always remained a gentle man. He loved his wife too much to divorce her but not enough to live with her. His long affair with Katherine Hepburn is the stuff of legends, but he cheated on her too. In short, his life was a series of inconsistencies that went all the way back to the very beginning.

Bibliography

Anderson, Christopher. An Affair to Remember: The Remarkable Love Story of Katharine Hepburn and Spencer Tracy (1997)

Curtis, James. Spencer Tracy: A Biography (2011)

Davidson, Bill. Spencer Tracy: Tragic Idol (1988)

Kanin, Garson. Tracy and Hepburn: An Intimate Memoir (2012)

Lowe, Brenda. Spencer Tracy Fox Film Actor: The Pre-C0ode Legacy of a Hollywood Legend (2009)

New England Vintage Film Society, Inc. Spencer Tracy, A Life in Pictures (2012)

Charlie Chaplin

Chapter 1: Tragedy and Performance

The story of Chaplin's childhood is highly incomplete, and even those aspects of his early life that have been uncovered are highly apocryphal. Although Chaplin wrote an autobiography, the validity of his recollections about his early upbringing has been heavily disputed and in certain respects contradicted altogether.

However, while Chaplin never had a birth certificate, it is generally agreed upon that he was born on April 16, 1889 to Hannah and Charles Chaplin, Sr. Charlie was the couple's first child, and in his earliest youth the family lived in East Street in Walworth, South London. They had virtually no money and subsisted on the scant money earned from the parents' careers as entertainers. Chaplin's impoverished upbringing led biographer David Robinson to refer to his life as "the most dramatic of all the rags to riches stories ever told". Chaplin himself would note, "I was hardly aware of a crisis because we lived in a continual crisis; and, being a boy, I dismissed our troubles with gracious forgetfulness."

Hannah Chaplin

On top of their poor financial condition, both Hannah and Charles Sr. had led troubled lives before their son's birth. Chaplin's father was a butcher's son and an alcoholic, while Hannah, the daughter of gypsy parents, had run away from home at the age of 16 and supported herself as a music hall performer. She gave herself the stage name Lily Harley in honor of Lily Langtry, her favorite Victorian music hall performer.

Although Charlie was born in 1889, Hannah had actually met her husband years earlier, after which she eloped to the gold mining region of the country with Sydney Hawkins, a con man who also served as a pimp. It is believed that Hannah worked as a prostitute during her relationship with Hawkins, and the two also conceived of an illegitimate child who would become Charlie's half-brother Sydney. Finally, in 1884, Hannah returned to London and improbably found Charles; the two would marry in 1886.

It is unclear whether Charlie ever knew that his mother had worked as prostitute, since he did not make mention of it in his autobiography and the information would likely never have surfaced were it not for the efforts of Dr. Stephen Weissman, Chaplin's recent biographer. The details surrounding Chaplin's mother are significant in that they illuminate some of the reasons for her conduct later in life. All throughout Chaplin's childhood, Hannah suffered from an unstable personality and had a fragile grasp of reality, a tendency that was compounded as Chaplin grew older. Hannah became devoutly religious and would preach at length before Charlie and his brother, sometimes even going so far as to act out scenes from the Bible. It is now believed that the reasons for the gradual deterioration of Hannah's mental state are actually symptoms of syphilis, which Hannah may have acquired as a result of her prostitution. Charlie would find himself on a different spiritual path, later writing, "I believe that faith is a precursor of all our ideas. Without faith, there never could have evolved hypothesis, theory, science or mathematics. I believe that faith is an extension of the mind. It is the key that negates the impossible. To deny faith is to refute oneself and the spirit that generates all our creative forces. My faith is in the unknown, in all that we do not understand by reason; I believe that what is beyond our comprehension is a simple fact in other dimensions, and that in the realm of the unknown there is an infinite power for good."

Although Hannah was mentally unstable for virtually all of Charlie's upbringing, she continued to work as an entertainer during his earliest childhood. She and her husband became estranged by 1891 when Charlie was still a toddler, and Hannah had difficulty providing for her sons since her husband neglected to provide any financial assistance until late in Charlie's childhood. Making matters worse, Hannah had an affair with a separate man, Leo Dryden, during which she gave birth to a third son, George Wheeler Dryden. Thus, despite having no means with which to provide for her children, Hannah had three sons by three different men. She was never tasked with providing for her youngest son, as Leo Dryden took sole custody of the child when he was just six months old, but she still couldn't care for her two eldest children, a problem exacerbated by the fact that Hannah could not secure consistent employment.

Due to her mental disability, Hannah was unsuccessful as an entertainer, and it was her own lack of success that led to Charlie receiving his first show business opportunity at age five. While there is no way of verifying whether or not the story is true, the legend holds that Charlie's mother had been booed off the stage during a performance, and in an act of desperation Charlie performed a rendition of a well-known dance hall tune. Exhibiting no signs of self-consciousness, he performed ably and the crowd showered him with coins in a demonstration of praise. Even if this well-known tale was embellished by Chaplin over the years, the story reflects the substantial talent held by Chaplin even early in his life.

Despite his love for his mother, Hannah's mental state grew increasingly worse, and she was eventually forced to relinquish control over her two sons. Charlie would later remember thinking, "Why had she done this? Mother, so light-hearted and gay, how could she go insane?" Consequently, at age seven, Chaplin moved to a workhouse (orphanage) and attended the Central London District School for Paupers, a Dickensian environment in which he was given little adult support. The experience in the orphanage, which he later termed a "forlorn existence", left Chaplin with an affinity for the environment of the poor that would remain with him and surface through such later films such as *City Lights* and *Modern Times*. Although he was given consistent shelter and nourishment, the seedy London environment was only a marginal improvement over the living conditions with his mother, and Chaplin and his brother left at the earliest opportunity.

Even though Hannah had never been able to provide sufficient economic support for Chaplin, he still preferred to live with her, so at age nine Charlie and his brother moved back in with her. Her health had improved, and Hannah had been able to find relatively consistent work as a seamstress, but she was still never quite able to provide adequate support, and she physically suffered from malnourishment. Just a few years after they had returned to live with Hannah, she was placed in an asylum, leaving Charlie and his brother under the custody of Charles Sr. This living situation proved to be the worst of all; Charles Sr.'s alcoholism made the environment unstable, and at one point during this period, the family was visited by the National Society for the Prevention of Cruelty to Children, a result of the fact that his father regularly abused Charlie and his brother. His father would die in 1901 from cirrhosis of the liver, a result of his hard drinking, leaving Charlie and his brother to be reassigned to a charity institution.

Chapter 2: Show Business Beginnings

"The summation of my character is that I care about my work. I care about everything I do. If I could do something else better, I would do it, but I can't." – Charlie Chaplin

In light of his harsh childhood, it may seem surprising that Chaplin would pursue a life in show business. After all, each of his parents had worked as entertainers, and they had both suffered severe health complications that rendered them unfit to care for their children. However, Chaplin relished his experience performing at age five, and he continued to have a desire for performing before an audience. Furthermore, it is important to remember that in late fin-de-siecle London, show business was not a glamorous profession; the music halls were seedy environments that were unlikely to enrapture a young adolescent such as Chaplin. Given those conditions, it is reasonable to believe that had Chaplin had a more affluent and bourgeois upbringing that never exposed him to those scenes as a youngster, he may never have been interested in pursuing a career as an entertainer.

Despite being exposed to the vulgarity of show business at a young age, Chaplin continued to refine his talent, and at 10 years old he joined the Eight Lancashire Lads clog dancing troupe. As he progressed into adolescence, Chaplin became increasingly negligent with regard to his academic studies, and at 13 he quit school altogether. The move was risky, but given his impoverished upbringing and background, show business provided perhaps his most plausible route to economic success. One year after quitting school, he formally entered the entertainment industry, registering with a theatrical agency in West London.

Chaplin's career as a traveling performer would last for a long while, and for someone who became such a notable giant of cinema, it may seem surprising that he did not work with movies until he had been an entertainer and theatrical performer for over a decade. While that career path is unlikely today, the cinema was still in its infant stages when Chaplin was a teenager, having just been introduced to the general public a decade earlier through the efforts of early cinematic luminaries like Thomas Edison, George Melies, and the Lumiere Brothers. People were not trained to act in motion pictures, and it would not be until his mid-twenties that Chaplin would enter the motion picture industry. Moreover, as a young adolescent in London, it is likely that Chaplin had little or no exposure to motion pictures, evidenced by the fact he continued to refine his technique in the vaudeville tradition. Even still, Chaplin would later recount that he "never lost sight of my ultimate aim to become an actor."

From 1903-1905, Chaplin toured with H.A. Saintsbury in Charles Frohman's production of *Sherlock Holmes*. Beginning in October 1903, Chaplin he played Billy the Page, and he subsequently performed other roles for a few years in the *Sherlock Holmes* production before shifting genres and working in comedy and burlesque. This included a stint with Casey's Court Circus, a company he toured with until 1907. During this time, his older brother had become a successful performer in his own right working in Fred Karno's comedy company, and through brother Sydney's advocacy, Charlie was able to sign with Fred Karno's company in February 1908. At the time, Karno remembered thinking Charlie was a "pale, puny, sullen-looking youngster" who "looked much too shy to do any good in the theatre."

Portrait of Charlie in 1912

During his time with Karno, Chaplin progressed through the ranks and began going on their extended tours throughout Europe. In late 1908 and 1909, he toured Paris, appearing in productions of *Mumming Birds* and *The Football March*. He enjoyed the opportunities for travel and retained a high level of ambition that would stick with him through the rest of his life. By working hard and catching the right breaks, things were finally looking up, and Chaplin would later write of the time, "What had happened? It seemed the world had suddenly changed, had taken me into its fond embrace and adopted me."

By 1910, Chaplin had become a significant star with the Fred Karno troupe, and after re-signing with Karno that year, he left for the troupe's American tour. The American tour lasted until June 1912, and Chaplin earned rave reviews, with one reviewer calling him "one of the best pantomime artists ever seen here." Chaplin had also perfected and popularized several kinds of comedic acts, playing a similar kind of character as the one he would eventually become famous for. Chaplin played a drunk known as the Inebriate Swell in Paris.

In the summer of 1912, Chaplin returned to England, but he would not be there for long. After quick stints in France and England, he returned to America in October 1912 on another tour. By this point, however, motion pictures had finally begun to seriously threaten the hegemony of the theatre, and Chaplin was intrigued by the possibility of acting in film. In September 1913, he signed with the Keystone Film Company at a salary of $150 per week. Having attained some semblance of financial stability, he left the Karno Company in November 1913. He would never perform in the theatre again.

Chapter 3: Early Film Career

"I remain just one thing, and one thing only — and that is a clown. It places me on a far higher plane than any politician." – Charlie Chaplin

Although Chaplin's early film career remains relatively unknown among the public today, his earliest years as an actor actually witnessed his most prolific output of films. From 1895-1915, the motion picture industry laid the very foundation for narrative cinema, and Chaplin's earliest films reflect an industry that was still engaged in the process of determining how to portray stories and distinguish itself from the theatre and vaudeville comedy, two mediums in which Chaplin had previously been employed.

In his essay on early silent cinema, Tom Gunning contends that cinema up until 1906 was concerned with simply showcasing the various visual attractions that were possible for the new medium; this "Cinema of Attractions," involved not only the spectacular (such as camera tricks) but also the relatively mundane. Directors like Edwin S. Porter, George Melies, and the Lumiere brothers all made films that fit under the classification of the Cinema of Attractions, which borrowed heavily from the vaudeville and were predicated on shocking the viewer. There was little camera movement, as the intent was for the film to be mostly analogous to the visual attractions viewers would get by visiting an amusement park or watching a magician. Instead of a narrative that absorbs the viewer, films were simply built around eliciting astonishment.

Over the following decade, however, film became more refined and gravitated away from its vaudeville influences toward actual narrative scenarios. Through the efforts of directors like D.W. Griffith, film also became more morally upstanding, and bourgeois members of society began to take the medium seriously. Early film stars, including Blanche Sweet and Lillian Gish, were respectable figures whose innocence resonated in their films. Even so, cinema continued to lag behind the theatre with regard to cultural respectability; in fact, the movie theatre was a dark locale and young girls were socially forbidden from attending by themselves.

It was during this period of marginal respectability that Chaplin began his career in the film industry. The Keystone Studios were so named because the films produced by the company involved the Keystone Kops, a lowly band of incompetent law enforcement officers. Before the onset of World War I, Chaplin would complete a full 57 films for the company, often producing multiple ones per week. While it should be noted that the films were especially short (often running fewer than ten minutes), Chaplin's output during this period was remarkable.

Chaplin's first film, *Making a Living*, was released on February 2, 1914. At this point, the 24 year old Chaplin had not yet created the Tramp persona that would make him famous, but his character in the film, a swindler with the Dickensian name Edgar English, wears a costume that anticipates that of the tramp. English dons a top hat, cane, mustache, monocle, and sport coat. Although his body is notably thinner and his frame more youthful than later Chaplin films, the mustache makes him appear as though he could be as old as 50, allaying boss Mack Sennett's concerns that Chaplin looked too young for the part.

Sennett

In the film, Chaplin's character tricks a journalist out of money and then delivers the news of an automobile accident to the press. Finally, the Keystone Kops realize that he is a con man and chase him at the film's conclusion. Chases were a major trope of cinema during the period of narrative integration, and it is even possible to refer to films involving chases as a genre unto themselves (the "chase film.") The chase provided an easy means for crafting a logical narrative, since it was not difficult to craft a plot outline out of one man running afoul of the law.

Despite the easy-to-follow narrative structure of *Making a Living*, the film nevertheless is edited in a sloppy manner, with errors in match-on-action that make it appear as though temporal lapses have occurred where they are not intended. However, such deficiencies would not have been glaring to an audience at that time, a reflection of the extent to which one's viewing experience was conditioned by the rapid changes within the film industry.

Chaplin constructed the Tramp persona for his second film, *Kids' Auto Race at Venice, California*, which was released on February 7, 1914, a mere five days after *Making a Living*. In explaining his influences for the Tramp, Chaplin noted that he wanted the character to reflect a number of contradictions:

"I wanted the clothes to be a mass of contradictions, knowing pictorially the figure would be vividly outlined on the screen. To add a comic touch, I wore a small mustache which would not hide my expression. My appearance got an enthusiastic response from everyone, including Mr. Sennett. The clothes seemed to imbue me with the spirit of the character. He actually became a man with a soul - a point of view. I defined to Mr. Sennett the type of person he was. He wears an air of romantic hunger, forever seeking death, but his feet won't let him."

Chaplin in his first appearance as the Tramp

The contradictions alluded to by Chaplin also relate to socioeconomic status. In particular, the hat, coat, and mustache suggest the attire of an affluent bourgeois society man, but the clothes are too baggy and the shoes too large, as though he were literally "unable" to inhabit the shoes of a wealthier man.

In *Kids' Auto Race*, Chaplin plays a spectator watching a kids' auto race. The event is being recorded by a film camera, and Chaplin repeatedly walks in front of the camera, even after he has been instructed to keep a distance. Because of the camera within the narrative, there are two cameras at work (counting the actual film camera), and in one scene late in the short film, the film camera itself is visible. This early example of cinematic self-reflexivity represents a strong example of the way in which the films during the period of narrative integration were concerned with showcasing the mechanical processes of the apparatus. Tom Gunning classified this tendency as the "Operational Aesthetic," a trope in which the narrative trajectory is constructed around a single gag with a machine. In this case, the machine represents the camera within the narrative, although other films of the period use machines such as cars or even household appliances, all of which function as surrogates for the cinematic apparatus.

Another notable film from 1914 was *His Trysting Place*, a film in which Chaplin's star persona as the Tramp became increasingly solidified. The film is a critique of domesticity, involving Chaplin meeting his friend Ambrose for a meal. Afterwards, the two grab each other's coats by mistake. Because Ambrose had a love letter in his coat pocket, Chaplin's wife accuses him of having an affair. Meanwhile, Chaplin's character had a baby bottle in his coat, resulting in Ambrose's wife suspecting that he had an illegitimate child. The plot is unrealistic and relies upon coincidences that offer little of the more nuanced plot trajectories that characterize Chaplin's mature directorial efforts. However, *His Trysting Place* is a useful film in analyzing the trajectory of Chaplin's career, as his character spends a significant amount of time performing before the camera. A notable example is the scene in the restaurant, during which Chaplin gnaws at a grotesque rib of meat. Throughout the film, it is clear that the premier attraction is watching Chaplin's body, with the formal plot largely extraneous. Biographer David Robinson would note that the actor had "a special mastery of telling stories in images", at a time when films largely lacked coherent narratives.

Decades later, Chaplin gave an interview in which he was asked at length about what made the Tramp a figure that managed to remain somewhat relevant in modern society despite the fact the films were completely antiquated:

"Interviewer: Can you talk about the moment you created the Tramp outfit?

Chaplin: It all came about in an emergency. The cameraman said put on some funny make-up, and I hadn't the slightest idea what to do. I went to the dress department and, on the way, I thought, well, I'll have them make everything in contradiction - baggy trousers, tight coat, large head, small hat - raggedy but at the same time a gentleman. I didn't know how I was going to do the face, but it was going to be a sad, serious face. I wanted to hide that it was comic, so I found a little moustache. And that moustache was no concept of the characterisation - only saying that it was rather silly. It doesn't hide my expression.

Interviewer: When you looked at yourself, what was your first reaction?

Chaplin: It'll do. It didn't ignite anything. Not until I absolutely had to play it in the presence of the camera. Making an entrance, I felt dressed; I had an attitude. I felt good, and the character came to me. The scene [from Mabel's Strange Predicament] was in a hotel lobby, and the Tramp was trying to pretend to be one of the guests just so he can get anchored on a soft seat and rest for a while. Everybody looked at him a little suspiciously, and I did all the things that the guests were doing in the hotel, looked at the register, took out a cigarette, lit it, watched the passing parade. And then I stumbled over the cuspidor. That was the first gag I ever did. And the character was born. And I thought, this is a very good character. But not every character I played followed the same format for all the comedy ideas after that.

One thing I intended to remain - not so much the dress of the Tramp, but the sore feet. No matter how rambunctious or exuberant he felt, he always had these very tired, big feet. I inquired of wardrobe that I wanted two large pairs of old shoes, because I had absurdly small feet, so I wanted these big shoes, and I knew they would give me a comic gait. I'm naturally very graceful, but trying to be graceful in big feet - that's funny.

Interviewer: Do you think the Tramp would work in modern times?

Chaplin: I don't think there's any place for that sort of person now. The world has become a little bit more ordered. I don't think it's happier now, by any means. I've noticed the kids with their short clothes and their long hair, and I think some of them want to be tramps. But there's not the same humility now. They don't know what humility is, so it has become something of an antique. It belongs to another era. That's why I couldn't do anything like that now. And, of course, sound - that's another reason. When talk came in I couldn't have my character at all. I wouldn't know what kind of voice he would have. So he had to go.

Interviewer: What do you think was the great appeal of the Tramp?

Chaplin: There is that gentle, quiet poverty. Every soda jerk wants to dress up, wants to be a swell. That's what I enjoy about the character - being very fastidious and very delicate about everything. But I never really thought of the Tramp in terms of appeal. The Tramp was something within myself I had to express. I was motivated by the reaction of the audience, but I never related to an audience. The audience happens when it's finished, and not during the making. I've always related to a sort of a comic spirit, something within me, that said, I must express this. This is funny."

Chaplin's first year in the motion picture was also notable in that Chaplin acted in his first feature-length film, *Tillie's Punctured Romance*. Released in November 1914, the film features Charlie as a character other than the Tramp. Instead, he plays a womanizer in the city who elopes with a rich girl from the country after getting her drunk, but after watching a morality tale in a movie theatre, he feels bad. Eventually, he is rejected by the girl's father after she decides that her social standing is too far above his. Although the film was directed by Mack Sennett, as many of the Chaplin films from 1914 were, the film has a moralistic message that would become a hallmark of Chaplin's own directorial efforts over the following year.

By the end of 1914, Chaplin had already become a popular figure, so much so that Keystone Studios was promoting him on both sides of the Atlantic. One advertisement that June asked Britons, "Are you prepared for the Chaplin boom? There has never been so instantaneous a hit as that of Chas Chaplin". But in November 1914 he left Keystone Studios to sign with Essanay. His primary reason for leaving Keystone was that he wanted to exert increased directorial control over his films. Although he had directed films while with Keystone, the films produced by that studio were generally formulaic and typically involved the Keystone Kops, and Chaplin wanted to convey more original narratives. According to Kevin Hayes, Essanay also had added appeal because it allowed Chaplin the opportunity to move to California: "He left Keystone for Essanay largely to exercise his creative freedom, to star in films that he would both write and direct. But wintertime in Chicago scarcely made for ideal filmmaking. After completing only one film here, he convinced Essanay management that sunny California was a much better place to make comedies."

With Essanay, Chaplin would reach the pinnacle of motion picture stardom in America. One of Chaplin's first films with Essanay was *The Champion* (1915), a film that continues the emphasis on narrative coincidence that characterized the Keystone films but also deployed Chaplin's own body in even more striking ways. As usual, Chaplin plays the protagonist of the film; after finding a "good luck horseshoe" while walking by a boxing gym, he decides to try his hand at becoming a boxer. Much of the pleasure of the film involves watching Chaplin dance around the boxing ring, dodging the punches of much larger fighters. He eventually defeats the world boxing champion, and he and the trainer's daughter fall in love.

As 1915 progressed, Chaplin became an increasingly greater star. In that era, films were not shown in isolation but were instead shown in succession with other short films. However, it was clear that Chaplin was the main attraction that brought audiences to the theatre on a regular basis. In *The Tramp* (1915), the last film Chaplin made for Essanay, viewers could quickly see how Chaplin's status had elevated. In addition to the fact Chaplin directed the film, it opens with a screen credit advertising his name. The film opens with his iconic Tramp character shown in medium shot, an implicit acknowledgment that he was the chief reason to watch the film.

Chaplin shows off a Tramp doll, 1916

Although Chaplin had refined the Tramp persona since as early as *Kids' Auto Race at Venice, California*, in *The Tramp* one sees the perfection of the Tramp identity. Specifically, the film marks the progression away from slapstick and towards a fusion of humor and pathos that to this day represents Chaplin's signature. Chaplin was driven by a desire to elevate film in the eyes of the public to the ranks of more culturally prestigious artistic forms such as opera or theatre, and he knew that the gag structure of his earlier films would not suffice in acquiring a more socially respectable following. With films such as *The Tramp*, Chaplin attracted a socially upscale audience while retaining his working-class demographic, giving him a much vaster audience than the theatre, as Schuyler Lynn noted: "'Chaplinitis,' as the writer dubbed the nation's fever, further heightened the awareness of silent filmmakers in all of the centers of production, from New York City and Fort Lee, New Jersey, to Philadelphia, Chicago, and Southern California, that their industry's position in American life was infinitely more powerful—and at the same time more vulnerable—than the theatre's."

Film was certainly more popular than theatre, but the vulnerability identified by Schuyler Lynn also explains the relative instability of the movies at the time. Chaplin's later efforts would involve the further maturation of the medium. He later explained how he came up with his ideas, and his philosophy on what was humorous:

"Interviewer: How does a gag sequence come to you? Does it come out of nothing, or is there a process?

Chaplin: No, there is no process. The best ideas grow out of the situation. If you get a good comedy situation it goes on and on and has many radiations. Like the skating rink sequence [in The Rink]. I found a pair of skates and I went on, with everybody in the audience certain that I was going to fall, and instead I came on and just skated around on one foot gracefully. The audience didn't expect it from the Tramp. Or the lamppost gag [in Easy Street]. It came out of a situation where I am a policeman, and am trying to subdue a bully. I hit him on the head with a truncheon, and hit him and hit him. It is like a bad dream. He keeps rolling his sleeves up with no reaction to being hit at all. Then he lifts me up and puts me down. Then I thought, well, he has enormous strength, so he can pull the lamppost down, and while he was doing that I would jump on his back, push his head in the light and gas him. I did some funny things that were all made off the cuff that got a tremendous laugh.

But there was a lot of agony, too. Miserable days of nothing working, and getting more despondent. It was up to me to think of something to make them laugh. And you cannot be funny without a funny situation. You can do something clownish, perhaps stumble, but you must have a funny situation.

Interviewer: Do you see people doing these things, or do they all come out of your imagination?

Chaplin: No, we created a world of our own. Mine was the studio in California. The happiest moments were when I was on the set and I had an idea or just a suggestion of a story, and I felt good, and then things would happen. It was the only surcease that I had. The evening is rather a lonesome place, you know, in California, especially in Hollywood. But it was marvellous, creating a comic world. It was another world, different from the everyday. And it used to be fun. You sit there and you rehearse for half a day, shoot it, and that was it...

Interviewer: Your comedy in part is a comedy of incident, too. It's not an intellectual thing, it's things that are happening, that are funny.

Chaplin: I've always thought that incidents related will make a story, like the setting up of a pool game on a billiard table. Each ball is an incident in itself. One touches the other, you see. And the whole makes a triangle. I carry that image a great deal in my work.

Interviewer: You like to keep a terrific pace going and you pack incidents one on top of the other quite a bit. Do you think this is characteristic of you?

Chaplin: Well, I don't know whether it's characteristic of me. I've watched other comedians who seem to relax their pace. I can feel my way much better with pace than I can with being slow. I haven't the confidence to move slow, and I haven't the confidence in what I'm doing.

But action is not always the thing. Everything must have growth, otherwise it loses its reality. You have a problem, and then you intensify it. You don't deliberately start with intensifying it. But you say, well, now, where do we go from here? You say, what is the natural outcome of this? Realistically and convincingly, the problem keeps getting more and more complicated. And it must be logical, otherwise you will have some sort of comedy, but you won't have an exciting comedy."

As the United States entered World War I, Chaplin was criticized for not enlisting, and though he was not drafted, there was a popular belief that he had a responsibility to enter the conflict overseas. However, Chaplin harbored anti-war sentiments in general, and in that he was hardly alone in America, where there was plenty of opposition to the war during its first few years. At the same time, Chaplin also provided a great deal of relief to the soldiers, who derived pleasure from watching his wartime films. In one film of Chaplin's from 1918, *Shoulder Arms* (which was made during Chaplin's time with First National Films), he even played a soldier in the war. Through providing relief to soldiers and civilians alike, it could be argued that he made a contribution to the war effort in his own right, and Hollywood stars like John Wayne would follow a similar path during World War II.

In 1916, Chaplin's contract with Essanay ended, and he signed with Mutual Studio. At this point, Chaplin's films were the most popular in the country, and he held the leverage to command whichever price he desired. Therefore, he signed with Mutual for $670,000 year, an incredible sum in that era, and particularly for someone just 26 years old. In response to the attention given the sum, Mutual's studio president, John R. Freuler, noted, "We can afford to pay Mr. Chaplin this large sum annually because the public wants Chaplin and will pay for him." He moved to Los Angeles, which by then was well into the process of becoming the epicenter for American moviemaking.

Chaplin made just 12 films for Mutual, each of them two-reel productions. Many of them, such as *Easy Street* (1917), are chase films centering on Chaplin's attempt to court the woman of his dreams. In *Easy Street*, the Tramp becomes a police officer and rescues his love interest after she has been kidnapped. On the surface, there is little remarkable about the films made for Mutual; the chase plot structure is a primitive narrative device, particularly in light of the films that were made during the period by D.W. Griffith, including *Birth of a Nation* (1915) and *Intolerance* (1916). However, the incorporation of a romantic plotline was significant in that it introduced a theme that would stay with Chaplin for the rest of his career. Harry Grace later noted that nearly 80% of Chaplin's film themes "concern relations between the sexes". Even if there is little of note in the Mutual films, their significance lies in the influence they would have on Chaplin's more mature works, many of which involved Chaplin rescuing a woman in danger.

The Mutual films are also notable because they involved Chaplin's most significant love interest up to that point in his life, Edna Purviance. Although she had starred in some of Chaplin's last films with Essanay, her own stardom escalated with Chaplin's during his tenure at Mutual, and she became one of the most popular silent film actresses of the time. In addition to starring in many of Chaplin's films for Mutual Studio, she was romantically involved with Chaplin through part of 1917. Even after splitting with Chaplin, she would continue to star in his films through as late as 1923.

Purviance

Chapter 4: The Star

Regardless of the fact the films with Mutual were not groundbreaking, Chaplin may have been the most recognizable man in the world by the end of the decade. Costume parties featured a majority of the men dressing up like the Tramp, and Chaplin's success spawned a wave of Tramp imitations that forced him to actually sue imitators at times. Minnie Maddern Fiske, one of the most famous female actresses of the era, wrote in Harpers Weekly that "a constantly increasing body of cultured, artistic people are beginning to regard the young English buffoon, Charles Chaplin, as an extraordinary artist, as well as a comic genius." Chaplin would later comment upon the label genius in an interview, asserting, "I've never known quite what a genius was. I think it's somebody with a talent, who's highly emotional about it, and is able to master a technique. Everybody is gifted in some way. The average man has to differentiate between doing a regular sort of unimaginative job, and the fellow who's a genius doesn't. He does something different, but does this very well. Many a jack-of-all-trades has been mistaken for a genius."

In the end, Chaplin's time with Mutual did not last long. By the end of the decade, he became increasingly interested in making feature-length films, and he signed with First National Studios in 1918. Employed at the unheard-of salary of one million dollars, Chaplin made nine films for First National from 1918-1923. In addition to making longer films, Chaplin continued to deviate from the overt slapstick that characterized his early Keystone Kops films, and though they were still humorous, Chaplin's films became more sentimental. The balance between humor and sadness captivated audiences, and the moral respectability of Chaplin's films with First National Studios made them appeal to a more upscale audience, even as the impoverished Tramp character made him appeal to the working class. Schuyler Lynn noted how Chaplin arrived at the ideal formula for elevating the respectability of the medium and giving him a mass audience:

> "The power inhered in the mass appeal of movies. At one end of the scale, they were now becoming fashionable among intellectually sophisticated young people at socially privileged colleges and universities; at the other, they continued to serve as the prime source of entertainment for underprivileged and uneducated immigrants; and in between lay the great heart of the moviegoing public, the millions of middle-class adults and children of varying levels of education from all regions of the country and a wide range of backgrounds...But precisely because of the indiscriminate seductiveness of the "house of dreams," as Jane Addams called the movie theatre, many religious leaders and lay reformers fervently believed that movies should be held to a higher moral standard than other forms of entertainment" (16).

Chaplin, along with D.W. Griffith, became an instrumental figure in the legitimizing of cinema as a respectable art form. In Chaplin's eyes, it was no longer acceptable to make films that mocked law enforcement, as he had done with Keystone studios, and in a sense the films Chaplin made with First National Films heralded his own maturation. The first film Chaplin made for First National Films was *A Dog's Life*, an oft-forgotten Chaplin film that bears many similarities with his later directorial efforts. In the film, the Tramp lives in a deserted lot and cannot find a job, but he finds a dog for companionship. The two wander the streets for food, but to no avail, and after they attempt to enter a dance hall, they are thrown out after they cannot pay the admission fee. Finally, the dog digs up a wallet, and when they go back to the dance hall they find that the dance hall singer (played by Edna Purviance) has just been fired. The Tramp then "rescues" Edna, and the film closes with Edna, the Tramp, and the dog united and poised for a successful future.

Although it relies heavily upon coincidence (the dog finding the wallet, Edna being fired at a fortuitous moment), *A Dog's Life* was a significant film for Chaplin in that it refined the balance between scenes of extreme sadness and humor. One of the scenes from the film also features a two-shot of Chaplin with the dog that would get reworked in a subsequent Chaplin film made for First National Films.

The Tramp in *A Dog's Life*

The shot is imbued with tragedy, and one can feel the despair of the Tramp's character, not only in his inability to sustain himself but also to provide for his dog. However, audiences could take heart in the fact that Chaplin redeems the tragedy of the plot through a happy ending; as Chaplin's career progressed, he began crafting endings that were more bittersweet, creating an even more emotionally complex reaction from the viewer.

By 1918, Chaplin's personal life had become controversial, and it would remain so for the rest of his life. He had terminated his relationship with Edna Purviance and began a relationship with a young woman who was considerably younger than himself. That September, 31 year old Chaplin married 17 year-old Mildred Harris, who became pregnant and gave birth to a child,

Norman Spencer Chaplin, in 1919. The child would die shortly after being born, and Chaplin's star image suffered as a result of his marrying someone so young. A contrast developed between the increasing acclaim of his films and the controversy of his romantic interests.

Many of the films Chaplin made for First National Films are no longer well-known, and the majority of the movies involve a romantic plot in which Chaplin's characters (not always the Tramp) overcome extreme obstacles to win over his love interest. In his most famous film and first feature-length one with First National Films, *The Kid* (1921), Chaplin reworked some of the plot elements from *A Dog's Life*. The film opens with the inter-title "A comedy with a smile— and perhaps a tear", a description that would come to encapsulate the essence of Chaplin's filmography.

In *The Kid*, Chaplin reprises his role as the Tramp and finds a baby in a garbage can. The baby had been placed in a limousine by a distressed mother (played by Edna Purviance), with the intention that the baby would be found by a rich couple who would raise the child to be successful. In addition to the baby, she had left a note dictating her desire for someone to safely provide for her child. However, the limousine is overtaken by criminals who discard the baby. After finding the young infant, Chaplin raises it until it is five years old, at which point the mother (who has become rich and spends her time conducting charity work in an effort to locate her lost son) calls a doctor to communicate her desire to find the boy. The doctor locates the note and assumes that Chaplin is a crook who has stolen the baby. However, in the end Chaplin is united with the mother and child in an image of stable domestic life, the exact opposite of his own childhood.

In many respects, *The Kid* is a lengthier version of *A Dog's Life*. Both films involve the Tramp caring for a surrogate son, and while there is plenty of slapstick and bodily humor, the film also incorporates numerous examples of tear-jerking scenes. One famous instance is reminiscent of the poster for *A Dog's Life*.

In this picture, viewers can see the refinement of Chaplin's directorial technique, or at least his attempt to elevate cinema to the status of traditionally prestigious art forms, particularly painting. In fact, the picture of Chaplin with the child represents a reworking of the symbolic Madonna with Child archetype that dominated Western art for centuries. Additionally, his storyline contained significant levels of drama, with none of the contrived *dues ex machine* devices that had characterized his early films; it was clear that Chaplin endeavored to make films that could compare with the most celebrated theatrical works, literary texts, and artistic compositions. Writing about *The Kid*, Kevin J. Hayes acknowledges the artistic ambition evinced by Chaplin, writing, "Though the film was an enormous accomplishment, its star and creator longed to be taken seriously as an artist. In conversation with De Casseres, he not only aligned his films with the works of Shakespeare, he also linked them to such important philosophers as Spinoza,

Schopenhauer, Nietzsche, and Pater. Furthermore, he expressed disgust that the cinema was not taken seriously as an art form, especially compared to the opera."

Although Chaplin earned considerable acclaim for *The Kid*, his relationship with First National Films soured, largely as a result of their attempt to pay him less than he had earned for the film. The studio attempted to pay Chaplin for just two reels despite the fact that the film was a full six reels in length, leading him to take the film reels out of California until they agreed to pay him the full $1.5 million. Although they finally acquiesced, the experience compromised his relationship with the studio. Chaplin would make three more films for First National Films, but he was already planning to operate as an independent filmmaker.

Chapter 5: The Maturation of Chaplin's Style

Even before making *The Kid*, Chaplin had decided that he wanted full authorship over the conception and production of his films, and in 1919 he had determined it would be preferable to head his own production studio. Alongside film actress Mary Pickford and directors Douglas Fairbanks and D.W. Griffith, Chaplin founded United Artists studio in February of 1919. The original agreement had been for each of them to produce five films per year, but this goal proved untenable with the rising costs for film production. Additionally, by the time United Artists actually began producing films in 1920, Griffith had already reached the nadir of his career. In the end, the pace of Chaplin's output would slow down considerably over the following decade.

Griffith

One of the reasons Chaplin had been inspired to head his own production studio was that it offered him the freedom to make films that were not comedies, as demonstrated by the first film he made for the studio. Titled *A Woman of Paris*, the film was released in 1923 and did not actually feature Chaplin himself. The plot involved a woman who is spurned by her fiancée, only to be reunited with him years later. However, her fiancée fails to grasp her intention to resume their relationship and commits suicide. *A Woman of Paris* stands out as an anomaly within Chaplin's oeuvre. It did not star Chaplin, and the heavy-handed plot recalls that of a 19th century novel rather than the playful mix of humor and pathos that characterized Chaplin's most acclaimed works. Realizing that his films had greater appeal when he starred in them, Chaplin would act in every one of the films he would make for the remainder of his career.

His following film for United Artists, *The Gold Rush* (1925), stands as one of his most famous films. In *The Gold Rush*, the Tramp is a gold prospector during the Alaskan gold rush that occurred at the end of the 19th century. The film contains many famous scenes that combine comedy with sorrow, including the famous scene in which the Tramp, distraught with hunger, attempts to eat his shoe. In another scene, Chaplin performs a celebratory dance with dinner rolls. In both instances, humor derives from the ability to transform the struggles of malnourishment into a fantasy of material prosperity. While Chaplin eventually wins the heart of a saloon girl, Georgia, the happy ending resonates almost as an afterthought, with the focus of the film dominated by the Tramp's ability to withstand adversity through the use of humor.

Chaplin would later discuss the shoe scene and the relationship between humor and tragedy:

"We had about two days of retakes on it. And the poor old actor [Mack Swain] was sick for the last two. The shoes were made of liquorices, and he'd eaten so much of it.

He said, 'I cannot eat any more of those damn shoes!' I got the idea for this gag from the Donner party. They resorted to cannibalism and to eating a moccasin. And I thought, stewed boots? There's something funny there.

I had an agonising time trying to motivate the story, until we got into a simple situation: hunger. The moment you've solved the logic of a situation, its feasibility, reality and possibility of being able to happen, ideas fly at you. It is one of the best things in the picture…

I think life is a very wonderful thing, and must be lived under all circumstances, even in misery. I think I would prefer life. Prefer the experience, for nothing else but the experience. I think humour does save one's sanity. We can go overboard with too much tragedy. Tragedy is, of course, a part of life, but we're also given an equipment to offset anything, a defence against it. I think tragedy is very essential in life. And we are given humour as a defence against it. Humour is a universal thing, which I think is derived from more or less pity."

In addition to showcasing the return of the Tramp, *The Gold Rush* is also significant for its autobiographical subtext. In particular, it is easy to see the rescuing of the saloon girl as a projection of Chaplin's desire to save his own mother, who had worked as a prostitute in a mining town that (while located across the globe) was not entirely dissimilar to the mining town featured in *The Gold Rush*. In reference to the theme of rescuing women that ran throughout Chaplin's career, Stephen Weissman believed the motif was a thinly-veiled projection of Chaplin's sadness towards being separated from his mother at an early age: "It was that loss and the scars it left that later shaped Chaplin's development of a screen character whose core identity (in the feature-length films) was the rescue and repair of damaged and fallen women" In this regard, the relationship between Chaplin and his lovers is a projection of his relationship with his own mother.

Despite using his films as a means through which to fantasize about a different life for his mother, Hannah's condition never recovered. Chaplin bought her a house in California and hired caretakers to watch over her continuously, but her mental health was destined to remain unstable until her death in 1928. Meanwhile, Chaplin's romantic life remained controversial. Having divorced Mildred Harris in 1920, he married film actress Lita Grey in 1924, and though Chaplin was never madly in love with Grey, he had impregnated her (the child was named Charles Jr.) and married her out of necessity. At the time, Grey was just 16 years of age, and again Chaplin created controversy due to the fact he was marrying a minor. Their relationship was conducted discreetly and they married in Empalme, Sonora, Mexico in an attempt to mitigate the negative press. However, Chaplin's affinity for underage women generated a stigma from which he was never fully able to separate himself.

Grey

The marriage with Grey was an unhappy one, and the two divorced in 1927, but by that time Grey had given birth to another child, a son named after Chaplin's brother Sydney. The large age gap limit their mutual interests, and Chaplin was an unfaithful husband who cheated on her repeatedly. Their divorce settlement, which was the most substantial up to that point in history, forced Chaplin to pay Grey over $600,000 and $100,000 for each child in trust. In an era in which divorce was frowned upon, Chaplin had already divorced twice, creating a significant public relations backlash.

After the rich pathos of *The Gold Rush*, Chaplin's next film was more lighthearted and in some respects a return to his pre-cinematic career as a vaudeville entertainer. Titled *The Circus*, the film was released in 1928 and stars Chaplin as the Tramp. The plot involves the Tramp as a vagrant who finds work with a circus, and there are a number of humorous gags, including one in which he walks a tightrope. In the end, Chaplin is primed to marry a woman who is berated by the circus boss, only to have her commit to his friend. The conclusion of the film involves Chaplin by himself walking along the road.

The failed romantic union between Chaplin and the girl with whom he is in love can be interpreted in a number of different ways. First, it represents the failure of his marriage to Lita Grey, as well as his sorrow over the death of his mother, which occurred the same year as the film's release. The Tramp is a solitary figure not destined for domestic life, and by ending the film as an isolated figure, the film's dominant tone is one of pathos rather than celebration.

By 1928, film comedy had progressed to a point in which it had become specifically cinematic and fully distinguished from the vaudeville theatre. The films of Chaplin and his rivals, Buster Keaton and Harold Lloyd, deployed sophisticated feats of timing that were not only hilarious but also specifically germane to the moving image that only cinema could provide. At the same time, there were distinct differences in style between the comedic rivals. While Chaplin's humor derived from the performance of the actors and their bodies, Keaton's films feature machines to a more significant degree. Meanwhile, the films of Harold Lloyd involve a greater amount of extreme physical stunts. In the case of each of the comedic directors, however, the comedic gags were structured around the precise organization of time and space, making full use of the movement inherent in the medium.

Following *The Circus*, the rate of Chaplin's filmic output continued to drop substantially, a byproduct of the fact he became more meticulous in devising his films, timing the comedic sequences, and editing the films. His next film, arguably the most famous of his career, was *City Lights*, which was not completed until 1931. By this point, cinema had already entered the era of synchronized sound, which posed serious challenges for Chaplin. Since all of his films had been silent, Chaplin's audiences had never heard his voice, and he was faced with the possibility that they would find his voice disagreeable. Chaplin's global fame was partly due to the fact that audiences from around the world could impose their own voice into Chaplin's character, making the Tramp a universal everyman for viewers worldwide. If viewers heard him speak, he would be identified as British, which threatened to abdicate his global appeal. Furthermore, as Chaplin boasted, "I was determined to continue making silent films...I was a pantomimist and in that medium I was unique and, without false modesty, a master." When asked about the advent of "talkies", Chaplin later said:

"I had experience, but not academic training, and there's a great difference. But I felt I had talent, I felt I was a natural actor. I knew it was much easier for me to pantomime than it was to talk. I'm an artist, and I knew very well that in talking a lot of that would disappear. I'd be no better than anybody else with good diction and a very good voice, which is more than half the battle... I've always said that the pantomime is far more poetic and it has a universal appeal that everyone would understand if it were well done. The spoken word reduces everybody to a certain glibness. The voice is a beautiful thing, most revealing, and I didn't want to be too revealing in my art because it may show a limitation. There are very few people with voices that can reach or give the illusion of great depth, whereas movement is as near to nature as a bird flying. The expression of the eyes - there's no words. The pure expression of the face that people can't hide - if it's one of disappointment it can be ever so subtle. I had to bear all this in mind when I started talking. I knew very well I lost a lot of eloquence. It can never be as good."

As a result, Chaplin eschewed making a "talkie," and *City Lights* is in many respects the defiant rebuttal of a silent film legend against the onslaught of sound cinema. The storyline for *City Lights* is also the most sentimental of any in Chaplin's entire canon. Reprising his role as the Tramp, he meets a blind girl with whom he falls in love, but she is also impoverished, and despite working as a flower vendor, she needs money in order to receive an operation that will restore her eyesight. In an effort to provide for her, the Tramp befriends a wealthy man who provides him with the money needed to subsidize her surgery, but after her operation, the girl sees that he is the Tramp and not the wealthy suitor she had envisioned. The film concludes with Chaplin staring sorrowfully into the camera, and the bittersweet ending recalls that of *The Circus*, leaving the Tramp destined to live alone.

In addition to the pathos of the ending and its selfless message concerning the need to help the disabled, *City Lights* is also one of the funniest films Chaplin made. There are a number of breathtaking sequences that involve precise timing, including a scene in which Chaplin narrowly avoids falling into a bed of water, as well as the opening scene, in which Chaplin entangles his body within a statue that is being unveiled. The use of timing is significant in that it is juxtaposed against sound, as though Chaplin were demonstrating to the audience that film does not require the use of dialogue in order to remain compelling.

Although *City Lights* is a silent film in that it does not involve any dialogue, it is not bereft of other forms of sound. For example, there are many instances in which noise is present, including a speech at the film's beginning in which muffled static emanates from the mouth of a city official. Music is also used throughout the film, and Chaplin uses the interplay between noise, music, and image to complex effect throughout the narrative. When Kevin J. Hayes writes (in reference to Chaplin's own life) that he "often preferred expressing himself in gestures instead of words," *City Lights* is perhaps the most telling example of this dynamic.

The human drama that characterizes the ending reflects the emphasis on social commentary that began to infiltrate Chaplin's cinema. At the time in which *City Lights* was made, the United States was in the early stages of the Great Depression and still reeling from the collapse of the economy, which had occurred just years earlier. Watching the Tramp selflessly help the blind girl even while he remained impoverished himself appealed to audiences that had little money themselves. Not only did the hilarity of Chaplin's comedic scenes provide relief to economically distraught viewers, but the humanistic message involving the need to help those less fortunate garnered mass appeal.

The Tramp in *City Lights*

Chapter 6: Social and Political Protest

"I am what I am: an individual, unique and different, with a lineal history of an ancestral promptings and urgings, a history of dreams, desires, and of special experiences, of all of which I am the sum total." – Charlie Chaplin

After the success of *City Lights*, Chaplin went an even greater amount of time between films. Immediately after the film's release, he left the United States for Europe, returning to London (including a visit to the school of his youth) and also spending time in France, Switzerland, and Japan. He later admitted, "I was confused and without plan, restless and conscious of an extreme loneliness." Although he considered permanently moving from the United States, he returned to Los Angeles in June 1932, and it was around then that he met Paulette Goddard, a 21 year-old actress who was roughly half his age.

Chaplin had returned to the United States in a state of depression, but his relationship with Goddard improved his spirits, and he began writing a record of his travels. It was also during this period that Chaplin was reticent to make another film and instead diverted his attention to politics, a direction that may have been motivated by both his exposure to other countries during his travels and the discrepancy between the wealth of the United States and the country's high rate of unemployment. He would note, "Something is wrong. Things have been badly managed when five million men are out of work in the richest country in the world."

Throughout the decade, Chaplin became fiercely liberal in his political views and supported President Roosevelt's New Deal. His next film, *Modern Times* (1936), not only stands as one of Chaplin's most famous and acclaimed films but also his most overt form of social protest. While every film is in some respect political, *Modern Times* addressed the contemporary socioeconomic injustice that pervaded America during the Great Depression.

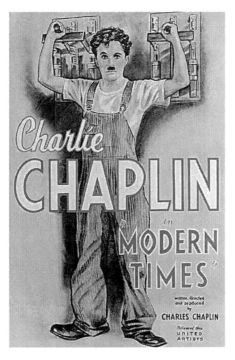

In *Modern Times*, which Chaplin labeled "a satire on certain phases of our industrial life", Chaplin again plays the Tramp, but the film differs from previous Tramp films because this time the character is employed. His job forces him to work at a machine for hours on end, to the point that his own body assumes the function of a machine. There are many famous scenes within the film in which Chaplin's own body becomes mechanized, including one in which a machine attempts to feed him. In another scene, Chaplin's arm movements become automated so that he cannot stop jerking his arm. The film portrays the effects of Taylorism, the industrial movement that was predicated on obtaining maximum productivity in the workplace, and critic Jérôme Larcher would note the film was a "grim contemplation on the automatization of the individual."

As a result of the work environment, Chaplin's character suffers a nervous breakdown and is hospitalized, after which he subsequently engages in a Communist labor protest and is arrested. After his release from prison, the Tramp meets a girl (Paulette Goddard) and attempts to start a domestic life, with both of them working at a restaurant. However, they lose their jobs, and the film ends with them walking along the road, an ending that directly recalls that of *The Circus*.

The Tramp in *Modern Times*

Modern Times is a monumental film, both within Chaplin's own career and film history more generally. It was the first film in which Chaplin spoke, during a scene where the Tramp performed an Italian dance hall tune while working as a waiter. While he would not speak any words until his next film, for the first time Chaplin revealed to his audience the sound of his voice. Chaplin's singing performance, which is conducted in an impromptu manner, also recalls his earliest stage performance as a five year-old boy in London, another example of the way in which autobiographical traits found their way into Chaplin's body of work.

On a broader level, *Modern Times* is remembered for its political message, initiating social protest at a time in which the vast majority of films shied away from expressing overt political views. The film appealed to the economically disenfranchised American public, and people superimposed themselves into the role of the Tramp laboring away at the machine. Although the scenes in the factory are undoubtedly hilarious, Chaplin used humor to spark political engagement in the viewer, an alienation device that was unseen in his earlier works. The association between humor and political protest makes *Modern Times* a capable example of Walter Benjamin's theory of collective laughter (expressed in "The Work of Art in the Age of Mechanical Reproducibility") as a means through which the viewer can witness their own subordination. Benjamin writes:

> "Collective laughter is one such preemptive and healing outbreak of mass psychosis. The countless grotesque events consumed in films are a graphic indication of the dangers threatening mankind from the pressures inherent in civilization. American slapstick comedies and Disney films trigger a therapeutic release of unconscious energies. Their forerunner was the figure of the eccentric. He was the first to inhabit the new fields of action opened up by film—the first occupant of the newly built house. This is the context in which Chaplin takes on historical significance."

Through watching the Tramp suffer at the hands of his machine, the contemporary viewer became confronted with his own injustice. Chaplin therefore utilized grotesque imagery to very serious ends, sparking sociopolitical engagement in the viewer. Chaplin had found a way to combine the humor that viewers sought when watching his films with a pronounced political commitment, demonstrating the possibilities for film as an instrument through which to effect social change. Even so, it came at a cost to his own popularity, as the overt politicization turned off plenty of viewers.

Following *Modern Times*, Chaplin and Paulette Goddard left the United States for an extended trip to Asia. While abroad, they married and would remain wedded until 1942. However, Chaplin again showed himself as unable to maintain a domestic relationship, and their marriage was not a close one. Although they remained amicable, they stopped living together very shortly after the marriage was consummated. Moreover, Chaplin grew increasingly disillusioned with the international political climate, and the onset of World War II drove him to become even more overtly political. After returning from his trip to Asia, Chaplin turned his attention to devising the script for *The Great Dictator*, a dark comedy protesting the nationalistic regime of Adolf Hitler. *The Great Dictator* would take over two years to produce, and it was not released until 1940. Fortunately for Chaplin, one of the advantages to writing, producing, and directing his films was that he was not tasked with adhering to the strict time frame imposed on directors hired by other studios.

In the film, Chaplin plays two roles: a Jewish barber and a Jewish dictator named Adenoid Hynkle. Although the film is set 20 years after the conclusion of World War II, it is clear that the dictator is a parody of Adolf Hitler, and Chaplin's own mustache resembles Hitler's.

Chaplin in *The Great Dictator*

The Great Dictator was a daring and controversial film on multiple levels. First, making a comedic film in the middle of World War II was especially risky, and Chaplin would later state that had he known the magnitude of the atrocities stemming from the war, he likely would not have made the film. Furthermore, the film involves the first time in which Chaplin spoke (the song in *Modern Times* notwithstanding), and the impact of the politically-charged message was heightened by the significance of the fact that it was the first time Chaplin had ever spoken in a film. In a speech at the end of the film, the Jewish barber is mistaken for the dictator, and while looking at the camera and addressing the audience directly, the barber states:

"I'm sorry, but I don't want to be an emperor. That's not my business. I don't want to rule or conquer anyone. I should like to help everyone, if possible, Jew, gentile, black man, white. We all want to help one another. Human beings are like that. We want to live by each other's happiness — not by each other's misery. We don't want to hate and despise one another.

In this world there is room for everyone. And the good earth is rich and can provide for everyone. The way of life can be free and beautiful, but we have lost the way. Greed has poisoned men's souls, has barricaded the world with hate, has goose-stepped us into misery and bloodshed. We have developed speed, but we have shut ourselves in. Machinery that gives abundance has left us in want. Our knowledge has made us cynical. Our cleverness, hard and unkind. We think too much and feel too little. More than machinery we need humanity. More than cleverness we need kindness and gentleness. Without these qualities, life will be violent and all will be lost.

The aeroplane and the radio have brought us closer together. The very nature of these inventions cries out for the goodness in men, cries out for universal brotherhood, for the unity of us all. Even now my voice is reaching millions throughout the world — millions of despairing men, women and little children — victims of a system that makes men torture and imprison innocent people. To those who can hear me, I say — do not despair. The misery that is now upon us is but the passing of greed — the bitterness of men who fear the way of human progress. The hate of men will pass, and dictators die, and the power they took from the people will return to the people and so long as men die, liberty will never perish.

Soldiers! Don't give yourselves to brutes — men who despise you — enslave you — who regiment your lives — tell you what to do — what to think or what to feel! Who drill you, diet you, treat you like cattle, use you as cannon fodder. Don't give yourselves to these unnatural men — machine men with machine minds and machine hearts! You are not machines! You are not cattle! You are men! You have the love of humanity in your hearts. You don't hate! Only the unloved hate — the unloved and the unnatural!

Soldiers! Don't fight for slavery! Fight for liberty! In the 17th Chapter of St. Luke it is written: "the Kingdom of God is within man" — not one man nor a group of men, but in all men! In you! You, the people have the power — the power to create machines. The power to create happiness! You, the people, have the power to make this life free and beautiful, to make this life a wonderful adventure.

Then, in the name of democracy, let us use that power! Let us all unite! Let us fight for a new world, a decent world that will give men a chance to work, that will give youth the future and old age a security. By the promise of these things, brutes have risen to power, but they lie! They do not fulfill their promise; they never will. Dictators free themselves, but they enslave the people! Now, let us fight to fulfill that promise! Let us fight to free the world, to do away with national barriers, to do away with greed, with hate and intolerance. Let us fight for a world of reason, a world where science and progress will lead to all men's happiness.

Soldiers! In the name of democracy, let us all unite!"

In this speech, one understands just how much Chaplin abhorred the nationalistic privileging of one race or culture above another. The address reflected a collectivist spirit that made clear his anti-war stance and would have appealed to viewers from around the world. Although it was argued that it was insensitive for Chaplin to direct a film mocking Hitler, one must recall that

Chaplin believed in the potential for humor to act as a political rhetorical device, and there is little doubt that he intended for *The Great Dictator* to arouse anti-Hitlerian sentiment rather than simply poking fun at the atrocities of World War II. Although the controversial subject matter engendered a mixed critical reception, the film did receive substantial acclaim in some areas, as it was nominated for five Academy Awards, including Best Picture.

After *The Great Dictator*, Chaplin continued to have difficulty in his personal life. Although he was still married to Paulette Goddard, he maintained an affair with Joan Barry. Barry had been hired by Chaplin in 1941 under the premise that she would star in a film of his, yet he was unable to offer a role for her. Barry claimed that he was the father of her child, and Chaplin vehemently denied that the baby was his. The allegation created a torrent of negative publicity directed toward Chaplin, and in 1945 he was determined to be the father and required to pay $75 per week in child support until the child, Carole Ann, turned 21 years of age.

On top of that, the FBI was keeping tabs on Chaplin, who J. Edgar Hoover had described as a "parlor Bolshevik" over a decade earlier. After Barry made her allegations, Chaplin was actually charged with violating the 1910 Mann Act, which forbid transporting a woman across state lines for "immoral purposes." While the legislation was clearly intended to stop prostitution, it was used as a catch-all to begin targeting anyone who authorities deemed as acting immorally with a woman. Since Chaplin associated himself with women half his age, and he was both famous and politically inclined, he was an attractive target. Chaplin would actually have to beat the charges in court, and he was acquitted after trial.

Despite the tumultuous episode with Joan Barry, Chaplin found contentment in his personal life after meeting 18 year-old Oona O'Neill. He married O'Neill in June of 1943, and the two would stay married until Chaplin's death nearly 35 years later. They would have eight children together: Geraldine (born 1942), Michael (1946), Josephine (1949), Victoria (1951), Eugene (1953), Jane (1957), Annette (1959), and Christopher (1961).

Chaplin and Oona

While adjusting to domestic life with Oona, Chaplin began work on his next film, *Monsieur Verdoux* (1947), a project that was originally to be directed by Orson Welles but for which Chaplin subsequently assumed authority. The film, based on the Bluebeard myth, involved Chaplin as a con man named Verdoux who marries wealthy elderly women and then murders them to support his own family. Although less overtly political than either *The Great Dictator* or *Modern Times*, the film still contained thinly-veiled political protest, highlighted by Verdoux's speech that "One murder makes a villain…millions a hero." Although the film's message was humanistic in nature, the public did not appreciate what they viewed as the autobiographical reference to Chaplin's own many wives, and Chaplin was viewed as having become the antithesis of the altruistic Tramp of his earlier films. The film had a highly abbreviated run in cinemas (it was even released twice, but was never able to find commercial success), and it became clear that Chaplin would have immense difficulty remaining profitable in the United States.

Following the production of *Monsieur Verdoux*, Chaplin's personal politics again stirred controversy. After World War II, the burgeoning Cold War between the West and the Soviet Union stirred a new red scare across the United States. Though anti-Communist sentiment in the 1950s is often derisively dismissed as McCarthyism, there was some basis for the era's fears.

The Communist Party in the United States was funded by the Soviet Union; its leaders were paid by the Soviets, and several were agents of the Soviet intelligence apparatus. During the 1930s, the Party had gained members who believed that the capitalist system was dying and the future lay with Communism, and those members also believed that the Communists were the only effective bulwark against Hitler and the rise of fascism. As a small elite group able to place individuals in positions of power, they did present a potential threat to the security of the country, and there were several spy rings operating in America at the time.

Of course, the real threat was exaggerated to a degree that comes across as completely farcical today. Shortly after World War II, Congress' House Committee on Un-American Activities began investigating Americans across the country for suspected ties to Communism, and U.S. Senator Joseph McCarthy made waves in 1950 by telling the Republican Women's Club in Wheeling, West Virginia that he had a list of dozens of known Communists working in the State Department. The political theater helped Senator McCarthy become the prominent anti-Communist crusader in the government, and the Rosenberg spy case only further emboldened him. McCarthy continued to claim he held evidence suggesting Communist infiltration throughout the government, but anytime he was pressed to produce his evidence, McCarthy would not name names. Instead, he'd accuse those who questioned his evidence of being Communists themselves.

The most famous victims of these witch hunts were Hollywood actors, including Chaplin, whose "Un-American activity" was being neutral at the beginning of World War II. An acknowledged political leftist, Chaplin was subpoenaed to appear in the McCarthy trials, but he was never actually called to testify, and when those who fingered him were called to testify under oath, they all refused to do so too. Even so, Chaplin publicly supported the Hollywood Ten and was unabashed in his objection to the increasingly conservative political climate in the United States. To his credit, Chaplin realized the perverse nature of the hysteria before most people, as he noted in his autobiography, "Friends have asked how I came to engender this American antagonism. My prodigious sin was, and still is, being a non-conformist. Although I am not a Communist I refused to fall in line by hating them. Secondly, I was opposed to the Committee on Un-American Activities — a dishonest phrase to begin with, elastic enough to wrap around the throat and strangle the voice of any American citizen whose honest opinion is a minority of one."

It is unclear exactly why Chaplin was targeted by the House Un-American Activities Committee, particularly because he was not open in advocating his Communist beliefs. Most likely, the Committee simply targeted him due to his fame and the publicity they would garner from implicating Chaplin. At the same time, however, Sbardellati and Shaw identify how their inability to actually find any conclusive grounds for which to accuse Chaplin reveals the flimsiness of the Committee itself:

"The Federal Bureau of Investigation targeted Charlie Chaplin because of his status as a cultural icon and as part of its broader investigation of Hollywood. Some of Chaplin's films were considered 'Communist Propaganda,' but because Chaplin was not a member of the Communist Party, he was not among those investigated by HUAC in 1947. Nevertheless, he was vulnerable to protests by the American Legion and other patriotic groups because of both his sexual and political unorthodoxy. Yet, although counter subversives succeeded in driving Chaplin out of the country, they failed to build a consensus that Chaplin was a threat to the nation. Chaplin's story testifies to both the awesome power of the countersubversive campaign at mid-century and to some of its limitations as well."

McCarthyism finally met its match when the Senator went after the Army. As chairman of the Senate Committee on Government Operations, McCarthy summoned decorated World War II veterans and challenged their loyalty. When he openly suggested World War II hero Brigadier General Ralph W. Zwicker was a Communist during one hearing, the military had had enough. In April 1954, the committee hearings were widely televised, and Americans watched Army members demand that McCarthy name names and provide evidence. On June 9, 1954, McCarthy was humiliated by the Army's legal representative, Joseph Nye Welch, who repeatedly demanded that McCarthy produce the list of alleged Communists in the U.S. Army. As McCarthy tried to wiggle out of the challenge, he finally named Fred Fisher, who had been affiliated with the National Lawyers Guild during law school, an organization Hoover himself tried to have the Attorney General designate a Communist front. Enraged, Welch responded, "Until this moment, Senator, I think I have never really gauged your cruelty or your recklessness. Fred Fisher is a young man who went to the Harvard Law School and came into my firm and is starting what looks to be a brilliant career with us…We know he belonged to the Lawyers Guild. Let us not assassinate this lad further, Senator. You've done enough. Have you no sense of decency, sir? At long last, have you left no sense of decency?" Welch received an ovation from the gallery, and McCarthyism had been publicly and permanently repudiated. After the hysteria had waned, former President Truman thunderously asserted in 1960, "I've said many a time that I think the Un-American Activities Committee in the House of Representatives was the most un-American thing in America!"

Unfortunately for Chaplin, by the time McCarthyism had been repudiated, the damage had been done to him. His outspoken stance against the persecution of the Hollywood Ten had made him even more unpopular among Americans, and though he completed his next film project, *Limelight* (1952) in Los Angeles, his sentiment toward the United States soured completely after his re-entry visa was revoked because he constituted a "security risk". After being informed that he would not be allowed back into the United States, he asserted, "I am not a political man and I have no political convictions. I am an individual and a believer in liberty. That is all the politics I have. On the other hand I am not a super-patriot. Super-patriotism leads to Hitlerism — and we've had our lesson there. I don't want to create a revolution — I just want to create a few more films."

Even more than his previous film, *Limelight* is filled with autobiographical references. Set in 1914 London, Chaplin plays a washed-up vaudeville performer named Calvero who rescues a female performer from suicide. Although the woman wants to marry him, he does not marry her but does accept her suggestion to return to the stage. Shortly after making a comeback, he dies of a heart attack. The plotline contains many references to both Chaplin's personal life and his past films. The rescuing of the young woman recalls the early Tramp films, and the role as a stage performer not only constitutes a surrogate for Chaplin's profession in the motion picture industry but also recalls his prior time with the theatre troupe and circus. With *Limelight*, Chaplin takes a somber, self-referential look at his personal and professional life.

Chaplin in *Limelight*

It was while attending the commercial release of *Limelight* with his family in London that Chaplin's re-entry visa to the U.S. was revoked by Attorney General James P. McGranery. Although it is likely that Chaplin would have won his appeal had he applied, he was satisfied to leave the country and moved to Vevey, Switzerland, where he would live for the remainder of his life. He remained politically active and was awarded the International Peace Prize by the communist-affiliated World Peace Council in 1954.

Despite being exiled and in the twilight of his career at 65 years old, Chaplin remained active with his film career and released his next film, *A King in New York*, in 1957. Continuing the self-referential spirit that characterized his previous two films, *A King in New York* contains many references to Chaplin's life and career. Chaplin plays the role of the protagonist, King Igor Shahdov, a deranged utopian king who intends to use atomic power to establish a peaceful society. The circuitous plot arc contains many attacks on American culture, with the focus directed especially toward the Red Scare in Hollywood.

The experience of making *A King in New York* left Chaplin dispirited and fatigued. The film had been shot and produced in England at Attica, the production company Chaplin had founded following his arrival in Europe. However, his increasing age and the fact he was working in exile created both material and personnel challenges, as Chaplin was forced to work away from his "home base" in Hollywood. After *A King in New York* was released, he took a long hiatus from making movies, concentrating instead on editing his past films and writing his autobiography, *My Autobiography*, which was published in 1964. In 1962, he was awarded an Honorary Doctorate from Oxford and Durham.

After completing his autobiography, Chaplin completed one final film, the satirical film *A Countess from Hong Kong* (1967). The film is a lighthearted romance starring Marlon Brando and Sophia Loren, and it is most notable for being the only film Chaplin would make in color. Already 78 years old, Chaplin did not star in the movie and instead made only a brief cameo near the end. Chaplin completed the film in England, but he also decided to release it in the United States, where it was distributed by United Artists.

Following the release of his final film, Chaplin's health suffered. He never formally retired, and in fact he worked on scripts that were never completed, but he suffered repeated strokes and was never up to the rigors of completing another film. During the 1970s, his mental faculties also began to leave him, and it is suspected that he suffered from dementia. He did manage to complete a pictorial autobiography, *My Life in Pictures*, in 1974, but as the decade progressed his health grew increasingly unstable. Chaplin died on Christmas Day in 1977, but controversy followed him to the grave, literally. Following his burial, his corpse was stolen, only to be later recovered in a nearby field. The two men who stole it were subsequently arrested.

Chapter 7: Chaplin's Legacy

Chaplin's life is remarkable for the imprint he made on cinema as a medium and the way in which his public image changed over his life. Given his upbringing, it is remarkable that he was ever able to enter the motion picture industry in the first place. At the same time, Chaplin's career was also filled with sadness, a fact that has been mostly obscured by the universal acclaim he has been the beneficiary of during the last 40 years. That fact is all the more ironic considering that the tragedies that were part of Chaplin's life also made their way into some of his most iconic works. To those who are interested in reading about Chaplin, the most noteworthy aspect of his life and career is the wide gulf between the warm public reception he received during the first three decades of his career and the vitriol inflicted upon him from 1940 onward. While it is true that there may be no director who made more people laugh or helped people through the harsh realities of the Great Depression more than Chaplin, it is also true that his career reflects the sorrows of working in exile and banishment from the United States.

Ultimately, Chaplin did not deserve his fate, although his legacy persists through this day. In the words of Rudolph Arnheim, a film theorist from Chaplin's early years, Chaplin was novel because "he is the poet of his films, that is, as director." Along with Griffith, Chaplin was instrumental in bringing a refinement to cinema, although where Griffith did so by invoking the novel, Chaplin brought respectability to the medium in a more expressive, poetic manner.

Although he may be one of the most recognizable actors and directors of all time, it's also apparent that Chaplin was misunderstood in his day and remains a somewhat elusive figure in death. He was idealistic and empathetic, but he had very stark shortcomings, particularly his neglect of his early wives and children, that should not be overlooked. Moreover, Chaplin's life story illuminates many themes that run throughout his films, including the relationship with his mother and the way in which he became more political as he matured. Even while certain aspects of his life continue to elude scholars and historians, the autobiographical nature of many of his films ensures that Chaplin's life and legacy will remain relevant for a long time.

Bibliography

Arnheim, Rudolph, Benjamin, Walter, and MacKay, John. "Walter Benjamin and Rudolph Arnheim on Charlie Chaplin. *The Yale Journal of Aesthetics and Art Criticism* 9.2 (Fall 1996): 309-314.

Benjamin, Walter. "The Work of Art in the Age of Mechanical Reproducibility." Eds. Michael W. Jennings, Brigid Doherty, and Thomas Y. Levin. Trans. Edmund Jephcott, Rodney Livingstone, Howard Eiland, and Others. Cambridge: Harvard University Press, 2008.

Chaplin, Charlie, and Robinson, David. *My Autobiography*. Brooklyn: Melville Press, 2012.

Grace, Harry A. "Charlie Chaplin's Films and American Culture Patterns." *The Journal of Aesthetics and Art Criticism* 10.4 (1952): 353-363.

Gunning, Tom. "Crazy Machines in the Garden of Forking Paths: Mischief Gags and the Origins of American Film Comedy." *Classical Hollywood Comedy*. Eds. Kristina Brunovska Karnick and Henry Jenkins. New York: Routledge, 1995.

Gunning, Tom. "The Cinema of Attraction: Early Film, Its Spectator, and the Avant-Garde." *Film and Theory: An Anthology*. Eds. Robert Stam & Toby Miller. Hoboken: Blackwell, 2000.

Hayes, Kevin J. *Charlie Chaplin: Interviews*. Oxford: University of Mississippi Press, 2005.

Sbardellati, John, and Shaw, Tony. "Booting a Tramp: Charlie Chaplin, the FBI, and the Construction of the Subversive Image in Red Scare America." *Pacific Historical Review* 72.4 (2003): 495-530.

Schuyler Lynn, Kenneth. *Charlie Chaplin: And His Times*. Rochester: Simon and Schuster, 1997.

Weissman, Stephen M. "Charlie Chaplin's Film Heroines." *Film History* 8 (1996): 439-445.

Weissman, Stephen M. *Chaplin: A Life*. New York: Arcade Publishing, 2008.

32128544R00203

Made in the USA
Charleston, SC
08 August 2014